DISPOSSESSION

THE AUSTRALIAN EXPERIENCE

ALSO IN THE SERIES
Geoffrey Sherington *Australia's Immigrants*
Geoffrey Bolton *Spoils and Spoilers*
Richard White *Inventing Australia*
Richard Broome *Aboriginal Australians*

COMPILED BY HENRY REYNOLDS

DISPOSSESSION
BLACK AUSTRALIANS AND WHITE INVADERS

ALLEN & UNWIN

© Henry Reynolds 1989

All rights reserved. No part of this book may be reproduced or transmitted in any form or by any means, electronic or mechanical, including photocopying, recording or by any information storage and retrieval system without prior permission in writing from the publisher. *The Australian Copyright Act 1968* (the Act), allows a maximum of one chapter or 10 per cent of this book, whichever is the greater, to be photocopied by any educational institution for its educational purposes provided that the educational institution (or body that administers it) has given a remuneration notice to Copyright Agency Limited (CAL) under the Act.

First published in 1989
Allen & Unwin Pty Ltd
9 Atchison Street, St Leonards, NSW 2065
Australia
Phone: (61 2) 8425 0100
Fax: (61 2) 9906 2218
Email: frontdesk@allen-unwin.com.au
Web: http://www.allenandunwin.com

National Library of Australia
Cataloguing-in-Publication entry:

Dispossession: Black Australians and white invaders,
Bibliography,
Includes index.
ISBN 1 86448 141 2

1. Aborigines, Australian—Treatment—Sources,
2. Australia—Colonization—History—Sources,
3. Land settlement—Australia—History—Sources,
4. Australia—Race relations—Sources. I. Reynolds,
Henry, 1988– . (Series Australian experience).

994.0049915

Library of Congress Catalog Card Number: 88-83857

Set by Graphicraft Typesetters Ltd, Hong Kong

10 9 8 7 6

*In memory of my father
the late John Reynolds*

CONTENTS

Illustrations viii
Abbreviations x
Acknowledgements xi
Introduction xii

1 WHITE AUSTRALIA: GUILTY OR NOT GUILTY? *1*
2 THE FRONTIER: PEACEFUL SETTLEMENT OR BRUTAL CONQUEST? *24*
3 THE LAND QUESTION: ARE WE A COMMUNITY OF THIEVES? *66*
4 THE IMAGE OF THE ABORIGINES: BLACK BROTHERS OR DEGRADED SAVAGES? *96*
5 ABORIGINES IN WHITE SOCIETY: CITIZENS OR OUTCASTS? *123*
6 MISSIONARIES: SAVIOURS OR DESTROYERS? *155*
7 GOVERNMENT POLICY: ASSIMILATION OR SEGREGATION? *182*

Bibliography *215*
Index *219*

ILLUSTRATIONS

'The old camping ground revisited'	8
Aboriginals on Bentinck Island, 1901	25
'The dangers of the Palmer'	32
The desertion of Gilberton	35
'The avengers'	42
A native police detachment in uniform, c. 1860	47
Native police rescuing beleaguered pioneers	50
Native police involved in a massacre of an Aboriginal camp	51
Blacks call a truce at Dagworth Station, Queensland	63
Batman's treaty with Port Phillip Aboriginals in 1836	75
Natives...being driven [to] the Police Court...1847	79
Ouriaga of Bruny Island	100
Illustration from an account of Governor Phillip's voyage to Australia	102
Scene in Sydney Street	103
Jinny, Manalargenna and *A Group of Aborigines, Van Dieman's Land*	112
Portrait of an Aboriginal, c. 1875	116
King Mickey Johnson, Illawarra, c. 1896	117
A Native Family of New South Wales... c. 1826	125
Aboriginal shepherds, c. 1884	128
'Going on the land'	135
Station homestead group portrait, c. 1890	136
Aboriginal stockman, Chadshunt Station, c. 1920	137
The colonised	139
Aboriginal trackers at work	141
Portrait of Aboriginal children	145
Aboriginal family outside their house, c. 1900	148
Last Tasmanian Aboriginals dressed for the Governor's Ball	150
Aboriginal men in a Queensland fringe camp	153
Salvation Army missionaries and their Aboriginal converts	162
Yarrabah Aboriginal Mission, North Queensland	168

ILLUSTRATIONS

Aboriginal mission, NSW;
Aboriginal women, mission inmates 176
Portrait of Samuel Kandwillen... Poonindie and
Portrait of Nannultera... Poonindie 178
'Proclamation to the Aborigines' 184
Blanket-giving ceremony, Herberton, Queensland 196
'Station Aborigines in Charters Towers for Christmas', c. 1920 201
Prime Minister Gough Whitlam and Vincent Lingiari, 1975 211

Illustration Acknowledgements

Permission is gratefully acknowledged for reproduction of material on the following pages:
Australian Information Service, p. 211
Australian Institute of Aboriginal Studies, p. 176
Dixson Library, State Library of NSW, p. 139
John Oxley Library, Brisbane, p. 25, 51, 116, 136, 153, 168, 176
Mitchell Library, State Library of NSW, p. 8, 32, 35, 42, 50, 63, 79, 112, 135, 184
Mortlock Library, South Australia, p. 162
National Library of Australia, p. 103, 117, 125, 141, 145, 148, 150, 178
South Australian Libraries Board, p. 102
Tasmanian Museum and Art Gallery, p. 112

ABBREVIATIONS

AJCP	Australian Joint Copying Project
CPP	Commonwealth Parliamentary Papers
HRA	Historical Records of Australia
ML	Mitchell Library
NSWLCVP	New South Wales Legislative Council Votes and Proceedings
NSWVP	New South Wales Votes and Proceedings
BPP	British Parliamentary Papers
QPD	Queensland Parliamentary Debates
QPP	Queensland Parliamentary Papers
SAPP	South Australian Parliamentary Papers
VLCVP	Victorian Legislative Council Votes and Proceedings
VPP	Victorian Parliamentary Papers
WAPD	Western Australian Parliamentary Debates
WAPP	Western Australian Parliamentary Papers

ACKNOWLEDGEMENTS

Many people have helped me with the research which forms the raw material for this book and in particular librarians and archivists all over the country. I have been assisted by research grants from the British Council, the National Library and the Australian Research Grants Committee. John Iremonger has provided encouragement, advice and a little judicious urging when enthusiasm flagged. Val Hicks has been an exemplary typist.

INTRODUCTION

Aboriginal and immigrant Australians have shared this continent for 200 years. Throughout that period their histories have been closely interwoven. The Aboriginal presence has been a central feature of white Australian historical experience since the beginning of settlement. Like the land, the indigenous people resisted the ready imposition of European culture and economy and in so doing have helped define Australian experience as something more than an extension of the old world. Nineteenth century writers were aware of the importance of the Aboriginal presence. Travellers, pioneers, explorers, all wrote about them. Their audience at home in Europe hungered for the exotic, the vicarious thrill of contact with 'wild' landscapes, 'primitive' people and 'savage' customs.

But when in the late 19th century the colonists began to write their own history the Aborigines were gradually eased out of the story. Frontier conflict was an embarrassment for writers who sought to highlight the peaceful nature of Australian settlement. The struggle with the land was far more appealing than conflict with the indigenous people for the land. Both scientific and popular opinion asserted that the Aborigines were a dying race, condemned to extinction by the iron laws of evolution. With an insignificant role in the past and none in the future it mattered little if they were overlooked in works which celebrated the triumph of progress and the emergence of a new nation. Some historians believed that there was no place at all for the Aborigines in Australian historical works. Walter Murdoch, one of the great literary figures of the first half of the 20th century, explained his standpoint in a school textbook:

When people talk about 'the history of Australia' they mean the history of the white people who have lived in Australia. There is a good reason why we should not stretch that term to make it include the story of the dark-skinned wandering tribes who hurled boomerangs and ate snakes in their native land for long ages before the arrival of the first intruders from Europe . . . He [the historian] is concerned with Australia only as the

INTRODUCTION xiii

dwelling place of white men and women, settlers from overseas. It is his business to tell us how these white folk found the land, how they settled in it, how they explored it, and how they gradually made it the Australia we know today.[1]

Historical neglect of the Aborigines persisted until the 1960s. In 1968 the celebrated anthropologist W.E.H. Stanner used his Boyer lectures on the ABC to berate the country's historians for their responsibility for what he dubbed 'the great Australian silence'. It was, he declared,

a structural matter, a view from a window which has been carefully placed to exclude a whole quadrant of the landscape. What may well have begun as a simple forgetting of other possible views turned under habit and over time into something like a cult of forgetfulness practiced on a national scale.[2]

By the time that Stanner spoke change was already underway. All over the country historians, archaeologists, and scholars in other disciplines were engaged in research that was to transform our picture of the role of the Aborigines in our history. Since the early 1970s increasing numbers of specialist studies have appeared concentrating on the relations of white and black. The journal *Aboriginal History* has flourished since it first appeared in 1977. General histories of nation, state, region and shire now deal seriously and sensitively with the Aboriginal experience. Gradually but inexorably our view of the past, our perception of ourselves and our place in the world has been transformed.

The editor's *Aborigines and Settlers: The Australian Experience, 1788-1939*,[3] was the first of a number of books of documents published in the early 1970s and dealing with white-Aboriginal relations. In 1988, it had been out of print for some years and it was decided that a new edition should be published. However as the work proceeded it became apparent that many of the original documents should be replaced or amended. The chapters were reorganized and eventually so much new material was included that the end product was a new book, rather than a fresh edition of an old one. But some features of the original book survived. The bulk of the documents still come from 19th and early 20th century sources. The emphasis is on the colonial heritage. However where

---
1 W. Murdoch, *The Making of Australia*, Whitcomb & Tombs, Melbourne, no date, p. 9.
2 W.E.H. Stanner, *After the Dreaming*, ABC, Sydney, 1968, p. 25.
3 Cassell, Melbourne, 1972.

the chosen themes have persisted into the contemporary period the documents chart the relevant developments, although not in a comprehensive manner.

Most of the documents deal with events which occurred beyond the reach of living memory and therefore fall outside the scope of the numerous books of personal reminiscences which have appeared over the past ten years. Of necessity the documents are practically all written by Europeans, but they range across a wide spectrum of opinion and belief. Many of them have provided raw material for three books published in the past six years—*The Other Side of the Frontier*, Penguin, 1982; *Frontier*, Allen & Unwin, 1987; *The Law of the Land*, Penguin, 1987. On reading the documents again in the course of selection for the present publication I was struck by the richness of ideas, the vigour of argument, the depth of moral concern which they display. Even in cases where parts of a document had been previously used it was obvious that the full extract had an importance in its own right. A few sentences, wrenched from their context, were invaluable props to an argument advanced elsewhere, but they often simplified a complex situation, or left out qualifications found in the original, or failed to fully display the intelligence or moral concerns of the author. Compiling this collection has, therefore, renewed my belief in the value of documentary collections. In this book our forebears speak for themselves and speak in many voices. Comments by the editor have been restricted to those which place documents in perspective and link together themes and chapters. All in all the reader will find a complex and fascinating picture of the way in which the European settlers and their Australian born descendants endeavoured to come to terms—emotionally, morally and intellectually—with the prior owners of the continent, the victims of the dispossession.

1

WHITE AUSTRALIA: GUILTY OR NOT GUILTY?

A visitor to the Australian colonies in the 19th century remarked that the right to Australia was a sore subject among the settlers and that they sought to satisfy their conscience in a number of ways. He was a perceptive tourist. Concern about the morality of settlement has run like an undercurrent through Australian life for 200 years. It re-emerged strongly in 1988 the Bicentenary year when the country focused on its past. It has always influenced white attitudes to the Aborigines and black attitudes to the settlers and their descendants. The large moral issues involved have also been linked with Australian attitudes to the Asian and Pacific environment—to our insecurity in being a European outpost in a non-European world. The documents to follow illustrate the debates which have punctuated public life since the 1820s.

The Problem Stated

Some of the most interesting comments on the moral problems associated with Australian settlement were made by a settler who, in 1826, wrote a report for the London-based Methodist Missionary Society.

A LETTER FROM A GENTLEMAN IN NEW SOUTH WALES, METHODIST MISSIONARY SOCIETY, IN CORRESPONDENCE: AUSTRALIA, 1812–26, AJCP.

New South Wales
October 1826

Dear Sir,

In venturing to state my Sentiments respecting the Aborigines of New South Wales, I am sensible that opinions formed during so short a residence must be more or less liable to error;—that I must, in some respects, betray a want of knowledge, which a more prolonged intercourse with the tribes of Natives could alone supply; but, as I know your competency to correct mistakes and to supply deficiencies, I shall merely commit to paper such thoughts as have arisen in my mind during my late excursion in search of land . . . When we look back on the past history of this unhappy race we find nothing to afford us consolation. If to the future, nothing to relieve the fearful foreboding . . . as to what will be if some expedient be not adopted to stay the waste of human life, which for now forty Years past has been diminishing such of the Aborigines as have been within the bounds of our population. Yes Sir, strange to say, Civilization has been the scourge of the Natives; Disease, Crime, Misery and Death, have hitherto been the sure attendants of our intercourse with them. Wherever we trace the steps of white population we discover the introduction of evil, the diminution of numbers, the marks of disease, the pressure of want, the physical and moral ruin of this people. If we inquire where are the tribes that once inhabited the places where Sydney, Parramatta, Windsor and other Towns now flourish, what will be the answer? Their existence is but a name. Assemble them and You will find a few miserable Creatures, Scarcely human in appearance, rise to bear witness that these spots were once peopled by Aborigines.

Could we but trace each poor individual's history, the lingering wretchedness of their conditions, what a tale would it unfold! Sir, it is a sad truth to assert that *our prosperity has hitherto been their ruin, our increase their destruction. The history of nearly forty years seals the veracity of this declaration.*

With such recollections as these fresh in our minds with what pleasure can we possibly survey the rapid encroachment of the Whites on these unhappy people. With what feelings can we look forward, but with those of deep regret, when we are assured that every new step which advances our interests is fatal to their existence. That every acre of land reclaimed by our industry is so much wrested from that pittance which Providence has bestowed on them.

If such be the truth the ruin of the Aborigines is inevitable, unless some expedient be devised to stay those evils. Tribe after Tribe must successively endure the same measure of sufferings until the total annihilation of the Natives of New Holland winds up the sad Catastrophe.

Should such a state of things be realized what will future generations think of our boasted Christianity, of our lauded Philanthropy, when our posterity read in the early page of Australia's history the misery and ruin which marked our adoption of this land;—when they find recorded that our proprietorship of the soil has been purchased at such a costly sacrifice of human happiness and life.

Truths like these, if recorded against us, will present a hideous picture of the present times! A picture which Mercy and Justice, Humanity and Religion would shudder to contemplate. And this guilty conduct we have reason to fear, will draw down the divine vengeance on the people who have so outraged the law of 'doing unto others what they would should be done unto themselves'...

Justice demands what humanity dictates and Christianity requires, that we should not usurp the possession of another's rights, however advantageous such may be to ourselves or however easy of accomplishment. Now we have usurped the rights of others in possessing ourselves of their land without even the offer of an equivalent. And we have thus done, also, at the heaviest possible cost to the rightful proprietors, viz. *their certain ruin.* We are therefore deeply indebted to this unhappy people; debtors beyond what money can repay or restitution compensate, for Property may be returned, but life cannot.

Deeply then are we in arrears to these injured Beings at whose expense we live and prosper. Their lands we have converted to our own use; their means of support we have destroyed, Kangaroos, and Oppossums, etc. have fled at the noise of the Axe, and the busy hum of civilized man. Have such a people then no cause for complaint,—No demand on our assistance? Can they not upbraid us with a want of principle, and for the evils we have introduced? Well may they adopt such language as this—'Where are our Ancestors'? 'Where is our Food'? 'Where are our Possessions'?... None can defend our Conduct towards the New Hollanders upon principle; let us not therefore persist in it, and let them yet receive from our hands some reparation for the wrongs we have done them.

* * * * * *

The colonists discussed the issues involved in private and public, in conversation, speeches, letters and diaries. A young man living on a pastoral station on the frontiers of settlement in southern Queensland in 1844 described an argument he had with three of his friends, in a letter to his mother and sister in England.

HENRY MORT TO HIS MOTHER AND SISTER, CRESSBROOK, 28 JANUARY 1844, MARY E. MCCONNELL, *JOURNAL FOR MY CHILDREN AND GRANDCHILDREN*, MSS, OXLEY LIBRARY.

Had a very animated discussion on the 'Moral right of a Nation to take forcible possession of a Country inhabited by savages'. John and David McConnell argued that it is morally right for a Christian Nation to extirpate savages from their native soil in order that it may be peopled with a more intelligent and civilized race of human beings etc. etc.

F. McConnell and myself were of the opposite opinion and argued that a nation had no moral right to take forcible possession of any place. What is your opinion on the subject? Don't you think it a most heinous act of any Nation however powerful, however civilized & however christianized that Nation may be—to take possession of a country peopled by weak & barbarous tribes, merely for the purpose of aggrandising the Christians at the expense of annihilating the unoffending & ignorant & Perhaps less avaricious savages? Yet I would say, let England increase her Colonial possessions, let her commerce be extended & let the Ministers of her Church carry out the sacred torch of civilization & religion so that the darkest & most remote recesses of heathen barbarism may be illuminated thereby.

* * * * * *

Harry Mort appeared to be having a bet each way. Over 40 years later a North Queensland miner, John Cook, had more definite ideas.

JOHN COOK TO S.W. GRIFFITH, 26 AUGUST 1891, QUEENSLAND STATE ARCHIVES, COL/A674, 11522 OF 1891.

Now I am not a bumtious [sic] sort of an individual and have stood a good deal of abuse from people on account of defending black people or the rightful owners of Australia—for even if we are born in Australia we are only usurpers here for if we take away the peoples' property without paying for it it does not matter much how we beautyfully [sic] try to cloak it it is and always must remain stolen property.

Subdue the Earth

The most popular justification for the settlement of Australia during the first part of the 19th century was to refer to the Bible and to God's instruction to humanity in the Old Testament to go forth and multiply and subdue the earth—or as the colonists argued—engage in agriculture.

C.P. HODGSON, *REMINISCENCES OF AUSTRALIA* ETC., LONDON, 1846, P. 75.

Thus far the Creator of the universe is just, in that he allows the superiority of civilization over barbarism, of intellect over instinct or brutish reason; thus far man is right, in that he has a legal right to improve the gifts of nature, and to convert barren and hitherto useless country into fruitful and productive territories; the world was made for man's enjoyment and created not as a beautiful spectacle, or spotless design, but as a field to be improved upon to the general interests of its inhabitants.

* * * * * *

Similar views were put forward by the famous radical clergyman, J.D. Lang, in a speech to a meeting of the Moreton Bay Friends of the Aborigines.

MORETON BAY COURIER, 19 JANUARY 1856.

They were certainly debtors to the Australian Aborigines, for they had ceased [sic] upon their land and confiscated their territory. In doing that, he did not think they had done anything wrong. God in making the earth never intended it should be occupied by men so incapable of appreciating its resources as the Aborigines of Australia. The white man had indeed, only carried out the intentions of the Creator in coming and settling down in the territory of the natives. God's first command to man was 'Be fruitful and multiply and replenish the earth'. Now that the Aborigines had not done, and therefore it was no fault in taking the land of which they were previously the possessors.

* * * * * *

A prominent Sydney barrister, Richard Windeyer, advanced similar arguments at a meeting of the Aborigines Protection Society in Sydney in 1838.

THE COLONIST, 27 OCTOBER 1838.

He entirely disagreed with the sentiments . . . that the natives had been usurped by *fraud and violence* by the Europeans, without paying any regard to the just rights of the natives. He could not look upon the natives as the *exclusive* proprietors of the soil. Nor could he entertain the ridiculous notion that we had no right to be here. He viewed colonization on the basis of the broad principle laid down by the first and great Legislator, in the command He issued to man 'to multiply and replenish the earth'. The hunting propensities of the natives caused them to occupy a much larger portion of land than would be necessary to their support, if it were under cultivation, and the only way to make them cultivate it, was by depriving them of a considerable portion of it. He thought the natives had no right to land. The land, in fact, belonged to him who should first cultivate it. Captain Sturt stated that he had travelled 300 miles, and only met one family. Now, he wished to know, whether these 300 miles belonged to this one family? No. *He* only had a title to lands, who first bestows labour upon it . . . He was himself a large landholder, and he certainly considered he had a good title to it. If we have no right to be here, we have nothing to do but to take ship and go home . . .

* * * * * *

Similar views were advanced by John West in his famous history of Tasmania written in 1852. In a section on the Aborigines he discussed the morality of settlement.

J. WEST, *HISTORY OF TASMANIA*, 2 VOLS., LAUNCESTON, 1852, II, PP. 92–6.

The original occupation of this country necessarily involved most of the consequences which followed: was that occupation, then, just? The right of wandering hordes to engross vast regions—for ever to retain exclusive property in the soil, and which would feed millions where hundreds are scattered—can never be maintained. The laws of increase seem to suggest the right of migration: neither nations nor individuals are bound to tarry on one spot, and die. The assumption of sovereignty over a savage people is justified by necessity—that law, which gives to strength the control of weakness. It prevails everywhere: it may be either malignant or benevolent, but it is irresistible. The barbarian that cannot comprehend laws or treaties, must be governed by bribes, or by force. Thus, that the royal standard was planted, need occasion no remorse . . .

It is common to speak of the guilt of this community; sometimes in variance with reason and truth. That guilt belongs only to the *guilty*; it cannot contaminate those who were helpless spectators, or involuntary agents. The doctrine of common responsibility, can only be applicable where all are actors, or one is the representative of all. The colonist may say, 'I owe no reparation, for I have done the native no wrong; I never contemplated aiding in his destruction: I have seen it with horror.' May the lesson of his sufferings become the shield of his race! Those who impute guilt to this colony, forget that its worst members are not stationary, and that many have borne away their guilt with their persons. That Being, who makes requisition for blood, will find it in the skirts of the murderer, and not on the land he disdained.

No man can witness the triumph of colonization, when cities rise in the desert, and the wilderness blossoms as the rose, without being gladdened by the change; but the question which includes the fate of the aborigines,—What will become of them?—must check exultation. The black will invade rights he does not comprehend; seize on stragglers from those flocks, which have driven off his game; and wound the heel which yet ultimately treads him to the dust. Such is the process—it is carelessly remarked, that the native is seen less often; that it is long since he ventured to cross the last line, where death set up landmarks in the slain. At length the secret comes out: the tribe which welcomed the first settler with shouts and dancing, or at worst looked on with indifference, has ceased to live.

If the accounts of discoverers have been too flattering to the native character, they are explained rather than contradicted by the early colonists. These describe with exultation, their new acquaintance, when writing to their friends: how peaceful, light-hearted, and obliging. They are charmed by their simplicity; they sleep among them without fear: but these notes soon changed; and passing from censure to hatred, they speak of them as improvident, importunate, and intrusive; as rapacious and mischievous; then as treacherous and blood-thirsty—finally, as *devils*, and beasts of prey. Their appearance is offensive, their proximity obstructive: their presence renders everything insecure. Thus the muskets of the soldier, and of the bandit, are equally useful; they clear the land of a detested incubus.

It is not in the nature of civilization to exalt the savage. Chilled by the immensity of the distance, he cannot be an equal: his relation to the white can only be that of an alien, or a slave. By the time astonishment subsides, the power of civilized men is understood, and their encroachment is felt. Fine houses garrison his country, enclosures restrict his chase, and alternately fill him with rage and sadness. He steals across the land he once held in sovereignty, and sighs for the freedom and fearlessness of his ancestors; he flies the track of his invaders, or surprises them with his vengeance;—a savage he was found, and a savage he perishes!

* * * * *

MITCHELL LIBRARY, STATE LIBRARY OF NSW. This illustration suggests that the artist felt considerable sympathy for the fate of the Aborigines, and that much may have been lost with the encroachment of neat huts and ploughed fields. 'The Old Camping Ground Revisited', *Illustrated Sydney News*, 12 November 1875.

When the conservative historian H.B. Turner reviewed relations between Aborigines and settlers at the beginning of the 20th century he had little difficulty in justifying colonization. He had dispensed with the appeal to the edicts of the Almighty and argued that Victorian progress alone was sufficient justification.

H.B. TURNER, *A HISTORY OF THE COLONY OF VICTORIA*, VOL. 1, LONGMAN, LONDON, 1902, P. 239.

The substitution of more than a million of industrious and peaceful people for a roaming, fighting contingent of six thousand cannot be said to be dearly purchased even at the cost of the violent deaths of a fraction of the most aggressive amongst them. The regrettable murders of harmless and inoffensive natives, which did occasionally take place, were the work of criminals, with which every community is infested, and which this community in its infancy was very especially exposed.

There is no serious stain necessarily resting upon the reputation of the colony from the retrospect of its treatment of the aborigines. It has been shown that costly and continuous efforts were made for the amelioration of their condition, and that these failed, not from neglect, but from the absolute incompatibility of the native character with even primary conditions of civilization.

Social Darwinism

By the time that Turner was writing, religious justification had been overtaken by the new secular faith in science. Social darwinism was the application to society of the evolutionary theories of Charles Darwin and first published in his great work *Origin of the Species* in 1859. These ideas came to dominate Australian thinking from the late 19th century until the 1940s and can be found in both popular and scholarly work.

THE AGE, 11 JANUARY 1888.

It seems a law of nature where two races whose stages of progression differ greatly are brought into contact, the inferior race is doomed to wither and disappear ... The process seems to be in accordance with a natural law which, however it may clash with human benevolence, is clearly beneficial to mankind at large by providing for the survival of the fittest. Human progress has all been achieved by the spread of the progressive races and the squeezing out of the inferior ones. No one can contend that it would have been better for the world had no European set foot on this continent and the blacks had been left to the chance of reaching civilization by a slow course of natural development. It may be doubted whether the Australian aborigine would ever have advanced much beyond the status of the neo-lithic races in which we found him, and we need not therefore lament his disappearance. All that can be expected of us is that we shall make his last days as free from misery as we can.

* * * * * *

Similar ideas were advanced by the historian Alexander Sutherland in his book *Victoria and Its Metropolis*, Melbourne, 1888, p. 29. It was written to celebrate the centenary of European settlement.

As to the ethics of the question, there can be drawn no final conclusion. Whether the European has a right to dispossess these immemorial occupants of the soil, or whether it is wicked that he should use his superior might in furthering his own interests at the expense of others, is a problem incapable of absolute determination. It is a question of temperament; to the sentimental it is undoubtedly an iniquity; to the practical it represents a distinct step in human progress, involving the sacrifice of a few thousands of an inferior race; he subtracts that as a small drawback to a vast good, and finds the balance enormously on the side of the good. But the fact is that mankind, as a race, cannot choose to act solely as moral beings. They are governed by animal laws which urge them blindly forward upon tracks they scarce can choose for themselves. If it is a divine law that the Anglo-Saxon people must double themselves every half-century, it must be a divine law that they are to emigrate and form for themselves new homes in waste lands. But every spot suitable for man's sustenance is held by some sort of human occupant; and, therefore, the Anglo-Saxon cannot choose but intrude upon the haunts of other races. When Victoria first felt the tide of immigration, England was peopled far beyond the then existing means of sustenance. Though trades extended and arts improved so as to yield employment for more and more, yet were there two hundred thousand human beings added to her population every year more than she could find food for. Had these stayed at home in deference to the claims which wandering savages might be supposed to have to forests that they merely hunted in, then for every savage so preserved, ten thousand human beings would have had to die by lingering deaths, the proximate causes many, but the ultimate cause the same distress from over-population; and the gloomy prospects that clouded the horizon in 1830 might have been a catastrophe of desperation in 1850. No Reform Bill could have prevented it.

In obedience to natural laws over which they had no control, seeing that they would not and could not brain their infants as the Australians did, the Anglo-Saxons sought these lands, and settled side by side with the natives. Their full justification lies in the fact that they recognized the claims of their sable brethren to subsistence from the soil, and though ruffianly individuals too often sullied the fame of their race by acts of cruelty, yet the wish of the whites as a community always was to secure, or, if necessary, to provide the means of subsistence to the aboriginals. Hence, as our future story will show, the appointment of protectors to guard the persons and rights of the native tribes; hence the formation of stations wherein the state supports and cares for them. But the altered conditions, which the white man's presence brought, have proved destructive to these poorly recuperative tribes. The vices which purge the civilized community of its inferior organizations, seized like a plague on the natives, and carried them off, as the smallpox did in the earliest years of settlement. Yet the actual hardship inflicted was not great. It was less a case of dying off than of failing to be born. The black man, indeed, paid the ordinary penalty we must all submit to; if he sadly regretted that he left none to inherit his blood we pity him, but our thoughts travel to the much harder scenes that would have been in city slums of the old world, and we are content with the balance.

Yet will there ever cling a pathos round the story of a vanishing race; and when we think of the agile forms that once held dominion over these widely forested lands; when we see them vanishing with terrible speed to be but a memory of the past, the contrast affects our feelings, even though our intellects refuse to be moved, recognizing the working of a law above that which man makes for himself.

The Rights of Conquest

Ever since the beginning of settlement there have been people who have argued that Australia was conquered by the British and that superiority in arms was in itself justification for everything that followed.

A correspondent in a Tasmanian newspaper raised many of the issues involved in the question.

LAUNCESTON ADVERTISER, 26 SEPTEMBER 1831

Are these unhappy people, the subjects of our King, in a state of rebellion or are they an injured people, whom we have invaded and with whom we are at war?

Are they within the reach of our laws; or are they to be judged by the law of nations? Are they to be viewed in the light of murderers, or as prisoners of war?

Have they been guilty of any crime under the laws of nations which is punishable by death, or have they only been carrying on a war *in their way*?

Are they British subjects at all, or a foreign enemy who has never yet been subdued and which resists our usurped authority and domination? . . .

We are at war with them: they look upon us as enemies—as invaders—as oppressors and persecutors—they resist our invasion. They have never been subdued, therefore they are not rebellious subjects, but an injured nation, defending in their own way, their rightful possessions, which have been torn from them by force.

* * * * * *

When faced with Aboriginal resistance settlers appealed to the right of the conqueror to impose his will by force.

MORETON BAY COURIER, 9 DECEMBER 1848.

If we hold this country by the right of conquest, and if that right gives us a just claim to its continual possession we must be empowered to enforce our claim by the strong arm, when necessary. One law *must* apply to all conquered nations.

QUEENSLAND GUARDIAN, 4 MAY 1861.

It must be constantly borne in mind that with the white man in this country, it is a question of forced occupation or none at all. We have decided beyond dispute that we are going to occupy the land and that all opposition must be overcome. This being our resolve, it remains only to be considered how we may do so with the smallest amount of violence— at the least expense of suffering.

* * * * * *

Some settlers thought that by accepting the reality of conquest they cut through the hypocrisy and ambiguity surrounding the question.

E.W. LANDOR, *THE BUSHMAN, OR LIFE IN A NEW COUNTRY*, LONDON, 1847, PP. 187—9.

Nothing could be more anomalous and perplexing than the position of the Aborigines as British subjects. Our brave and conscientious Britons, whilst taking possession of their territory, have been most careful and anxious to make it universally known, that Australia is not a conquered country; and successive Secretaries of State, who write to their governors in a tone like that in which men of sour tempers address their maladroit domestics, have repeatedly commanded that it must never be forgotten 'that our possession of this territory *is based on a right of occupancy*'.

A 'right of occupancy!' Amiable sophistry! Why not say boldly at once, the right of power? We have seized upon the country, and shot down the inhabitants, until the survivors have found it expedient to submit to our rule. We have acted exactly as Julius Caesar did when he took possession of Britain. But Caesar was not so hypocritical as to pretend any moral *right* to possession. On what grounds can we possibly claim a *right* to the occupancy of the land? We are told, because civilized people are justified in extending themselves over uncivilized countries. According to this doctrine, were there a nation in the world superior to ourselves in the arts of life, and of a different religious faith, it would be equally entitled (had it the physical power) to the possession of Old England under the 'right of occupancy'; for the sole purpose of our moral and social improvement, and to make us participants in the supposed truths of a new creed.

We have a right to our Australian possessions; but it is the right of Conquest, and we hold them with the grasp of Power. Unless we proceed on this foundation, our conduct towards the native population can be considered only as a monstrous absurdity. However Secretaries of State may choose to phrase the matter, we can have no other *right* of occupancy. We resolve to found a colony in a country, the inhabitants of which are not strong enough to prevent our so doing, though they evince their repugnance by a thousand acts of hostility.

We build houses and cultivate the soil, and for our own protection we find it necessary to declare the native population subject to our laws.

This would be an easy and simple matter were it the case of conquerors dictating to the conquered; but our Secretaries of State, exhibiting an interesting display of conscientiousness and timidity, shrink from the responsibility of having sanctioned a conquest over a nation of miserable savages, protected by the oracles at Exeter Hall, and reject with sharp cries of anger the scurrilous imputation. Instead, therefore, of being in possession by right of arms, we modestly appropriate the land to ourselves, whilst making the most civil assurances that we take not this liberty as conquerors, but merely in order to gratify a praiseworthy desire of occupying the country. We then declare ourselves seized in fee by right of occupancy. But now comes the difficulty. What right have we to impose laws upon people whom we profess not to have conquered, and who have never annexed themselves or their country to the British Empire by any written or even verbal treaty?

Frontier Realism

When confronted by humanitarian criticism settlers often adopted the stand that there was no middle way between conquest on the one hand and abandonment of the country on the other. All settlers, they argued, were equally to blame, all were beneficiaries of frontier violence.

'W.B.' IN THE *SOUTHERN AUSTRALIAN*, 8 MAY 1839.

It is useless now to speak about our right to come to New Holland and appropriate a part of it for our subsistence. It is now in vain to talk about the *injustice* of dispossessing the natives of part of their territories, though it were granted that they ever possessed them; every one of us by coming here, has, in reality, said that we either had such a right—or, not having the right, that we, at least, have the might, and resolved to exercise it. Let us therefore hear no more about the *right* or *justice* of our proceedings in this respect; or let every sincere objector on this ground, prove his sincerity, by at once leaving the country which he thinks he has so unjustly taken from another.

This therefore, by a short cut brings us to this point in the argument, viz. that whether by right or by might we are now located on a part of New Holland, beside a tribe of savages, whose manners and customs differ so much from ours, that we cannot live in peace with each other if they are permitted to follow their own inclinations. In short we must conform to *their* customs, or they must conform to *ours*; and there can be no difficulty in seeing, that it is them that must submit to us. I say must, not because I think that we have any right to force our laws and customs upon them, far less that they are under the slightest obligation to obey us unless they chose; but it is useless to disguise the fact—that we find it necessary, after taking their country, to force our laws upon them, to enable us to retain our possession. We have no better right to do so, however, than we have to occupy their country. It is, however, not necessary to discuss even this point; the sole question now being 'how can we most easily bring the natives under our dominion'? . . .

Some of your other correspondents talk with a laudable zeal for the honour of the English name and nation; thinking these compromised by the injustice done to the natives in taking possession of their country, but with strange inconsistency maintain, that the Aborigines should be punished and punished with severity when found guilty of aggressions upon the lives and property of the whites and (begging your pardon Mr. Editor) you state in your last leading article the same idea in other words. Now, I say, that upon the *principles of justice*, that we have *no right whatever* to punish the natives for spearing our sheep; or if we have they have an equally good right to inflict punishment on us for killing their kangaroos. May I question very much *our right* to punish them for killing ourselves—in doing so they may be following exactly their own laws, which are, no doubt as much respected by them as our laws are by us. Let us not flatter ourselves therefore, that we are acting from higher motives towards the natives than we really are. Our conduct towards them, will be, and has been, regulated upon the principle of expediency and self-interest. I should be as happy as anyone could be, to think it was otherwise, but I cannot lay the flattering unction to my soul.

* * * * * *

In a letter to the *Queenslander*, 8 May 1880, a correspondent using the nom de plume 'Never-Never' hit out at both the paper and other correspondents who had launched an attack on frontier violence.

Nothing is easier than to sit down at desk or table, and—on paper—work out a civilizing code that shall make the savage a docile tractable being, anxious to work and eager to please; and nothing harder than to take one's flocks and herds and go out into the desert and carry the theory into practice. As I intend to speak decidedly and openly on this subject, I may say that I have lived for sixteen years in this colony, and as a rule in outside country always; that I have been at the settlement of North and West, and have had to hold responsible situations where blacks had to be utilized for want of other labour. I think I may say that I have been as successful in getting as much work as possible out of them as other men; and that my experience pretty well comprises the boundaries of Queensland. I say this merely to show that I am not writing on a strange and unknown subject, but one that has been continually under my notice. Furthermore, I am what would be called a 'white murderer', for I have had to 'disperse' and assist to disperse blacks on several occasions . . . The question then arises, What lives are we to sacrifice—black or white? Are we to protect the black or protect the white? Shirk it as we will, this is the question. So long as we have country to settle, so long as men have to trust their lives to their own right hands, so long shall we come in contact with the natives, and aggressions and reprisals will take place . . . Is there room for both of us here? No. Then the sooner the weaker is wiped out the better, as we may save some valuable lives by the process. If the blackfellow is right in murdering white men for invading and taking possession of his country, then every white man, woman, and child who sits at home at ease in our towns and townships is a murderer, for if they had the courage of their opinions they would not stop on in a colony built up on bloodshed and rapine. Do they do this? do our black protectors—our philanthropists of today—go out and enquire into the truth of the many stories that are brought in from the back country, or do they rather sit in the high places, and partake of the corn and oil, leaving it to the sinful to go out and bear the heat and burden of the day? I rather think they do the last. Hide it as you will, our policy towards the black is bad, but it is only the game we played all over the world; and it starts with the original occupation of the country, and any other policy would be equally outrageous that entailed the taking of the land from the blacks. Say that we make reserves, and put the natives on them—have them guarded, and watched, and cared for—is not that just as arbitrary and high handed as shooting them? Would *we* recognize the justice of a superior race coming here, curtailing our boundaries, picking out our best country for their own use, and instituting a fresh code of religion, law, and morality for our benefit? Would we submit tamely, or prefer a quick and easy death to it? By its very presence and publication here the *Queenslander* recognizes the utility, to put it mildly, of dispossessing the blacks, and until it takes its departure to another country, and there preaches its sermon, its voice has a very hypocritical ring about it. We all want to get on here, and we all want to get somebody else to do the work needful; and if there is any dirty work necessary we are the first to cry out against it—when we are in a position to do so. This is the black question, as put forward by the protectors of the poor savage, I know full well that I shall hear of atrocities, of barbarities, and other disgraceful proceedings committed by the whites; but that does not touch the point at issue. The unanswerable fact remains that by overrunning this or any other country we expose the natives to the chances of suffering the rigours of guerrilla warfare— always the cruellest and worst—and, knowing that, we come here and take up our quarters with our eyes open; by our very presence in the land justifying the act of every white ruffian in the outside country. We are all savages; look beneath the thin veneer of our civilization and we are very identical with the blacks; but we have this one thing not in common— we, the invading race, have a principle hard to define, the harder to name; it is innate in us, and it is the restlessness of culture, if I dare call it so. The higher we get in the educated scale, the more we find this faculty; and if we do not show it in one shape we do in another. We work for posterity, we have a history, and we have been surrounded by its tales and legends since infancy. We look upon the heroes of this history as familiar friends, and in all our breasts there is a whisper that we too by some strange chance may be known to posterity. This brings us here to wrest the lands of a weaker race from their feeble grasp, and build up a country that our children shall inherit; and this feeling is unknown to the native of Australia. He has a short history, but it is more a matter of gossip than anything else, and only goes back one generation. He has no thought of the future, because he never knew of anyone being remembered more than a lifetime, therefore he has no interest but to pass through life as easily as possible, and he never seeks to improve land for those who will come after him. This justifies our presence here; this is the only plea we have in justification of it, and having once admitted it we must go the whole length, and say that the sooner we clear the weak useless race away the better. And being a useless race, what does it matter what they suffer any more than the distinguished philanthropist, who writes in his behalf, cares for the wounded half-dead pigeon he tortures at his shooting matches. 'I do not see the necessity,' was the reply of a distinguished wit to an applicant for an office who remarked that 'he must live'; and we virtually and practically say the same to the blacks and with better reason. We are pursuing the same policy in Zululand and Afghanistan, and, I suppose, on a more barbarous scale; the recital of all the atrocities going, of all the shooting and slaying by the Native Police, never alters the fact that, once we are here, we are committed as accessories, and that to prove the fidelity of our opinions we should leave the country.

Twentieth Century Debate

The anthropologist W.E.H. Stanner discussed the questions underlying Australian settlement in his chapter 'The Aborigines' published in J.C.G. Kevin, *Some Australians Take Stock*, London, 1939, pp. 3–6.

A tragedy underlies the rise of Australia from convict colony to Dominion Status. Often shamefully, and always miserably, the black tribes have died out wherever the whites have overrun the continent. The process of extinction still goes on in the remoter parts of the outback, out of sight of the white urban populations, and out of mind.

Year by year since 1788 the tribes have gone downhill. When the colony was founded the aborigines probably numbered at least 300,000, but have now dwindled to about 50,000. Their decline was most rapid in the nineteenth century, in the years when the upward surge of the white Australian population widened the inner frontiers of the settlement at great cost of body and spirit, no less to the invaders than to the dispossessed tribes whose lands they seized. Officially, there are supposed to be 60,000 natives still alive, but this guess (it is little more) is almost certainly wrong. No proper aboriginal census has ever been undertaken. A national headcount would probably show that 50,000 is a generous estimate. In any case it is a fact that about five-sixths of the original black population have been wiped out in 150 years, a rate equivalent to the death every year since 1788 of two large tribes totalling 1,700 souls.

The position today is that if every person of any degree of native blood now alive in Australia (including the wretched half-caste remnant in the eastern States) were brought together in the Northern Territory, there would be only one person to every ten square miles. The rest of the Commonwealth—six States, including Tasmania—would be completely empty of the former native population. About the only traces of them which would remain would be a few not-too-well-preserved rock carvings and paintings, a midden or two, some scanty records and collections in universities and museums, and a handful of inferior books. As it is, the old tribesmen of New South Wales and Victoria might as well have been shadows moving in the trees of the eighteenth century for all the imprint they have left behind. Will history be content to record their disappearance, and leave it at that?

The Australian point of view about it is shapeless. There are a few vestigial regrets appearing here and there in a mass of solid indifference. Implicitly, perhaps, this may mean that the loss of the primitive tribes is held, after all, to be heavily outweighed by the gain of the wealthy democracy which has replaced them; and it is true that there are now nearly 7,000,000 white Australians and a materially rich civilization where formerly there were 300,000 Stone Age aborigines and a wilderness. The material and social achievements of the 150 years since 1788 have indeed been unparalleled. It is also true that we embrace futility by piously wishing that the liberal regrets of today had been operative yesterday. The acquisitiveness and eagerness for progress drunk or sober were the driving incentives to colonial effort, and *laissez-faire* was still the golden rule on frontiers as well as in cities. Most of the conquest of Australia, and thus most of the obliteration of the tribes, took place between 1830 and 1890, the period in which economic expansionism, land hunger and pioneering were at their strongest. In such a period nothing which was then politically practicable could have been done to isolate the simple Australian tribes. They went down like ninepins, and made no mark on the ground.

There are few signs that the life and death of the tribes have made any mark at all on Australia; the thought, culture, even the literature of the dominion, have scarcely been affected. The native tragedy does not yet serve as the motif of dramatic, literary, or artistic work of any consequence. There are no epics on the last of the tribes. There are no national monuments to a vanishing people; yet there is a monument to a mythical Dog on a Tucker-Box nine miles from Gundagai. There are not even a great many writers commercializing the disappearance of a quaint and at least tourist-worthy race. Spurious boomerangs are still made for tourists, and others only slightly less spurious for innocents who visit the encampment at La Perouse, but most of these artefacts are so inferior that even tourists pass them by. Each year in the golden winter of north Australia motor-tourist parties are visiting some of the more accessible aboriginal camps, but they see little and take away less. The aboriginal languages have enriched the Australian vocabulary with such words as *boomerang, kangaroo, billabong, woomerah, warrigal, wallaby*, and some hundreds of others. Some of the Australian slang has its roots in the east-coast native dialects. A few hundred towns are known by more or less corrupted versions of improperly preserved native names, spelt in barbarous phonetics which cannot wholly corrupt the original and underlying euphony of the words. Yet for every Wooloomooloo and Dee-Why there is a second-hand Kensington and an imitation Kew.

* * * * * *

The distinguished historian Geoffrey Blainey considered the validity of the Aboriginal rights movement in 'Why the Aborigines Do Protest Too Much'.

WEEKEND AUSTRALIAN, 10–11 OCTOBER 1987.

I have a deep respect for many facets of Aboriginal history and many Aboriginal achievements. I also support the case for reasonable grants of land to Aborigines, though I do not see it as a right.

But I do not accept the picture often painted by those Aborigines demanding vast areas of land as well as a signed compact, with its undertones or proclamations of guilt.

In their claim for compensation, the Aborigines depict themselves as one nation, living in peace and harmony until the British arrived. They portray themselves as a people declining largely through the newcomers' firearms and cruelty, rather than by infectious diseases.

They also claim that the Aborigines were unique among colonial or modern peoples in that they lost their sovereignty without even the recognition of a treaty.

In my view that picture is mistaken.

The case for massive compensation also rests on the idea that any injustice committed far into the past can be publicly resurrected, with blame apportioned and reparations assessed.

The history of the world, sadly, is laced with injustices. Many of the worst examples in the past 150 years could be investigated.

Should we, for example, re-examine the plight of the 160,000 British convicts transported to Australia after 1788?

Perhaps half of the convicts, especially the women and children, were sent into permanent exile for reasons that we would now see as unjust or even outrageous.

Should we now search for their descendants in Australia and pay them an annual compensation? For while the Aborigines sadly lost their lands, the convicts suffered a similar loss—the loss of a homeland.

Do we also go back to World War I and decide that the relatives of those Australians who lost their lives should be paid continuous compensation, generation after generation, for the serious losses they suffered?

And do we reopen the wounds of World War II and decide that Germany and Japan and Italy should pay massive compensation, now that they are far wealthier than they were in 1945?

In international affairs, as in civil affairs, there normally has to be a kind of statute of limitations—a limiting of the time during which long-gone events can be revived and turned into litigation. Otherwise, countless wars of the past could well be fought again.

Some say that the Aborigines were victims of a unique injustice. Certainly it was devastating and tragic—but not, perhaps, unique.

Some commentators argue that the Aboriginal tragedy was unique because it harmed 'an entire race'. But that does not make it unique either.

In the persecution of racial minorities in China, Africa and Europe in the last seven centuries, infinitely larger numbers were killed or displaced than in Australia.

To be invaded and dispossessed of lands or culture has been a common experience in human history. It has been inflicted without a treaty, and even with a treaty, which the losers were forced to sign under protest.

I find it astonishing, therefore, that a constitutional committee set up by Canberra has now recommended that in 1988 we should proclaim to the whole world that Australia's right to this continent is dubious, and amend the Constitution to read: 'Australia is an ancient land, previously owned and occupied by Aboriginal peoples who never ceded ownership'.

On the other hand, a strong and compassionate case can be made that Aborigines, more than most other peoples, found it unusually painful and slow to adjust to the regime of their displacers or conquerors.

Certainly, they suffered long and hard from the loss of their lands, culture and, above all, their self respect.

I accept the argument that large numbers of Aborigines still suffer to an unusual degree, partly because of the European occupation of their lands.

The nation should certainly help and foster them, not because they are Aborigines, but because they are Australians.

Many Aborigines and their white supporters want a sweeping and permanent compensation for all Aborigines. But that argument rests more on racial criteria and a distorted view of history than on real need.

There is an irrefutable case, which is in the interests of all Australians, for a strong attempt to improve the daily life of many Aborigines.

In most facets of life, this will succeed only if that attempt is made primarily by Aborigines.

Their health will probably not be improved unless they themselves are determined that it should improve, and unless they have a powerful say in formulating the plans for that improvement.

The future of the Aborigines lies in looking to the 21st century, not to the 18th century.

Even if a minority of Aborigines succeed in keeping alive parts of their traditional culture, their future and success will be more as Australians than as Aborigines.

I am sure that some Aboriginal leaders, especially women, accept this view of their future.

The argument by white and black Australians that the events of 1788 are primarily to blame for the plight of many Aborigines is far too negative.

The solutions which have been proposed—massive land rights, white confessions of guilt and the granting of hereditary privileges to Aborigines—essentially look backwards.

Moreover, these solutions are based on a version of history which is much less valid than its exponents believe.

* * * * * *

Henry Reynolds turned his attention to the same question in the conclusion of his book.

THE OTHER SIDE OF THE FRONTIER, PENGUIN, RINGWOOD, 1982, PP. 200−2.

For many years white Australians have used Aboriginal words, symbols and designs to heighten their national distinctiveness and underline their separate identity. We can scarcely wonder if others judge us in this light and use our attitude to the Aboriginal historical experience as the acid test when they come to judge if white Australians have assimilated to the continent or are still colonists at heart. If we are unable to incorporate the black experience into our national heritage we will stand exposed as a people still emotionally chained to our nineteenth century British origins, ever the transplanted Europeans.

Much of Aboriginal history since 1788 is political history. Recent confrontations at Noonkanbah and Arukun are not isolated incidents but outcrops of a long range of experience reaching back to the beginnings of European settlement. The Tent Embassy of 1972 did not launch Aborigines into Australian politics but rather reminded white Australians of old truths temporarily forgotten. The questions at stake—land, ownership, development, progress—arrived with Governor Phillip and have been at the pivot of white–Aboriginal relations ever since. They are surely the most enduring issues of Australian politics and will in the long run prove to have been of much greater consequence than many questions which since the middle of last century claimed the attention of parliaments and public for a season or two.

Frontier violence was political violence. We cannot ignore it because it took place on the fringes of European settlement. Twenty thousand blacks were killed before federation. Their burial mound stands out as a landmark of awesome size on the peaceful plains of colonial history. If the bodies had been white our histories would be heavy with their story, a forest of monuments would celebrate their sacrifice. The much noted actions of rebel colonists are trifling in comparison. The Kellys and their kind, even Eureka diggers and Vinegar Hill convicts, are diminished when measured against the hundreds of clans who fought frontier settlers for well over a century. In parts of the continent the Aboriginal death toll overshadows even that of the overseas wars of the twentieth century. About 5,000 Europeans from Australia north of the Tropic of Capricorn died in the five wars between the outbreak of the Boer War and the end of the Vietnam engagement. But in a similar period—say the seventy years between the first settlement in north Queensland in 1861 and the early 1930s—as many as 10,000 blacks were killed in skirmishes with the Europeans in north Australia.

How, then, do we deal with the Aboriginal dead? White Australians frequently say 'all that' should be forgotten. But it will not be. It cannot be. Black memories are too deeply, too recently scarred. And forgetfulness is a strange prescription coming from a community which has revered the fallen warrior and emblazoned the phrase 'Lest We Forget' on monuments throughout the land. If the Aborigines are to enter our history 'on terms of most perfect equality', as Thomas Mitchell termed it, they will bring their dead with them and expect an honoured burial. So our embarrassment is compounded. Do we give up our cherished ceremonies or do we make room for the Aboriginal dead on our memorials, cenotaphs, boards of honour and even in the pantheon of national heroes? If we are to continue to celebrate the sacrifice of men and women who died for their country can we deny admission to fallen tribesmen? There is much in their story that Australians have traditionally admired. They were ever the underdogs, were always outgunned, yet frequently faced death without flinching. If they did not die for Australia as such they fell defending their homelands, their sacred sites, their way of life. What is more the blacks bled on their own soil and not half a world away furthering the strategic objectives of a distant Motherland whose influence must increasingly be seen as of transient importance in the history of the continent. Mother England has gone—the Empire too—yet black and white Australians have still to come to terms almost two hundred years after the British established their first beach-head at Sydney Cove.

2

THE FRONTIER: PEACEFUL SETTLEMENT OR BRUTAL CONQUEST?

The story of the exploration and settlement of the land is the central theme of Australian history. It is met with in school text-books, novels, poems, stories and films. It is a significant part of the 'legend' by which we define our Australian identity. The traditional account is of peaceful settlement, of a struggle against the land, not against other human beings for possession of the land. The bloodshed has often been conveniently forgotten. Yet the issue of frontier violence was frequently at the forefront of public debate during the 19th century. Explorers and pioneers were often quite frank about their part in the violent dispossession of the Aborigines. Some glorified the struggle, seeing it as one of the achievements of settlement. On the other hand there

THE FRONTIER

> *were always colonists who were horrified by the events on the frontier. The ensuing debate can be traced throughout the 19th century.*

Overview

The Victorian pioneer and author Edward Curr studied the question of Aboriginal–White relations in all parts of the continent. He wrote the best overview of frontier conflict.

JOHN OXLEY LIBRARY, BRISBANE. There are very few photographs of early contact with the Aborigines. This one is therefore unusually interesting. Taken on Bentinck Island in 1901 it may represent a first meeting at close quarters of white and black. The European extends a hand of friendship but keeps his gun ready for instant use. The women have picked up their children and retreated to the edge of the water. The one closest to the white man looks terrified. The one on the left hides her face in her hands.

E. CURR, *THE AUSTRALIAN RACE*, 3 VOLS. MELBOURNE, 1886, VOL. I, PP. 100–6.

In the first place the meeting of the Aboriginal tribes of Australia and the White pioneer, results as a rule in war, which lasts from six months to ten years, according to the nature of the country, the amount of settlement which takes place in a neighbourhood, and the proclivities of the individuals concerned. When several squatters settle in proximity, and the country they occupy is easy of access and without fastnesses to which the Blacks can retreat, the period of warfare is usually short and the bloodshed not excessive. On the other hand, in districts which are not easily traversed on horseback, in which the Whites are few in number and food is procurable by the Blacks in fastnesses, the term is usually prolonged and the slaughter more considerable. In the early days of our colonization, the area taken up by a squatter was small, from twenty thousand to one hundred thousand acres being the average extent of runs. At that period, also, a great many more men were employed in the management of a given number of sheep or cattle than at present, the result of which was that the settlers and their servants were not only able to cope with the Blacks, but their numbers inspired respect, and comparatively few were shot down. At that time, also, Government endeavoured, and in many cases, succeeded, in affording its protection to the Blacks. After stock had increased in the colonies, flocks became larger and population more disseminated, small bodies of mounted police were enlisted from the White population, and were employed to punish outrages committed by the Blacks. Subsequently, it became the custom to supplement the White police with a few Black troopers, who were found of great service in tracking their offending countrymen to their retreats.

Hence the meeting of the White and Black races in Australia, considered generally, results in war. Nor is it to be wondered at. The White man looks on the possession of the lands by the Blacks as no proper occupation, and practically and avowedly declines to allow them the common rights of human beings. On the other hand, the tribe which has held its land from time immemorial and always maintained, according to native policy, the unauthorized digging up of one root on its soil to be a *casus belli*, suddenly finds not only that strangers of another race have located themselves permanently on their lands, but that they have brought with them a multitude of animals, which devour wholesale the roots and vegetables which constitute their principal food, and drive off the game they formerly hunted. Besides this, the tribe finds itself warned by the more merciful settler, that as cattle will not remain on a run about which Blacks seek their daily food in the usual way, as they are alarmed at their very smell, that they must give up that practice, or take the consequence and be shot down whenever met. The tribe, being threatened with war by the White stranger, if it attempts to get food in its own country, and with the same consequences if it intrudes on the lands of a neighbouring tribe, finds itself reduced to make choice of certain death from starvation and probable death from the rifle, and naturally chooses the latter.

An Explorer Explains

The famous explorer Edward Eyre set out to explain why Aborigines attacked frontier settlers. He gave seven reasons.

E.J. EYRE, *JOURNALS OF EXPEDITIONS OF DISCOVERY* ETC., 2 VOLS., LONDON, 1845, 1, PP. 167–72.

First, That our being in their country at all is, so far as their ideas of right and wrong are concerned, altogether an act of intrusion and aggression.
Secondly, That for a very long time they cannot comprehend our motives for coming amongst them, or our object in remaining, and may very naturally imagine that it can only be for the purpose of dispossessing them.
Thirdly, That our presence and settlement, in any particular locality, do, in point of fact, actually dispossess the aboriginal inhabitants.
Fourthly, That the localities selected by Europeans, as best adapted for the purposes of cultivation, or of grazing, are those that would usually be equally valued above others, by the natives themselves, as places of resort, or districts in which they could most easily procure their food. This would especially be the case in those parts of the country where water was scarce, as the European always locates himself close to this grand necessary of life. The injustice, therefore, of the white man's intrusion upon the territory of the aboriginal inhabitant, is aggravated greatly by his always occupying the best and most valuable portion of it.
Fifthly, That as we ourselves have laws, customs, or prejudices, to which we attach considerable importance, and the infringement of which we consider either criminal or offensive, so have the natives theirs, equally, perhaps, dear to them, but which, from our ignorance or heedlessness, we may be continually violating, and can we wonder that they should sometimes exact the penalty of infraction? do not we do the same? or is ignorance a more valid excuse for civilized man than the savage?
Sixthly, What are the relations usually subsisting between the Aborigines and settlers, locating in the more distant, and less populous parts of the country: those who have placed themselves upon the outskirts of civilization, and who, as they are in some measure beyond the protection of the laws, are also free from their restraints? A settler going to occupy a

new station, removes, perhaps, beyond all other Europeans, taking with him his flocks, and his herds, and his men, and locates himself wherever he finds water, and a country adapted for his purposes. At the first, possibly, he may see none of the inhabitants of the country that he has thus unceremoniously taken possession of; naturally alarmed at the inexplicable appearance, and daring intrusion of strangers, they keep aloof, hoping, perhaps, but vainly, that the intruders may soon retire. Days, weeks, or months pass away, and they see them still remaining. Compelled at last, it may be by enemies without, by the want of water in the remoter districts, by the desire to procure certain kinds of food, which are peculiar to certain localities, and at particular seasons of the year, or perhaps by a wish to revisit their country and their homes, they return once more, cautiously and fearfully approaching what is their own—the spot perhaps where they were born, the patrimony that has descended to them through many generations;—and what is the reception that is given them upon their own lands? often they are met by repulsion, and sometimes by violence, and are compelled to retire again to strange and unsuitable localities. Passing over the fearful scenes of horror and bloodshed, that have but too frequently been perpetrated in all the Australian colonies upon the natives in the remoter districts, by the most desperate and abandoned of our countrymen; and overlooking, also, the recklessness that too generally pervades the shepherds and stock-keepers of the interior, with regard to the coloured races, a recklessness that leads them to think as little of firing at a black, as at a bird, and which makes the number they have killed or the atrocities that have attended the deeds, a matter for a tale, a jest or boast at their pothouse revelries; overlooking these, let us suppose that the settler is actuated by no bad intentions, and that he is sincerely anxious to avoid any collision with the natives, or not to do them any injury, yet under these even comparatively favourable circumstances, what frequently is the result? The settler finds himself almost alone in the wilds, with but few men around him, and these, principally occupied in attending to stock, are dispersed over a considerable extent of country; he finds himself cut off from assistance, or resources of any kind, whilst he has heard fearful accounts of the ferocity, or the treachery of the savage; he therefore comes to the conclusion, that it will be less trouble, and annoyance, and risk, to keep the natives away from his station altogether; and as soon as they make their appearance, they are roughly waved away from their own possessions: should they hesitate, or appear unwilling to depart, threats are made use of, weapons perhaps produced, and a show, at least, is made of an offensive character, even if no stronger measures be resorted to. What must be the natural impression produced upon the mind of the natives by treatment like this? Can it engender feelings otherwise than of a hostile and vindictive kind; or can we wonder that he should take the first opportunity of venting those feelings upon his aggressor?

But let us go even a little further, and suppose the case of a settler, who, actuated by no selfish motives, and blinded by no fears, does not discourage or repel the natives upon their first approach; suppose that he treats them with kindness and consideration (and there are happily many such settlers in Australia), what recompense can he make them for the injury he has done, by dispossessing them of their lands, by occupying their waters, and by depriving them of their supply of food? He neither does nor can replace the loss. They are sometimes allowed, it is true, to frequent again the localities they once called their own, but these are now shorn of the attractions which they formerly possessed—they are no longer of any value to them—and where are they to procure the food that the wild animals once supplied them with so abundantly? In the place of the kangaroo, the emu, and the wallabie, they now see only the flocks and herds of the strangers, and nothing is left to them but the prospect of dreary banishment, or a life of misery and privation. Can it then be a matter of wonder, that under such circumstances as these, and whilst those who dispossessed them, are revelling in plenty near them, they should sometimes be tempted to appropriate a portion of the superabundance they see around them, and rob those who had first robbed them? The only wonder is, that such acts of reprisal are so seldom committed. Where is the European nation, that thus situated, and finding themselves, as is often the case with the natives, numerically and physically stronger than their oppressors, would be guilty of so little retaliation, of so few excesses? The eye of compassion, or of philanthropy, will easily discover the anomalous and unfavourable position of the Aborigines of our colonies, when brought into contact with the European settlers. They are strangers in their own land, and possess no longer the usual means of procuring their daily subsistence; hungry, and famished, they wander about begging among the scattered stations, where they are treated with a familiarity by the men living at them, which makes them become familiar in turn, until, at last, getting impatient and troublesome, they are roughly repulsed, and feelings of resentment and revenge are kindled. This, I am persuaded, is the cause and origin of many of the affrays with the natives, which are apparently inexplicable to us. Nor ought we to wonder, that a slight insult, or a trifling injury, should sometimes hurry them to an act apparently not warranted by the provocation. Who can tell how long their feelings had been rankling in their bosoms; how long, or how much they had borne; a single drop will make the cup run over, when filled up to the brim; a single spark will ignite the mine, that, by its explosion, will scatter destruction around it; and may not one foolish indiscretion, one thoughtless act of contumely or wrong, arouse to vengeance the passions that have long been burning, though concealed? With the same dispositions and tempers as ourselves, they are subject to the same impulses and infirmities. Little accustomed to restrain their feelings, it is natural, that when goaded beyond endurance, the effect should be violent, and fatal to those who roused them;—the smothered fire but bursts out the stronger from having been pent up; and the rankling passions are but fanned into wilder fury, from having been repressed.

Seventhly, There are also other considerations to be taking into the account, when we form our opinion of the character and conduct of the natives, to which we do not frequently allow their due weight and importance, but which will fully account for aggressions having been committed by natives upon unoffending individuals, and even sometimes upon those who have treated them kindly. First, that the native considers it a virtue to revenge an injury. Secondly, if he cannot revenge it upon the actual individual who injured him, he thinks that the offence is equally expiated if he can do so upon any other of the same race; he does not look upon it as the offence of an individual, but as an act of war on the part of the nation, and he takes the first opportunity of making a reprisal upon any one of the enemy who may happen to fall in his way; no matter whether that person injured him or not, or whether he knew of the offence having been committed, or the war declared. And is not the custom of civilized powers very similar to this? Admitting that civilization, and refinement, have modified the horrors of such a system, the principle is still the same. This is the principle that invariably guides the native in his relations with other native tribes around him, and it is generally the same that he acts upon in his intercourse with us.

Shall we then arrogate to ourselves the sole power of acting unjustly, or of judging of what is expedient? And are we to make no allowance for the standard of right by which the native is guided in the system of policy he may adopt? Weighing candidly, then, the points to which reference has been made, can we wonder, that in the outskirts of the colony, where the intercourse between the native and the European has been but limited, and where that intercourse has, perhaps, only generated a mutual distrust; where the objects, the intentions, or the motives of the white man, can neither be known nor understood, and where the natural inference from his acts cannot be favourable, can we wonder, that under such circumstances, and acting from the impression of some wrong, real or imagined, or goaded on by hunger, which the white man's presence prevents him from appeasing, the native should sometimes be tempted to acts of violence or robbery? He is only doing what his habits and ideas have taught him to think commendable. He is doing what men in a more civilized state would have done under the same circumstances, what they daily do under the sanction of the law of nations—a law that provides not for the safety, privileges, and protection of the Aborigines, and owners of the soil, but which merely lays down rules for the direction of the privileged robber in the distribution of the booty of any newly discovered country.

The Impact

Aboriginal attack was a serious hazard for frontier settlers. Some settlers were financially ruined. An early Victorian settler, David Waugh, wrote to the government in 1840 describing how local Aborigines had ransacked his station and had driven him into bankruptcy.

PAPERS RELATIVE TO THE ABORIGINES: AUSTRALIAN COLONIES, *BPP*, 1844, PP. 114–16.

On his return from Melbourne, where he remained for about 18 days, disposing of his cattle, taking out his licence, and procuring supplies, he learned that the blacks had visited the station in his absence, murdered the two men in charge of the sheep, most of which they had carried away, plundered the head station of almost everything valuable and compelled the two men in charge of it to entirely abandon it.

The loss which the petitioner has sustained upon this occasion is so great as to exhaust all he has acquired during the six years he has been in the colony, and near to entirely ruin him in his means and prospects. He cannot estimate his direct loss as less than 900 pounds the particulars of which will appear from the schedule hereto annexed besides an indirect loss of 300 pounds, and the consequent derangement of all his plans, and nearly the complete loss of the season.

LIST OF ARTICLES taken by the Blacks from the station of D.L. Waugh, on the Dallatite or Devil's River.
Sheep destroyed or died from wounds:

Ewes in lamb	490
Rams	18
Wethers	30
Lambs, about	100
	638

The men killed were—
John Kyly, immigrant, native of Cork; Emmanuel Haly, per 'Recovery,' 1836, native of Yorkshire; sentence, life.
All their clothing and bedding, &c. &c. (of which a more detailed list was submitted to his Excellency).

* * * * * *

MITCHELL LIBRARY, STATE LIBRARY OF NSW. Early contact with the Aborigines and the recurrent skirmishing took place on the outskirts of European settlement. Few colonists had any personal experience of frontier life. They learnt of such events from the newspapers and from imaginative drawings produced by artists who may or may not have had any direct experience themselves. But such etchings were important because they shaped the perception of large numbers of people living in urban Australia. *Illustrated Sydney News*, 22 July 1876. The original caption follows:

The Dangers of the Palmer—A Native Attack

One of the greatest obstacles to the development of the Queensland goldfields, is the hostility displayed by the blacks to the miners who come amongst them in search of the precious metal. On the Palmer these treacherous foes have lately been very troublesome, and several of the enterprising prospectors have fallen victims to their clubs and spears. Our illustration depicts an occurrence that is unfortunately but too common. The man in the foreground, whose bronzed countenance and swarthy features show him to be no new chum at the wash-pan, has, assisted by

At times whole communities felt the impact of Aboriginal hostility. The small Queensland town of Maryborough was very vulnerable. It was surrounded by dense forest and local Aborigines could escape to nearby Fraser Island after carrying out robberies in or near the town. A local government official prepared a list of hostile Aboriginal activity over a six week period in November and December 1855.

ANNUAL REPORT OF CROWN LANDS COMMISSIONER FOR 1855, LETTERBOOK OF CROWN LANDS COMMISSIONER, WIDE BAY AND BURNETT, 1855–57, QUEENSLAND STATE ARCHIVES, 30/11.

November 7 Mrs. Whites's house robbed of a quantity of flour.
         9 Mr. Palmers stores robbed of tobacco.
       12 Cahills dray robbed of 200 lbs of flour.
       13 Hughes dray robbed of 200 lbs of flour, and a quantity of rations.
       18 Mr. Melvilles house robbed 60 lbs sugar.
       19 Jas. Frectius house robbed of tea, sugar and flour.
          Thos. McCrudden robbed of 100 lbs of sugar and 48 lbs of Flour.
       22 J. Church robbed of wearing apparel and rations.
          Mrs. Gadd—laundress robbed of linen, clothes etc.
       25 Mr. Reid's dray robbed of 70 lbs of Flour.
       26 Two of Mr. Reid's bullocks speared.
       27 Dowdle (?) speared by the Blacks. Denny and (?) beaten

---

his mate, pitched their rough tent in the centre of a clump of trees, which serve to protect them from the fierce rays of the mid-day sun. For some days their operations have been progressing undisturbed, but the alarm has just been given of the approach of the dusky foe. Hastily dropping the pans that they have been working with, they rush to the tent, and prepare to defend their little home. In these times their arms are always kept loaded. Snatching their rifles, they quietly await the approach of the invader. The war cry becomes louder and louder, and some eight or ten naked blacks are seen approaching with threatening gestures, brandishing their spears aloft. As the leader of the attack comes wildly on, and is preparing to discharge one of his weapons with the unerring skill of his race, the miner lifts his rifle to his shoulder and takes a steady aim. Probably they will be victorious, as the blacks seem to have only their native weapons to rely upon, in which case a few well-aimed shots will quickly cause them to retreat and give the objects of their attack time to shift quarters before they return in numbers that would ensure the carrying out of their murderous designs.

and ill used by the Blacks and robbed of Blankets clothing 145 lbs of Flour, 45 lbs of Beef, 50 lbs of Sugar, 2 lbs tea and a quantity of cooking utensils.
28 Jas Western robbed of 4 sovereigns and beaten.

December 2 Walsh's dray robbed.
5 George Furber and Jos. Wilmshurst murdered and a large quantity of rations blankets clothing and Tomahawks stolen.
6 Michael Joyce nearly murdered being left for dead and his hut robbed of rations, clothing etc.
7 Dowzer and (?) store broken into and robbed.
8 Mr Uhr's house and garden robbed.
9 Comm. C. Lands garden robbed.
10 Herberts drays robbed of 800 lbs of sugar and 600 of Flour.
11 Martins house entered.
17 Mr. Landrigans house entered and robbed at night.
18 J. Arthurs carrier dray robbed of a quantity of sugar and flour.
19 J. Leitchs house entered and robbed during the night.
20 Mrs. Bennet assaulted and head cut with a Tomahawk.
21 Mr. Uhrs store attempted to be broken into.
22 Powers store entered and robbed.

* * * * * *

A more comprehensive 'list of atrocities committed by the natives' was prepared by an official committee in Tasmania. It covered a 20 month period in 1830 and 1831.

J. WEST, *THE HISTORY OF TASMANIA*, EDITED BY A.G. SHAW, ANGUS AND ROBERTSON, SYDNEY, 1971, PP. 289—92.

1830.—January 1. William Smith, in the employ of—Triffet, jun., killed near the river Ouse. Piper's hut, at Bark Hut Plains, broken open and plundered of a musket, blankets, sugar, &c. Captain Clark's hut, at Bark Hut Plains, robbed, and his house entered by the natives.

February 1st. Mr. Brodie's hut, near the Clyde, was attacked while he was in it; he was speared in several parts of his body, but not mortally; they stole blankets, tea, sugar, &c. 9th. Mr. Mazetti's hut robbed; Lawrence Dering, servant to Mr. Bell, killed. 11th. Mr. Bell's house and servants attacked on Great Jordan Lagoon; the natives kept at bay from the house, but one man received a spear through the thigh. Mr. Hopley murdered about a mile from Mr. Betts'; James M'Carthy desperately

THE FRONTIER

MITCHELL LIBRARY, STATE LIBRARY OF NSW. At Gilberton, in 1873, the population of a hundred or so miners abandoned the town through fear of the Aborigines. The exodus began when the local clans drove the Chinese miners away from the river. The picture of Chinese diggers decamping with unseemly haste, pigtails flying, tells us much about contemporary attitudes to the Chinese as well. For an account of the desertion of Gilberton see the editor's book *Frontier*, Allen & Unwin, Sydney, 1987, pp. 20–22. *Illustrated Sydney News*, 15 February 1873.

---

wounded. 12th. Mr. Howells' dwelling hut burned, Mrs. Howells and her children narrowly escaping the flames. Twenty of Mr. Espie's sheep killed and maimed. Mr. Thomson's hut attacked by forty or fifty. Mr. Paterson's shepherd pursued by the natives. 17th. John Bluchaby and Philip Norby killed at Dysart parish, Oatlands, at noon day. Lawrence Murray, servant to Mr. Bell, killed. A child killed at Bagdad, near the road side. 20th. Mr. M'Rae's house, near Bothwell, plundered of flour, and within a mile of the military station, at Bothwell. Mr. Sherwin's house burned to the ground, with the greater part of his property; his servants' hut and fences also consumed. The Weazle Plains Hut burned down; a black man wounded, in the act of setting fire to it. 22nd. Captain Clark's barn and corn stacks consumed, containing 1,200 bushels of grain.

March 2nd. A hut, near Captain Clark's, fired. A hut, at Davis' Marsh, plundered. 9th. A mob of natives appeared at Captain Smith's hut, at his run; a part of them killed 100 of his sheep. 10th. Piper's hut fired, and partly destroyed. 11th. Captain Wood's hut, at Poole's Marsh, robbed. Mr. Jones' hut, Side Line Marsh, threatened. Mr Bisdee's hut attacked; also Mr. Thomson's stock hut, and Mr. Brodribb's, at the Black Marsh. Mr. Denholme's hut, at the same place, attacked, and his servant speared. 13th. M'Gennis' hut, Richmond district, plundered of muskets, powder, and ball, and every thing of value in the house. 15th. A hut, near the mouth of the Carlton River, attacked, a man and woman dangerously wounded; four spear wounds, and a cut on the head, supposed mortal. Another woman speared through the arm. 19th. About forty natives attacked the house of Mr. Brodribb, Black Marsh: they were divided into small parties, and made their attacks simultaneously: one man speared. On their being driven back, they proceeded to the hut of Mr. Thomson, which they robbed of every thing in it. On the same day, a man was speared in bed, at E. Danoven's, Black Marsh.

April 1st. John Rayner speared in several places, and dreadfully beaten by natives, at Spring Bay.

May 18th. Mr. Lord's hut, at Eastern Marshes, attacked; of two men in it, one was dangerously speared, and the other dreadfully beaten. The natives then plundered the hut, and retired.

June 1st. Mr. Sherwin's hut, Weazel Plains, plundered by the natives. 15th. The aborigines plundered the Den hut on the Lake River, of every thing in it, and murdered Mary Daniels, and her two infants, in cold blood.

August 7th. S. Stockman's hut, Green Pounds, plundered by natives. 9th. The death of Mr. Sharland (surveyor) and his men robbed of muskets, powder, and shot, by the natives; on the same day, government hut, between Bothwell and Blue-hill, robbed by natives, as well as the houses of Mr. Wood and Mr. Pitcairn. A man servant of Mr. Barrs, wounded. About forty natives met by Mr. Howells' party: a woman wounded. 23rd. The huts of J. Connell and Mr. Robertson attacked; the latter plundered. Mr. Sutherland's shepherds attacked, and their arms taken; one of them speared: arms taken from Mr. Taylor's hut. 24th. James Hooper killed, and his hut plundered of everything in it. The huts of Lieutenant Bell and Watts attacked by natives, who were repulsed from both.

September 8th. Captain Clark's shepherd attacked, but escaped. 13th. One man killed, and one man wounded, by the natives, on the banks of the Tamar. 14th. A man, employed by government at the lime kilns, near Bothwell, chased by natives, but escaped. 18th. A private, of the 63rd regiment, killed by natives: two sawyers speared, one of whom died of his wounds. 27th. Francis Broken speared and killed. 28th. Three men, at

THE FRONTIER

Major Grey's, wounded by natives, and one dangerously wounded with stones. 30th. Mr. G. Scott's house attacked by a mob of natives; they speared one man, and killed another—the body of whom they threw into the river. They ransacked the house of every thing they could find, and even went up stairs, and broke the doors open—a proceeding to which they had never before resorted. They took away blankets, shirts, sheets, knives, 600 or 700 lbs. of flour (which they tied up), half a basket of tobacco, 100 lbs. of sugar, a bag of tea, and a considerable quantity of slop clothing: so great ingenuity was displayed in the attack, that for some time it was supposed that Europeans had conducted it. On the same day, the natives plundered a hut, opposite to Mr. Scott's, of all the tea, sugar, flour and bedding, that were in it.

October 16th. The settlement at Sorell, attacked by natives: one severely wounded; four houses plundered of blankets, flour, tea and sugar, and clothes of every description. 18th. Captain Stewart's shepherd wounded by spears, and Mr. Guildas, a settler, killed by two spear wounds. 19th. Natives showed themselves on the farms of Messrs. Gatehouse and Gordon, and attacked the house of Mr. Gough, whom they wounded severely.

November 16th. Two huts robbed on the Ouse. 18th. Captain Wight's shepherd killed by natives; dreadfully mangled twenty-seven sheep. A hut on the South Esk attacked by natives: every thing portable sent off.

February 3rd, 1831. The natives attacked Mr. Bursby's house, on the Tamar; speared Mr. Wallace in several parts of the body, and inflicted several severe and dangerous wounds on his head: they likewise wounded a child. The hut of Allright attacked by them; plundered of every thing it had in it. The hut of Mr. Sutherland, North Esk, robbed: three horses speared, three others wounded. A woman, named M'Haskell, killed at Retreat, near Westbury: house robbed of 300 lbs of flour, knives and forks, blankets, chest of tea, 100 lbs. of sugar, tobacco, two casks of butter, three muskets, and powder. 7th. Stewart's house attacked by natives, who were beaten off.

March 8th. Two sawyers attacked by natives; severely wounded. Two huts, near New Norfolk, plundered. 12th. Mrs. Cunningham's hut, at East Arm, robbed by natives: she and the child wounded, very dangerously. 21st. Mr. Lawrence's servant murdered, and three men dangerously wounded by the natives, on Norfolk Plains.

April 5th. J. Ralton speared through the body, whilst at work splitting wood. 6th. N. Fitzgerald speared twice through the body, whilst sitting reading at the door of his cottage; the house plundered by the natives of guns, blankets, and other things. 7th. The same house again attacked.

May 10th. Hut on Patrick's Plains, containing government stores, burnt to the ground, by natives. Mr. Kemp's establishment, at Lake Sorell, attacked by a considerable mob of natives: the fire arms carried away, buildings totally consumed by fire; two men murdered, and one wounded.

June 6th. Several huts attacked, near Hunter's Hill; J. Triffits speared. Mr. Baretti's hut robbed, likewise Mrs. Bell's of every thing in it, and the wife of N. Long murdered. Mr. Clark's hut plundered.

September 5th. Thomas Smith, hut-keeper, at Tapsly, murdered: hut plundered. John Hignston speared, and hut robbed; four sawyers' huts robbed. 7th. B.B. Thomas, Esq., and his overseer, Mr. Parker, murdered near Port Sorell, by a mob of natives, whilst, actuated by the most humane views, they were endeavouring to carry the conciliatory measures of government into effect. Mr. Thomas had received ten spear wounds, and Mr. Parker eleven. Stocker's hut desperately attacked: a child wounded; a man, named Cubit, speared. 22nd. Mr. Dawson's hut, on Brushy Plains, attacked, and his servant severely beaten with waddies. 23rd. Mr. Dawson's servant, Hughes, severely beaten by natives, nearly losing his life.

October 3rd. The natives, having possession of fire-arms, attacked and robbed the premises of constable Bird, and plundered the house of Mr. Amos, jun.

The Settler Response

The colonists were not necessarily antagonistic to the Aborigines they came into contact with. Some frontier settlers were able to establish friendly relations with neighbouring clans; others began with good intentions but ended up with blood on their hands. The British scientist J.B. Jukes had considerable experience with Aborigines around the coast of Australia during a surveying voyage of the *HMS Fly* in the 1840s. Jukes began with a humanitarian interest and engaged in a series of friendly encounters at various points along the Queensland coast. The spearing of one of the ship's company radically changed his attitude.

J.B. JUKES, *NARRATIVE OF THE SURVEYING VOYAGE OF* HMS FLY, LONDON, 1847, PP. 109–14.

After meeting the rest of the party, and telling those unarmed to get out of the bushes, which were thin straggling trees about eight feet high, I met Yule limping along, and asked him if there was any one behind. 'Yes,' said he, 'one man,' whom I immediately saw pushing through the bushes, about fifteen yards from me, and a little on my right . . .

At the same time I saw a black fellow standing in the bushes about twenty-five yards from me, and a little on my left. I called to our man to come on, and looked towards him to enforce it by gesture, and on turning my eyes again to the black, I saw him with his spear quivering over his head fixed in the throwing stick, and in the act of taking aim. I had my gun cocked in my hand, and immediately drew both triggers, but, alas! they both missed fire, the spear flew, and our man fell. The black fellow paused an instant, looking intently to see if his spear had taken effect, giving me time again to cock both barrels and cover him, but with the same ineffectual result, when he dived into the gully at his back and disappeared. Yule, who, when I met him, had guessed there was something wrong by the tone of my voice, and stopped, ran forward to pick up our man, whose name was Bayley. After rushing to the edge of the ravine, shouting for muskets, and finding no black fellow to be seen, I went to him and found Yule breaking off the long end of the spear, which was deeply fixed in the back between the shoulder blades, and the poor fellow writhing on his hands and knees in great pain, begging us to take it out. This could not now be done, and on M'Clatchie saying he must be taken on board first, he was carried down to the boat, while the Doctor and myself, with another man, kept guard at the edge of the ravine. In order to try my gun, I fired into the bushes of the ravine, and this time, although I had done nothing to it, not even put on a fresh cap, both barrels went off. I had hardly loaded again before we saw the black fellow emerge from some bushes on the other side the ravine, and walk across a sandy plain about 150 yards off, with a jaunty step, as if congratulating himself on his prowess. Three bullets whistling about his ears, and striking up the dust of the plain before him, soon made him change his pace, and he rapidly disappeared. This time, when it was of little moment, the gun went off at the first trial; after this we saw no more of them, and the party having reached the boat we slowly retired, burning with vexation. It was the first time in my life in which I had seen wounds (and, as it turned out, death) inflicted in open field, or in any kind of strife, and the sensations were as new to me as they were unpleasant. A burning feeling of mixed rage and grief, and a kind of animal craving for revenge, seemed to take possession of the heart, and a reluctance to leave the spot till some kind of amends had been obtained. A glance at the broken nature of the country, however, full of scrubs and gullies, shewed how impotent any pursuit would be; and Yule, who hastened off with the Doctor and the wounded man in the first boat, gave us positive orders not to remain behind, but to follow immediately.

It was not till we got on board that we thought of the canoe, or we might at least have gone and brought off that, as some slight punishment, and it might have drawn them from their lurking-holes to receive a greater.On getting on board, we had great difficulty in withdrawing the spear from the wounded man, and when we did so, we found that the point and barb had remained behind. Bayley lingered till the third day, when he died. He was an excellent man: quiet and attentive to his duty, with a good character in every respect.

It appeared from the account of the cockswain of the boat, that, while we were on the hill, the natives came down about the boats unarmed; that they were treated kindly, without any dispute or apparent offence given them, except that they were prevented taking several things out of the boats, which they attempted to do; that they went away together, and were again returning to the boats with their spears, apparently to attack and plunder them, when our coming down the hill stopped them. Annoyance at being thus frustrated in their hopes of plunder was the only reason we could assign for this treacherous and cowardly attack upon us. Cowardly, as they waited till the last man's back was turned, and ran as soon as they had speared him. I have always joined in reprobating the causeless injuries sometimes inflicted by civilized, or quasi-civilized man, upon the wild tribes of savage life; and many atrocities have doubtless been committed in mere wantonness, and from brutality or indifference. I have always looked, too, with a favourable eye on what are called savages, and held a kind of preconceived sentimental affection for them, that I believe is not uncommon. I had been inclined to suppose that they were rarely the aggressors, and were always more sinned against than sinning. One such practical example as this, however, wrought a great change in my feelings on these points; and though far, I hope, from abetting cruelty, I could make great allowances for any one who, under such circumstances as I have detailed, took a larger revenge than the strict justice of the case demanded. I felt that the life of one of my own shipmates, whatever his rank might be, was far dearer to me than that of a wilderness of savages, and that to preserve his life or avenge his death I could willingly shoot a dozen of these black fellows; and I could read the same feelings in the eyes of those around me. Nor was this feeling very transient; for many days or weeks after, it would have been felt as a relief by all those who saw Bayley's fall, to have come into collision with any party of black fellows they could have been justified in firing on.

Punitive Expeditions

Privately organized parties of settlers rode out to 'punish' the Aborigines for spearing stock or to seek revenge for attacks on Europeans. They were a feature of all parts of Australia from the late 18th century to the early 20th century.

G.S. Lang's pamphlet provided one explanation of settler behaviour.

THE FRONTIER

THE ABORIGINES OF AUSTRALIA MELBOURNE, 1865, P. 42.

When white men are murdered, it is indispensable to punish the murderer; but still the ordinary law is powerless, as the blacks never leave any survivor who might give legal evidence. The frontier settlers, however, can always obtain conclusive evidence from the natives themselves, and upon such testimony they are often obliged to act. The usual course is then for a party of whites, guided by blacks usually of another tribe, to start during the night, creep up close to the enemy's camp, wait till daybreak, and then commence the onslaught, in which, even when the greatest possible care is taken to avoid it, the women and children are sometimes shot. Everything in the camp is then destroyed, the blacks are scattered, destitute of the means of existence, and, of course, perfectly desperate. I must say this for the whites, however, that (although I have known brutal exceptions) whenever they can bring the blacks to a fair fight they do fight them fairly, and not unfrequently have been beaten, for the chances of such a contest are not so unequally divided as may be supposed. A blackfellow, with some eight or ten spears in his hand and some paddy-melon sticks, will throw them all while a white man is reloading after firing two shots; and I have known one man to be pierced in the thigh by two spears successively, thrown at seventy yards off. The attacks of the natives on the other hand are always sudden, and so carefully arranged, that when a white man is attacked his escape is almost hopeless, while his murderers are equally certain of escaping with impunity, and the whites become so furious that they often come in time to follow the treacherous tactics of the blacks with even greater cruelty than themselves. How aggravating these atrocities are, few can conceive who have not experienced and lived in the daily and hourly risk of them. A friend told me that when he came upon two fine young men lying murdered, whom he had induced to come from his father's estate to enter his service, he could have eaten the blacks, and from that time killed ruthlessly, yet was a most benevolent man. Bloodthirsty as the blacks are, the whites have quite or more than equalled them . . .

* * * * * *

Despite the widespread activity of punitive expeditions such attacks on the Aborigines were illegal and killing them was murder. Not surprisingly, then, few eye witness accounts of punitive expeditions have survived and those that have are often deliberately vague as to time and place and participants. The following account comes from a book of reminiscences relating to northern New South Wales in the 1840s.

42   DISPOSSESSION

MITCHELL LIBRARY, STATE LIBRARY OF NSW. The punitive expedition was a common feature of frontier life. This etching, taken from a Sydney newspaper, was accompanied by a short explanatory note:

> An ordinary scene in bush life. Some natives having attacked a station and murdered some of their mates, are followed by a couple of their companions. Our engraving represents the moment when the pursuers are just on the eve of firing on the natives.

Illustrated Sydney News, 16 March 1866

F. ELDERSHAW, *AUSTRALIA AS IT REALLY IS*, LONDON, 1854, PP. 63–73.

Towards the close of the autumn of 41 after a beautiful and most prosperous season, we were miserably startled from the unconscious lull of security which long continued inpunity from harm invariably produces, by the appalling intelligence that one of my out-stations had been attacked, its three unfortunate occupants brutally massacred, and the sheep, two thousand in number, carried off as spoils, together with whatever stores and implements the station had been provided. Accompanied by three neighbours, I immediately proceeded to reconnoitre the spot of this atrocity. The tracks, camp fires, and numerous *gunyahs* indicated clearly the recent presence of a tribe numbering, we surmised at least two hundred. The hut was empty, but we could plainly perceive, by blood and other evidences of deadly struggle, that one at least of the unfortunate fellows had here met his dread end. A still further and more minute examination of every track and indication around revealed to our practiced eyes, mysteriously, but unmistakably, full evidence of the conduct of the whole catastrophe. The watchman, it was apparent, had been sneaked upon in his hut, and while in the act of turning or in some way attending to a 'damper' baking in the ashes, speared in the back. The shepherds, had been waylaid on their return with the flocks, and destroyed probably without the chance of an effort for their lives.

Possessed of all the information which it was possible thus to obtain, we returned to arrange a party for immediate pursuit. Each of our men was savagely anxious to be chosen for this painfully imperative task; the thought of their butchered comrades, with sundry vivid reminiscences of personal escapes from a fate as dreadful, made them pant for an opportunity of vengeance on the heads of their wily and dangerous enemy. We made our selection from among them, however, upon other and I hope sounder grounds than could be gathered from the noisiest ebullition of excited feeling. Including my neighbouring friends, we mustered a party of ten, well mounted and accoutred, and taking with us ten days provisions, we started at day break on the following morning in pursuit.

[The party tracked the Aborigines and attacked their camp, which was on the edge of a cliff, from both above and below.]

Pouring in, therefore, upon the eager but unconscious crowd below the contents of ten barrels, a fearful charge was effected in their savage glee; a scream of mingled consternation and surprise, a rush in reckless despair towards the only means of escape from their exposed and dangerous elevation, a murderous and tumultuous struggle amongst themselves, their yells of mingled hate and agony, as grappling together in the last grasp of death the foremost of them fell, urged over the ledges' brink by the pressing crowd behind that madly hurried on, into the yawning sepulchre beneath, was all of the horrid scene that the increasing darkness of the night enabled us clearly to perceive.

We had now reloaded, and our party from below, pushing forward to the scene of conflict, poured in a deadly volley upon the thronging crowds that lined the rocky entrance to this fatal ledge—back flew the despairing wretches from that dreadful spot—again a volley from our party on the heights dealt frightful havoc in their ranks. The utmost wildness of despair now ceased upon them all; some actually dashed themselves in frantic violence to the depths beneath . . . Such of the horrid carnage below, I fain would have retired from the dreadful spot, but all my efforts and entreaties, threats were utterly useless. Shot after shot, with curses wild and deep, the excited fellows launched at their hated foes—their butchered comrades' blood was that night fearfully avenged.

Official Violence

As well as the private punitive parties the Aborigines were subject to a variety of government sponsored 'police' actions. During the early history of New South Wales, Tasmania and Western Australia the resident military forces were used. The so called Battle of Pinjarra saw a concerted attack on the Aborigines on the outskirts of the Swan River settlement.

G.F. MOORE, *DIARY OF TEN YEARS' EVENTFUL LIFE OF AN EARLY SETTLER IN WESTERN AUSTRALIA*, LONDON, 1884, PP. 240—3.

Crossing the ford, where the river had an average depth of 2½ feet, and was running about 1½ miles an hour to the north, an Easterly course was taken for the purpose of looking at the adjoining country, but the party had not proceeded more than a quarter of a mile over the undulating surface of the richest description, covered with nutritious food for cattle, when the voices of many natives were heard on the left. This being a neighbourhood much frequented by the native tribe of Kalyute, which had long been indulging in almost unchecked commission of numerous outrages and atrocious murders on the white people resident in the district, and which had hitherto succeeded in eluding the pursuit of the parties that had been searching for them since their treacherous murder of Private Nesbitt of the 21st Regiment, and the spearing of Mr. Barron only a few weeks ago—the moment was considered propitiously favourable for punishing the perpetrators of such and other diabolical acts of a similar nature, should this prove to be the offending tribe. For the purpose of ascertaining that point, His Excellency rode forward 200 or 300 yards with Messrs. Peel and Norcott, who were acquainted both with the persons of the natives and with their language, and commenced calling out and talking to them for the purpose of bringing on an interview. Their own noise, was however, so loud and clamorous, that all other sounds appeared lost on them, or as mere echoes.

No answer being returned, Captain Ellis, in charge of the mounted police, with Mr. Norcott, his assistant, and the remaining available men of his party, amounting to three in number were despatched across the ford again to the left bank, where the natives were posted, to bring on the interview required. The instant the police were observed approaching at about 200 yards distance, the natives, to the number of about 70, started on their feet, the men seized their numerous and recently made spears, and showed a formidable front, but finding their visitors still approached, they seemed unable to stand a charge, and sullenly retreated, gradually quickening their pace until the word 'forward' from the leader of the gallant little party brought the horsemen in about half a minute dashing into the midst of them, the same moment having discovered the well-known features of some of the most atrocious offenders of the obnoxious tribe. One of these, celebrated for his audacity and outrage, was the first to be recognized at the distance of five or six yards from Mr. Norcott, who knew him well, and immediately called out, 'These are the fellows we want, for here's that old rascal Noonar,'—on which the savage turned round and cried with peculiar ferocity and emphasis, 'Yes, Noonar me,' and was in the act of hurling his spear at Norcott, in token of requital for the recognition, when the latter shot him dead.

The identity of the tribe being now clearly established, and the natives turning to assail their pursuers, the firing continued, and was returned by the former with spears as they retreated to the river. The first shot, and the loud shouts and yells of the natives, were sufficient signal to the party who had halted a quarter of a mile above, who immediately followed Sir James Stirling, at full speed, and arrived opposite Captain Ellis' party just as some of the natives had crossed and others were in the river. It was just the critical moment for them. Five or six rushed up the right bank, but were utterly confounded at meeting a second party of assailants, who immediately drove back those who escaped the firing. Being thus exposed to a cross fire, and having no time to rally their forces, they adopted the alternative of taking to the river, and secreting themselves amongst the roots and branches and holes on the banks, or by immersing themselves with the face only uncovered, and ready with a spear under water, to take advantage of any one who approached within reach. Those who were sufficiently hardy or desperate to expose themselves on the offensive, or to attempt breaking through the assailants, were soon cleared off, and the remainder were gradually picked out of their concealment by the cross fire from both banks, until between 25 and 30 were left dead on the field and in the river. The others had either escaped up and down the river, or had secreted themselves too closely to be discovered except in the persons of eight women and some children, who emerged from their hiding places (where, in fact, the creatures were not concealed), on being assured of personal safety, and were detained prisoners until the determination of the fray. It is, however, very probable that more men were killed in the river, and floated down with the stream.

Notwithstanding the care which was taken not to injure the women during the skirmish, it cannot appear surprising that one woman and several children were killed, and one woman amongst the prisoners had received a ball through the thigh. On finding the women were spared, and understanding the orders repeatedly issued to that effect, many of the men cried out they were of the other sex; but evidence to the contrary was too strong to admit the plea. As it appeared by this time that sufficient punishment had been inflicted on this warlike and sanguinary tribe by the destruction of about half its male population, and amongst whom were recognized, on personal examination, fifteen very old and desperate offenders, the bugle sounded to cease firing, and the divided party reassembled at the ford, where the baggage had been left in charge of four soldiers, who were also to maintain the post. Here Captain Ellis had arrived, badly wounded in the right temple by a spear at three or four yards distance, which knocked him off his horse, and P. Heffron, a constable of the police, had received a bad spear wound above the right elbow. No surgical aid being at hand, it was not without some little difficulty the spear was extracted, and it then proved to be barbed at the distance of five inches from the point.

Having recrossed the river in good order with the baggage on three horses, the whole party formed a junction on the left bank, fully expecting the natives would return in stronger force, but in this were disappointed. After a consultation over the prisoners, it was resolved to set them free, for the purpose of fully explaining to the remnant of the tribe the cause of the chastisement which had been inflicted, and to bear a message to the effect that, if they again offered to spear white men or their cattle, or to revenge in any way the punishment which had just been inflicted on these for their numerous murders and outrages, four times the present number of men would proceed amongst them and destroy every man, woman and child.

* * * * * *

By far the most lethal force used against the Aborigines was the Queensland Native Mounted Police. It was first used on the northern frontier of New South Wales in 1848 and was still being used in modified form in the more remote parts of the state in the early 20th century. The force was officered by Europeans, who

THE FRONTIER

A Native Police detachment posing for a photograph in the 1860s in full uniform. The three European officers are a study in themselves. The Sub-Lieutenant in the middle looks cold and sadistic. One sergeant is large and lecherous, the other diminutive but full of self importance. Source: E. B. Kennedy, *The Black Police of Queensland*, London, 1902, frontispiece.

---

controlled a body of Aboriginal troopers over 200 strong in the 1870s. The Aborigines were recruited far from the districts of the forces' operations and had no cultural or kinship links with frontier tribes. Few official records of the force have survived but it is possible to learn something about its activities from instructions issued by the Commandant in January 1858.

INSTRUCTIONS OF THE COMMANDANT TO OFFICERS AND CAMP SERGEANTS, SELECT COMMITTEE ON NATIVE MOUNTED POLICE, *QVP*, 1861, PP. 151–52.

It is the duty of the Officers at all times and opportunities to disperse any large assemblage of blacks; such meetings, if not prevented, invariably lead to depredations or murder; and nothing but the mistaken kindness of the Officers in command inspired the blacks with sufficient confidence to commit the late fearful outrages on the Dawson River [the attack on Hornet Bank Station in 1858]. The Officers will therefore see the necessity of teaching the aborigines that no outrage or depredation shall be committed with impunity—but on the contrary, retributive justice shall speedily follow the Commission of crime; nevertheless the Officers will be careful in receiving reports against the blacks, as it frequently happens that mistakes are made as to the identity of the aggressors. In case of any collision with the aborigines a report is to be forwarded to the Commandant without delay.

(Signed) E.V. Morisset
Commandant Native Police

* * * * * *

Public opinion was deeply divided over the activities of the Queensland Native Police. Controversy surrounded it throughout its history. In 1880 the Colony's leading newspaper, the *Queenslander*, observed that 25 per cent of the population were strong supporters of the force, another 25 were as strongly against it. The 50 per cent in the middle were indifferent to the moral issues involved. Conflicting opinion can be illustrated by three extracts from local newspapers. In the first, the writer refers to the attack on Maryborough's 'town-blacks' by the Native Police under Lieutenant Bligh.

LETTER TO EDITOR, *MORETON BAY COURIER*, 25 APRIL 1861 FROM 'A BELIEVER IN GASSON'S STATEMENT'.

On the morning of the 3rd February . . . Mr. Bligh, with a party of the police, rode into town early, and fired several shots at a few blacks encamped near Cleary's; then came into East Maryborough, charged a camp near Mr. Melville's, drove the poor creatures from it—some through the town, some into the river—and commenced butchering them forthwith. 'Darkey,' who had been constantly employed in the town—who could have been apprehended at any moment, had there been any desire, or occasion, was shot down opposite Mr. Palmer's, where his body was left, and subsequently roasted. 'Young Snatchem,' an excellent and industrious black, was driven into the river, near the public wharf,— scores of men, women, and children stood by, and Lieut. John O'Connell Bligh stationed himself in the bow of a boat, which was in readiness, and forty or fifty shots were actually fired, five or six by Mr. Bligh himself. The boat overtook him (the black) in an exhausted state, and [Bligh] lowered his carbine, and shot the defenceless, tired, unresisting wretch, in the back. 'Yankine,' who was then wounded, has since recovered. Against him, there never was a single charge. Another poor fellow, blind in one eye, an old grey headed man, was taken prisoner, triumphantly marched in handcuffs through the town, led out some miles by these bloodthirsty

THE FRONTIER

brutes, and has never since been seen. The blacks immediately brought in word that he had been shot near the Six-Mile Creek, and as the old creature was well known here, and a frequent visitor at certain houses, it is beyond doubt that he too had been, if possible, more barbarously murdered than the others. Thus terminated the foulest deed—and shall I say, the foulest day—Maryborough ever witnessed.

* * * * * *

Six years later a miner in the small community of Morinish wrote to the local press describing another Native Police attack.

'A MINER ON MORINISH', *ROCKHAMPTON BULLETIN*, 18 JUNE 1867.

Sir,—The inhabitants of the quiet New Township of Morinish were startled this morning, a little before sunrise, by hearing a volley of eight shots fired in quick succession, in the direction of the Blacks' Camp, which for some weeks past has been located a few hundred yards to the east of the township.

The first surmise was that it was some early kangaroo hunter, but the crack was too sharp for that, and the number of discharges too numerous to allow of such a supposition bearing a second thought, and a rush in the direction of the camp was immediately made by those who were so early a-foot, where a scene presented itself alike brutal on the part of the perpetrators, and revolting to the feelings of those who saw it. The native camp was deserted, but around the fires nearest to the township lay the scanty garments of men, gins, and piccaninnies, many of them saturated with blood, while the track of the fugitives could be easily traced by the trail of blood leading from the fires in every direction. At the fire nearest the Creek, which separates the camp from the township, and around which a number of blacks apparently had been sleeping, two pools of blood and brains showed where foul murder had been perpetrated, and a gin's clothing, all stained with blood, was also found, exactly as if the unfortunate blacks had just left the articles on finding herself wounded. A little further on, close to a fire, where one person, probably an old man, had passed the night, another puddle of blood and brains was found, and the surrounding ground bore all the traces of the flight of wounded men, and of dead bleeding bodies having been dragged over it. The first body discovered was that of a black boy called Tommy, and better known as 'Mr. Pattison', from having been a stockdriver in the employment of Mr. Joseph Pattison, which led him jocularly to adopt the name, and stamped him as a well-known character in the district. The poor fellow was found lying in a water hole with three wounds, one through the arm, another through the chest, and a third

MITCHELL LIBRARY, STATE LIBRARY OF NSW. This illustration casts the Native Police in a favourable light, riding heroically to the rescue of beleaguered pioneers. *Illustrated Sydney News*, 12 October 1876. The original caption read:

A Skirmish With Aborigines At Creen Creek, Queensland.
We have been favoured by a gentleman (who was travelling in the vicinity) with the drawing for our engraving of a skirmish between the Aborigines and the Native Police of Queensland, on the Normantown-road, at Creen Creek, about 150 miles from Georgetown. It appears that several hundred blacks had been holding a place called Bora, near Creen Creek, and had attacked the telegraph station there. Two detachments of the Queensland Native Police went to the rescue, under the command of Inspectors Armit and Peingdestre, and they attacked the blacks, who resisted: the fight lasted a considerable time, but the blacks eventually were dispersed. Inspector Armit's horse was killed under him, and numerous spears passed under the horse of Inspector Peingdestre. A gentleman coming on to Georgetown had a very narrow escape; he leant forward just as a spear passed through the seat of his saddle, the horse bucking and throwing him, but Inspector Armit rescued him. The police officers say that they have never met with such a determined resistance from the blacks, and that the Normantown-road is a dangerous one for travelling, as the aborigines are numerous and vindictive.

THE FRONTIER

JOHN OXLEY LIBRARY, BRISBANE. A very different view of the force. Here they are involved in a massacre of an Aboriginal camp. A baby has been killed and lies on the ground. The women are being carried off for 'immoral purposes'. *Queensland Figaro*, January 1885.

through the brain. The next corpse found was a little lubra, stiff and stark, concealed under a bush, but up to the present time no trace of any other dead bodies has been found; several of the wounded, however, have made their appearance, amongst whom is a girl with a bullet through her thigh, a little boy also wounded in the leg, and a poor lame old man (since dead) who could scarcely hobble along, from the effects of disease. The body of the old man has since been found dead, on one of the heights in the neighbourhood of the town, amongst the scrub, where he had either been shot down or had attempted to conceal himself.

Scattered over the bush, were to be seen several black troopers, belonging to the Native Police, in close pursuit of the fugitives, and who, by way of recreation, amused themselves by shooting with their revolvers at the dogs, which were either running masterless or following the general stampede. It was only too evident that a fearful slaughter had been committed, and report gave as its cause, that on the previous day a shepherd's hut, on one of Mr. Archer's stations, had been entered by the blacks, the shepherd murdered, mutilated, and disembowelled, and the hut robbed of the rations it contained. One of the troopers is said to have told this tale to more than one person, and to have added that their instructions were to 'spare none'. Be this as it may, there was not a word of truth in it, with the exception, that two stray blacks of a different tribe had entered a shepherd's hut and stolen some sugar and tea, but had used no violence, nor committed any outrage.

The facts, as I have been able to ascertain them, simply are that a robbery of rations from a shepherd's hut having been committed the Native Police were called upon to follow up and capture the thieves, and with the services of a black tracker, they supposed that they had been able to find them in the neighbourhood of Morinish. Camping out for the night, the troopers and their commandant must have started before daylight, and caught the all unsuspicious natives asleep at their camp, and the horrible tragedy and disgraceful butchery I have described, followed before the sun had risen, which has been palliated by calling it 'a warning to the blacks not to rob shepherds' huts in future.'

* * * * * *

But many people supported the Native Police and applauded their attacks on the Aborigines. The Burketown correspondent of the *Port Denison Times* made his views clear in a report published on 4 June 1868.

I much regret to state that the blacks have become very troublesome about here lately. Within ten miles of this place they speared and cut steaks from the rumps of several horses. As soon as it was known, the Native Police, under Sub-Inspector Uhr, went out, and, I am informed, succeeded in shooting upwards of thirty blacks. No sooner was this done than a report came in that Mr. Cameron had been murdered at Liddle and Hetzer's station, near the Norman. Mr. Uhr went off immediately in that direction, and his success I hear was complete. One mob of fourteen he rounded up; another mob of nine, and a last mob of eight, he succeeded with his troopers in shooting. In the latter lot there was one black who would not die after receiving eighteen or twenty bullets, but a trooper speedily put an end to his existence by smashing his skull . . . Everybody in the district is delighted with the wholesale slaughter dealt out by the native police, and thank Mr. Uhr for his energy in ridding the district of *fifty-nine* (59) myalls.

The Public Debate

Controversy over the Native Police was just one example of an intense public debate that continued throughout the 19th and into the 20th century. In letters, magazines, newspapers, speeches,

THE FRONTIER

lectures, and sermons the settlers wrestled with the fundamental moral problems arising from the relations of black and white and especially the violence of the frontier. It was perhaps the most enduring and most important debate in Australian history. The conflicting views can most easily be traced in the 'letters to the editor' columns of the newspapers. Many of the issues dealt with throughout the 19th century were discussed by three correspondents writing to the *Sydney Gazette* in 1824. At the time settlers were pushing out into the country around Bathurst. Aboriginal resistance was met by the declaration of martial law and punitive expeditions led by the military. The exchange of opinion in the *Gazette* was perhaps the very first public controversy relating to frontier conflict.

LETTER FROM 'FIDELIS', *SYDNEY GAZETTE*, 29 JULY 1824.

Sir,
The present unhappy state of hostility that prevails amongst the Aborigines, in the western country, is doubtless a matter of serious concern to many individuals in this Colony. To hear the lamentable fate of so many defenceless and unprotected fellow-men, stationed beyond the reach of succour, inhumanly murdered, robbed, or pillaged, must be galing [sic] to the feeling ... and awaken the spirit of justice in every British heart. The adoption of the most determined measures must be speedily resorted to, to effect the suppression of such wanton atrocity and horrid murder—to allow its continuation would indeed be heart-rending—human nature shudders at the idea. The kind, generous and benign Administration under which we are fortunately placed will afford us prompt and decisive support, to avenge the loss of our murdered *countrymen*. Do not the acts of inhumanity already committed, call aloud for the extirpation of such lawless marauders? And do not the lacerated remains of the unburied corpses, and mangled limbs of individuals, who have breathed their last in agony, in the lonely sequestered forests ... kindle feelings indescribable in the breast of every generous member of our community and demand immediate punishment? ...

I unhesitatingly affirm, that to reason with those offenders would be attended with as much success, as would the application of eloquence to subdue or command any kind of undomesticated cattle; and that, in my humble opinion, they should meet the same fate, while the present illegalities are continued ... at present, I think, mercy ought to be unquestionably laid aside ... until by a true sense of our superiority they would discontinue their murder and rapacity ...

* * * * * *

LETTER FROM 'PHILANTHROPUS', *SYDNEY GAZETTE*, 5 AUGUST 1824.

Sir,
Considering myself a member of the great human family, I feel that you have injured me. But, as I believe it to be done unintentionally, I therefore, without being solicited, very sincerely forgive you.—The injury is this; viz. you have admitted into the last week's Gazette, a letter, which is not favorable to the happiness or well being of the aborigines . . .

I suppose the New Hollanders to be *human creatures*, and that their Maker has taught them more than the beasts of the earth. I think they have with myself, and all other men, one *common ancestor*. I am therefore willing to call them brethren, and to acknowledge them entitled to my compassion and fraternal respect. Hence, I have been led to estimate *even* the least one of these, my despised and injured brethren, at more value than all the sheep and cattle on Bathurst Plains; than all the flocks and herds in the territory of New South Wales than all the animals in the whole world!

In the sight of the *Creator*, their souls I believe to be of infinite importance. For, so precious is the soul of man declared to be, that no one, by any means, can redeem his brother, nor give to God a ransom for him.—'What,' is the unanswerable question, 'what shall man give in exchange for the soul?' If we therefore now hasten their destruction, or neglect to promote their salvation, shall we be innocent, or without blame?

If we are depriving the aborigines of any earthly enjoyment, or natural support, and also disregarding their comfort and intellectual improvement, are we not committing two evils? And, for these violations of 'the law of kindness,' must we not give account unto Him who sees and judges not as partial man?

Attempts will be made to restore and preserve peace, but should not something more be done for the melioration of these black people? To these original proprietors of the country for what we may possess, are we not, in common justice, bound to render an equivalent, in such kind and manner as may afford or secure to them the greatest benefit? If we do not approve of their conduct in molesting our people or property, how can we approve of our own conduct, in having first invaded their land, and, in a great measure, deprived them of their pleasure and subsistence? Rather than trespass any further, should we not endeavour now to make reparation, and so prove to them, and to all mankind, that we are not in principle, or in practice, less honorable than heathens; but that, on the contrary, we are humane and generous Christians—and really concerned for the welfare of these aborigines? I would have it made manifest, that by our superior endowments we are taught to sympathize with those who are in the lowest condition, and to exercise our benevolence for their present and eternal felicity. In good will to you and your Correspondent, Mr. Editor, and in the purpose of never ceasing regard to the Aborigines.

* * * * * *

LETTER FROM 'AMICITIA' IN *SYDNEY GAZETTE*, 26 AUGUST 1824.

Sir,
The total extermination of the blacks, which is the measure *Fidelis* seems to recommend, would it is true, effectually prevent any future molestation; but it would be a needless, unmerited, and consequently a murderous destruction of our fellow men. The extinction of human life is an act so transcendantly awful in its consequences, that it can only be justified by extreme necessity—as the only possible method of avoiding evils of at least equal magnitude, or as the legal penalty of the most flagrant and pernicious offences. Before we determine on the excision of several thousand individuals, we should scrupulously enquire into the justice and necessity of so dreadful a doom. In the present case, we should first be fully satisfied that this fate is deserved by the crimes already committed, or is indispensably requisite for the protection of our lives and property. Unless one of these points can be established, the massacre of the blacks would be a foul and unpardonable murder. Let us however examine the views of *Fidelis* on this subject. His 'humble opinion is, that these offenders should meet the same fate as any kind of undomesticated cattle, while the present illegalities continue' . . . But we cannot treat the blacks in this way, because, 1st they are not cattle, but human beings, whose life is infinitely more valuable than that of beasts, and, secondly, though now undomesticated, they are capable of being gendered as harmless and *humane* and perhaps as useful, as *Fidelis* himself. But you hope Government will assist you 'to avenge the loss of our murdered countrymen'. Pray, what do you mean by vengeance? If you mean any thing more than legal punishment, you mean more than you ought, more than can be sanctioned in a civilized and Christian country. Punishment, to be legal must be inflicted only upon the guilty, and even then must be proportioned to the enormity of the crime. But 'the extirpation of these lawless marauders', which is the vengeance you appear to wish for, and for which you think 'the acts of inhumanity, already committed loudly call', would involve many, especially of the children and females, who were not at all concerned in those acts. And even of those who actually committed them, something can be said in mitigation of their guilt. They were incensed by the wanton cruelty and shameful brutality with which some of the whites had treated them, and particularly their women; and, though the door of legal redress is open to them as well as us, yet they are probably ignorant of it . . .

In enquiring how we ought to act, we must first consider that the aborigines of this country are our *fellow subjects*. They are recognized as such by the British Government, which has taken them under its control, and extends to them its protection. It is not now necessary to show the principles on which Government has adopted these children of nature as its own: the fact is incontrovertible; they are regarded, legislatively, as British subjects; they are governed and defended by the same laws as ourselves, so far as those laws are applicable to their condition . . . The general rule of our conduct towards the blacks must therefore be, to treat them in precisely the same manner as we should treat any other British subjects in the like circumstances.

'Taming the Niggers'

Over 80 years after the debate in the *Sydney Gazette* between *Fidelis, Philanthropus* and *Amicitia* there was a similar on-going controversy in the Townsville weekly paper, the *Townsville Herald*. It was prompted by a series of specially commissioned articles on the settlement of North Australia by a correspondent calling himself 'H.7.H.' The second article of the series was called 'Taming the Niggers'.

TOWNSVILLE HERALD, 2 FEBRUARY 1907.

In the early days of settlement on the northern rivers of Australia many means were adopted for taming the nigger and making him respect the white man and his laws—the principal of which was the rifle. The nigger was not always a very apt pupil, however, and partly from ignorance, but principally by desire to give the white man trouble he committed murder, fired the grass, killed cattle, and generally played up 'old Harry' . . . and as a result the rifle was introduced into the argument, and the nigger most times got on the losing side. On a property on one of the rivers flowing into the western coast of the Gulf of Carpentaria many and bloody were the battles fought between the white man and his black brother. The latter were continually hunting and killing cattle, and the herds were getting as wild as hawks, and the boss decided to teach the sons of the forest a lesson. No one had been allowed to shoot a myall until evidence was forthcoming that they were spearing cattle, but we had not long to wait for such evidence, for one day the boss and a few of the hands were out on tracks and came across the trail of a mob of cattle that had been galloping, and running the trail up came across the carcase of a fine fat bullock with the best of the meat hacked off, and tracks of myalls everywhere. By the fact that the niggers had not stopped to take the whole of the meat from the carcase it was evident that they were on the move, and that their camp was some distance away, so we returned to the station, and got all the available hands together (including some 40 half-civilised 'bucks' who loafed on the creek and sponged for their tucker from the offal heap, etc. about the killing yard). The former were armed with Winchesters and the 'bucks' with their own weapons, and with pack-horses and tucker we set out to give the darkies their first lesson in white man's law as relating to the killing of 'free beef,' and one that they were never to forget, and which the children of that time (now grown to be men and women) refer to even to this day as 'the finish of the blackfellow.'

[The revenge party tracked the Aborigines and in the dark crept up to within 100 yards of their camp and waited for first light.]

Having arranged not to attack until the camp awoke at daylight, and also that gins and piccaninnies were as far as possible to be spared the slaughter, it was decided that the boss should give the signal by firing the first shot. After this we began our climb up the rocks and after many stumbles and curses for scratches and bruises received in the climb we took up our positions and awaited events. All was quiet as death in the gorge below us, nothing moved and only the twinkle of a live coal in a dying fire here and there, and the plaintive wail of a young piccaninny as it awoke from its slumbers to doze off again almost immediately told that the niggers were camped below us. It seemed ages before we saw the morning star shoot up bright and smiling away in the east in the direction of civilisation, and where our loved ones at the time were no doubt sleeping soundly and perhaps dreaming of us, little thinking that our hands were so soon to be stained in the blood of our fellow-man—even though he were a wild uncivilised myall, against whom every man's hand was turned, and who was doomed to extermination that the white man might take his country for his own use. Such thoughts were mine as we lay there with our rifles pointed towards the niggers' camp, and our magazines full, every bullet meaning the end of one of the poor black devils so peacefully sleeping below us, and little dreaming of the storm of lead that was to greet him as he awoke from his slumbers. Thinking this the time went by and I must have been half asleep or else in a deep reverie, when the bang of a rifle shot awoke me from my dreams and this was followed by others to left and right of me, and mingled with the noise of the rifles were the shrill screams of the gins and piccaninnies as the bucks fell around them in dozens. Taken by surprise and totally demoralised the myalls for a few moments stood as though galvanised into stone, and then with a wild yell of fear they broke in all directions . . . while others tried to scramble up the face of the gorge, and thus escape by the hills, but they were shot down before they had ascended the almost perpendicular face of the rocks for any distance. It was estimated that over 150 myalls 'bit the dust' that morning, and unfortunately many women and children shared the same fate. In that wild yelling, rushing mob of black people it was hard to avoid shooting the women and babies, and there were men in that mob of whites who would ruthlessly destroy anything possessing a black hide—man, woman, or child—and after considering one or two of the blood-thirsty murders committed by the niggers in the Northern Territory that was almost excusable.

[H.7.H's article continued with an account of the killing of a station owner called Leonard and the revenge which followed.]

When Leonard's mate arrived at the head station with news of the murder there was a call to arms, and every white man on the run was enlisted in a force to avenge the death of their comrade. The party left the station the same night, and rode to Leonard's camp. Next day they went out in search of Leonard's body, but could find no trace of it, the only thing that remained of the dead man being a pool of blood at the spot where he fell. For several days the tracks of these niggers were followed until on the evening of the fourth day, the avengers came upon a camp of old feeble gins and bucks, who had been members of the camp where Leonard met his death, but had been compelled to fall behind, the pace at which the stronger members of the tribe travelled in their endeavor to get away from the vengeance they knew awaited them being too much for the old people, and they accordingly dropped behind. Being satisfied that none of these poor old wretches took an active part in the murder, they were not molested, but the pace was increased on the tracks of the leaders until sundown that night, and all next day those tracks were followed. Late on the evening of the sixth day of the chase we were in the vicinity of the head waters of the anabranch of the Lemman River and the country was beginning to get very rough and travelling was difficult. Here the tracks of the fugitives were very hot and we expected to run into the rear guard at any moment. The pace was beginning to tell on the myalls, who must have been travelling day and night and several of them had abandoned what little property they had in order to accelerate their speed in the hope of outpacing the grim vengeance they knew full well would be sure to pursue them. Before sundown that day the country having become very rough, it was decided to form a camp and send out scouts to ascertain the position of the maylls, for it was evident that they could not be far ahead, their tracks not being more than an hour old. Accordingly four of our best white trackers and one nigger, all armed with Winchester repeaters, were sent on ahead, and travelling as rapidly as the nature of the country would allow they came upon the main body of the niggers just about to fix a camp on the scrubby side of a creek that came in from the hills ... It was evident that the myalls had begun to fancy themselves more secure in this rough country, as a large number of them were in the water fishing, while others were preparing fires, and others still in doubt were on the prowl looking for other tucker, for at the pace they had been travelling it was not likely that they had devoted much time to hunting during their march. The news our scouts brought back put heart into the pursuers, who had begun to think that the niggers would get into the hills before we overtook them. Rifles were looked to afresh, cartridges were put into the magazines, and everything made in readiness for the attack which was to be by moonlight, as it was likely that if we waited until daybreak we would find our 'birds' had flown. We moved up under cover of the darkness to within a few hundred yards of where the niggers' camp lay, and there we awaited the rising of the moon to witness one of the greatest slaughter of murdering myalls that ever took place in the North of Australia. Having arranged our force in the form of a half moon round the myalls' camp and made everything ready for the attack we waited for old Luna to get up and lend her light, that the slaughter might be more effective ... Steadily she climbed her course, gliding up and up until the shadows shortened and she was fairly overhead. Then from the centre of our half-circle up rose the massive form of our old man, and before you could say Jack Robinson every man was on his feet and creeping silently and steadily in towards where the nigger camp was situated. They slept soundly those myalls after their long march, and could have had no thought of us being so close to them, for we were within revolver shot of them before our presence was discovered, and then it was too late, for muddled with sleep, sore-footed, weary, and panic-stricken they offered no resistance, and many of them were 'wiped out' before they could gain their feet. Talk of the 'Furies of Hell,' that night's work amongst those myalls with the white man's rifle and tomahawk would make 'Hell's Furies' blush. How those gins and kiddies shrieked when we got amongst them. The blood of the white man was up and nothing with a black hide escaped death that night. One or two of the bucks may have escaped, but one or two only, for when we had finished our work and drawn off, and in daylight came to view the white man's work of vengeance bucks, gins, and piccaninnies were lying dead in all directions, and not a thing in that camp moved or breathed ...

The foregoing will serve in some way to give an idea of the manner in which the myalls were originally tamed and taught to obey the law of the white man. It may appear cold-blooded murder to some to wipe out a whole camp for killing, perhaps a couple of bullocks, but then each member of the tribe must be held equally guilty, and therefore, it would be impossible to discriminate. I do not wish to make out that the pioneer white men of this north land were in any way heroes, although they to a certain extent needed pluck to face such odds as they were pitted against in the myalls, although the niggers were only armed with spears. The nigger is a treacherous, lying, double-dealing, thieving black brute, with no sense whatever of honor, gratitude or fair play, and he has been known to stalk the white man for months until an opportunity occurred to get him unarmed and then the nigger's spear settled the argument, most often when the white man was asleep, or otherwise unconscious of the black devil's presence. The writer never held a man guilty of murder who wiped out a nigger. They should be classed with the black snake and death adder, and treated accordingly.

* * * * * *

H.7.H's article led to an exchange of letters which were printed over the following two months. Three of them are printed below.

LETTER FROM 'AMICUS NIGRORUM', *TOWNSVILLE HERALD*, 14 FEBRUARY 1907.

Sir,
In your issue of the 4th I notice an article with the above headline. I am surprised that you should allow your paper to be contaminated with such an article. Is 'H.7.H.' a lunatic? or does he intend to boast of his many cold-blooded murders? He gives an account of the murder of 150 blacks because they speared a bullock. What is the penalty a white man would pay for a similar offence? two or three years' imprisonment and not the murder of himself together with all his friends and relatives. Then, in Leonard's case, who was responsible for his death? 'H.7.H.' thinks that the murder of hundreds was quite justifiable as revenge for one man's death. I consider that the aboriginal was quite within his rights to take the other's life. It was a case of either kill or be killed. Had the black attempted to run away he would certainly have been shot. Had he remained inactive the same fate would have overtaken him. I would like to ask what 'H.7.H.' would have done if he had been in the place of the blackfellow? Just think for a moment! Your correspondent says that while waiting among the rocks for daylight so that they could begin their slaughter, they thought of loved ones. Surely had such been the case, they would have held their hands, or at least not boasted of their crime ... To read the article from your correspondent's pen would make any Christian wish he were not of the same nationality as 'H.7.H.' Are we living in the enlightened 20th century and allowing this to go on? What are the Government and Chief Protector [of Aborigines] doing? The evidence given in your publication should surely be sufficient to set the

machinery of the law in motion. If not, then Justice must indeed be
blind, as well as blindfolded. I should strongly advise 'H.7.H.' to say no
more about it publicly, but to give his conscience—if he has any left—a
chance. I sincerely hope that the experiences he recounts are at an end
so far as he is concerned.—Yours, etc.

* * * * * *

LETTER FROM 'THEODORIC', *TOWNSVILLE HERALD*, 23 FEBRUARY 1907.

Sir,
A correspondent signing himself 'Amicus Nigrorum' takes strong
exceptions to the narrative of 'H.7.H.' in his 'Taming of the nigger.'
I believe that the majority of your readers will side with the
correspondent's remarks which oppose the brutal treatment received by
the blacks at the hands of 'H.7.H.' and his friends on the stations. To me
it seems incredible that such blood-thirsty deeds should have been
carried on, and only, it appears, as late as the eighties. Was the
administration of Queensland in a state of paralysis that it did nothing to
stop these uncalled-for murders? However, I don't agree with the above
writer when he urges that we should have no more of that kind of
literature. Why does he plead in that way? I cannot understand it. Let us
have the truth, no matter how painful it is to us. We, the rising generation,
at any rate, will demand sooner or later that the history of our State shall
be written, whether it has numerous stains or not. So let 'H.7.H.' keep on
relating stories of the brutality that the blacks suffered from the
selfishness of the whites. We don't want to be kept in the dark about the
past doings of some of our pioneers. We want to know what kind of men
our bush conquerors were. I think it is absurd to exclude any kind of
information because it deals with 'man's inhumanity to man.' On the
same grounds we should not allow knowledge to be spread of the early
struggles of religious bodies, who aimed at the ruling of the State, with
the bloody disputes that followed. The Thirty Years' War was the
outcome of the difference between powerful religious institutions. So I
conclude—do not refrain from publishing those cruel facts which
constitute after all parts of our history.—Yours, etc..

* * * * * *

'H.7.H.' replied to his critics in the issue of *Townsville Herald*, 9
March 1907.

Sir,
In your issue of 15th February, I note that a correspondent under the nom
de plume of 'Amicus Nigrorum' makes an attack on 'H.7.H.' regarding his

account of how the niggers in certain districts of the Commonwealth were tamed by the early settlers, and your correspondent, actuated no doubt by a strong religious fervor asks certain questions of 'H.7.H.' and regarding that 'cold-blooded brute,' that the cold-blooded brute will answer if you will allow him space in your valuable journal. In the first place, I take exception to 'Amicus Nigrorum's' expression of surprise that you should allow your paper to be contaminated by the publication of such an article. I would remind 'A.N.' that the article to which he takes such exception, and which appears to have stirred such a strong feeling of disgust, is no more blood-curdling than many accounts of battles fought by the Empire's forces in the Soudan and in Zululand, when the British Government was doing just what the squatter was doing in my case—simply acquiring property, or, to put it in another way, extending the Empire. Whereas the Zulus and the Soudanese at both Ulundi and Omdurmann were armed with little more formidable than a yamstick, the results of the engagements were acclaimed throughout the English-speaking world as 'glorious victories,' and great honors and much gold fell to the lot of the respective commanders, Chelmsford and Kitchener. In the case of the man who tamed the Australian nigger, the circumstances were altogether different, for the pioneer white man was almost alone in the wilderness, and was pitted against a treacherous, cunning, and blood-thirsty foe who killed for killing sake, and was never so happy as when shedding blood, whether human or animal. It is all very well for men of the class of 'Amicus Nigrorum' to rush into print at this late hour because a few plain facts of a score of years ago are given to the public. If 'Amicus Nigrorum' is as horrified as he would like people to believe, he has only to go out into the back country—the Northern Territory in particular—and keep his ears and eyes open, and he will find enough of horrors of various descriptions to keep him letter-writing for a life-time. The city man knows nothing of the ways of the 'untrodden' north. Present and past it has been a sealed book to him—and, judging by the effect of my 'Taming the Nigger' article on 'Amicus Nigrorum,' that gentleman must be either a new chum in this country, or else, his education, so far as any knowledge of the early settlement days of the back-country is concerned, has been sadly neglected . . . I would like to state right here that 'H.7.H.' is not a lunatic, but only a man who has travelled this country and poked his nose into the more outlandish places, and in a way 'done his bit' towards opening the country up, that 'Amicus Nigrorum' and other gentlemen of the tender conscience variety, might come after. Furthermore 'H.7.H.' does not believe in the wholesale slaughter of niggers except when circumstances make it compulsory. In the days of which I wrote the rifle was the only known law in the Northern Territory, when black and white came into conflict, and it has been so throughout the world when the white man has 'moved out' to acquire territory and make room for the white races to expand. It has always been an unwritten law that wherever the white man sets his foot the black man must go, and as the latter never cares to go quietly, there is always an argument, and the white man comes out on top. It is amusing to old timers, who risked their lives and their fortunes to open up the country for the benefit of posterity, to hear ink-slingers like 'Amicus Nigrorum' giving his opinion of how things should be done. Right enough for that gentleman twenty years after the country has been settled to talk of and criticise the men who opened up the country.

Keeping Them in Their Place

Conflict came to an end in every district in one way or another. The Aborigines 'came in' to white society to live on pastoral stations or in camps on the fringes of the pioneer townships. But the legacy of frontier violence lived on. The Aborigines had been forced into submission. Insecurity and fear continued to dominate their relations with Europeans. The whites were often willing to employ Aboriginal labour or to co-habit with black women but they too bore the scars of the past. A tradition of brutality lived on, a fear of

MITCHELL LIBRARY, STATE LIBRARY OF NSW. An artistic recreation of events on Dagworth Station in Queensland. Such attempts to come to terms with the Europeans and to call a truce in the ongoing conflict were quite common. 'Arrival of Blacks with Flags of Truce at Dagworth Station, Queensland', *Illustrated Sydney News*, 26 January 1878.

revenge, an underlying sense of guilt. All came together in the belief that the Aborigines must 'be kept in their place'. A most interesting discussion of these issues took place in the small Queensland town of Bowen in the late 1860s just after local clans had been 'let in'. The editor of the local paper outlined the situation as he saw it.

PORT DENISON TIMES, 12 JUNE 1869.

The aboriginal question is again asserting its claim to our attention on all hands and in louder tones than ever.

First and foremost we see daily in the midst of us numbers of the former lords and ladies of the soil in almost their native costume marching about with that lordly air that so distinguishes them and apparently taking stock diligently spying out the nakedness of the land and the weak points, maybe, of its holders. So far no one can have any objection. Indeed it is far better to see them coming thus fearlessly amongst us than to know they are skulking in the scrubs cowering from fear of the white man's bullet, their hand against every [white] man and every [white] man's hand against them. But on the other hand it becomes us as invaders to enforce submission to our laws on the part of the conquered. We have hitherto done this by the strong hand, that is to say, to unhesitating recourse to powder and ball. Against this system all right feeling men have thoroughly revolted and it has lately been hoped that the time had come when, with regard to our own safety, a milder system might be inaugurated and more friendly relations established between us and those whom we have supplanted. How to effect this is the problem now before us and it is needless to say that it is by no means an easy one. In the first place of course it would be absurd under any circumstances to expect any kindly feeling to exist towards us in the breasts of the blackfellows especially so shortly after the reign of terror by which they have hitherto been kept in subjection. In whatever plan we may adopt with respect to them we shall do well to bear in mind that their feelings towards us are and must be those of resentment and hostility and that however the exhibition of those feelings may be restrained by motives of policy on their part they do exist and probably will continue to do while the race lasts, and that this smouldering fire will be ready to burst into flame when favourable conditions offer.

Whilst therefore it is one of our foremost duties to escape as soon as possible from the terrible necessities which our position has forced upon us, we must not cease to be firm and must take especial care to show our black neighbours that whilst we are willing, nay anxious, to hold our hands from slaughter, we are at the same time determined to enforce at all hazards and by *any* means submission to our laws and that any infraction of them will be met by retribution prompt and severe. If we do not we will be failing in our duty alike to them and to ourselves. For we shall not only endanger the safety of our own citizens, which after all should be our first care, but we shall render inevitable a return to the bloody system, the possible termination of which we have all regarded with so much hope and pleasure. Upon the attitude we now assume depends in very great degree the amount of success we may hope to achieve in the solution of this problem. Times of change from one system to another, that is of revolution, have in all cases their peculiar elements of danger. One of the first maxims of such periods is principius obsta—that is, check anything that appears likely to disturb the working of the new system at the outset. It is by far the wisest and most merciful plan. For this reason we hold that the action taken by the sergeant of police as described in our last issue, we mean that the flogging of the gin who had stolen the child's petticoat, was, though perhaps not strictly legal, quite the right thing to do under the circumstances. We should not perhaps have alluded to this but that during the past week there have come under our notice several instances of offences committed by the blackfellow which though not in themselves of a very heinous nature are just such as if allowed to pass unchecked will embolden the savages and lead to more serious outrages and eventually to the undoing of whatever progress has been made in the direction of placing our blackfellow policy on a better footing than heretofore. One of the instances to which we refer occurred at Muller's garden the other day, when one of them cut down a valuable peach tree, we suppose from the fancy that it would make a good waddy, and perhaps being unaware that it was good for anything else; and another broke, we do not know exactly under what circumstances, a grindstone belonging to M. Muller; but assuming that both deeds were committed without malice, we maintain that in both cases they ought to have been punished, if only to teach them better for the future, but chiefly to teach those principles of submission which our position renders it so necessary for us to enforce... We would however, before leaving this part of our subject, utter one word of warning to our white fellow citizens, and that is not to forget, as we said above, that the blackfellows are by force of circumstances our enemies and that their feelings towards us, however much fear or policy may smooth the behaviour, are those of undying hostility. In fact they hate a white man and the very sight of him and we do not see how they could do otherwise. Gratitude, except as 'a lively sense of favours to come', or perhaps a fear of future punishment, they have none, and it would be very odd if they had... The moral of all this is that we should not allow ourselves to be thrown off our guard in our dealings with them.

3

THE LAND QUESTION: ARE WE A COMMUNITY OF THIEVES?

The famous novelist Xavier Herbert presented a challenge to his fellow countrymen a few years ago when he wrote:

Until we give back to the black man just a bit of the land that was his, and give it back without strings to snatch it back, without anything but generosity of spirit in concession for the evil we have done to him—until we do that we shall remain what we have always been, a people without integrity, not a nation, but a community of thieves.[1]

---

1 Quoted by S. Harris in J. Wright, *We Call for a Treaty*, Fontana, Sydney, 1985, p. xiii.

> *Most Australians are aware of the issues involved in the land rights question and feel strongly about them regardless of what side they take. But contemporaries who discuss the issue think that it is a relatively new development which emerged during the turbulent years of the late 1960s and early 1970s. The historical record proves otherwise. The issues so keenly debated today were discussed just as strongly in the 1830s and 1840s. The land question has accompanied Australian settlement for 200 years, as the following documents will indicate.*

Terra Nullius

The single most important feature of the British expropriation of Aboriginal land was the belief that Australia in 1788 was a *terra nullius*, a land without owners. This enabled the settlers to convince themselves that they had a legal and moral right to the land because Australia had never actually become the property of the resident Aborigines. This idea had become accepted legal doctrine in the first generation of settlement and it has played a central role in relations between black and white Australians ever since.

LAW OFFICERS [OF THE BRITISH GOVERNMENT] TO EARL BATHURST [SECRETARY OF STATE FOR THE COLONIES], 15 FEBRUARY 1819, *HRA*, 4, 1, P. 330.

That part of New South Wales possessed by His Majesty, not having been acquired by conquest or cession was taken possession of by him as desert and uninhabited, and subsequently colonized from this country...

* * * * * *

The idea that Australia was waste land had become a central doctrine of the colonial courts by the middle of the 19th century.

CHIEF JUSTICE STEPHEN IN THE CASE WILSON V. TERRY, NEW SOUTH WALES SUPREME COURT, 1849 IN J.G. LEGGE (ED.), *A SELECTION OF SUPREME COURT CASES*, 2 VOLS., SYDNEY, 1896, 1, P. 508.

The circumstances of newly discovered and unpeopled territories, claimed by and vested in the Crown, on behalf of all its subjects, are so widely different from those of a populated and long-settled country, in which the lands never practically belonged to the Crown... have for centuries been owned and cultivated by its subjects, that a moment's reflection would present them to the mind even of a stranger. The lands in new territories are unoccupied and waste, until granted by the Crown to some individual, willing to reclaim them from a state of nature.

* * * * * *

'Terra nullius' received the sanction of the Privy Council, the British Empire's highest court of appeal, in 1889. The Council determined that in 1788 Australia had been 'practically unoccupied, without settled inhabitants'. When determining his judgement in 1971 in the Gove Land Rights case, Mr Justice Blackburn argued that the Privy Council decision 80 years earlier was still binding on Australian Courts. Blackburn's judgement was very important for the history of the land rights question because it was the first case in Australian legal history which fully explored the fundamental issues created by the colonization of the continent and the expropriation of Aboriginal land.

MILIRPUM V. NABALCO [THE GOVE LAND RIGHTS CASE], *FEDERAL LAW REPORTS*, 13 OCTOBER 1971, P. 245.

On the foundation of New South Wales, therefore, and of South Australia, every square inch of territory in the colony became the property of the Crown. All titles, rights, and interests whatever in land which existed thereafter in subjects of the Crown were the direct consequence of some grant from the Crown.

The Law of Nations

In developing their justification for taking Aboriginal land the Australian colonists made use of international law which they assumed, probably wrongly, favoured their case. Above all other writers they referred to the book *The Law of Nations*, written in the middle of the 18th century by the Swiss jurist Vattel. His work was quoted by Mr. Justice Willis in his judgement on an Aboriginal offender in New South Wales.

PUBLISHED IN *PP: ABORIGINES—AUSTRALIAN COLONIES*, 1844, PP. 152–53.

According to the commission whereby this colony is governed, the sovereignty of the Crown is asserted over the whole of the territory

THE LAND QUESTION

comprised within the limits it defines ... There does not appear to be any specific recognition in this commission of the claims of the aborigines, either as the sovereigns or proprietors of the soil: although it is in the recollection of many living men that every part of this territory was the undisputed property of the aborigines. Whether the sovereignty thus asserted within the limits defined by the commission of His Excellency the Governor legally excludes the aborigines, according to the law of nations, as acknowledged and acted upon by the British Government, from the rightful sovereignty and occupancy of a reasonable portion of the soil, and destroys their existence as self-governing communities so entirely as to place them, with regard to the prevalence of our law among themselves, in the unqualified condition of British subjects; or whether it has merely reduced them to the state of dependent allies, still retaining their own laws and usages, subject to such restraints and qualified control as the safety of the colonists and the protection of the aborigines required (subject to that right of pre-emption of their lands which is undoubted), is the point upon which the present question mainly rests. Much will depend on the manner in which this colony is considered to have been acquired; and this brings me, in the second place, to advert to the law of nations as acknowledged by the British Government, with regard to colonial possessions. 'Colonies,' says Mr. Clark, in his summary of Colonial Law ... 'are acquired by conquest, by cession under treaty, or by occupancy. By occupancy, where an uninhabited country is discovered by British subjects, and is upon such discovery adopted or recognised by the British Crown as part of its possessions. In case a colony be acquired by occupancy (he adds) the law of England, then in being, is immediately and *ipso facto* in force in the new settlement.' He further states, 'New South Wales and Van Diemen's Land were acquired by discovery or simple occupation.' New South Wales was not, however, unoccupied, as we have seen, at the time it was taken possession of by the colonists, for 'a body of the aborigines appeared on the shore, armed with spears, which they threw down as soon as they found the strangers had no hostile intention'. This being the case, it does not appear there was any conquest; and it is admitted there has hitherto been no cession under treaty. Protectors, indeed, have recently been appointed, and certain lands set apart, by order of Government, within this district, for the location of the aborigines; but no more. This colony, then, stands on a different footing from some others, for it was neither an unoccupied place, nor was it obtained by right of conquest and driving out the natives, nor by treaties. Indeed, as M. Vattel very justly says, 'whoever agrees that robbery is a crime, and that we are not allowed to take forcible possession of our neighbour's property, will acknowledge, without any other proof, that no nation has a right to expel another people from the country they inhabit in order to settle in it herself.' But in a preceding page the same author declares, in the passage quoted by the learned crown prosecutor, 'that those who pursue an erratic life, and live by hunting rather than cultivate their lands, usurp more extensive territories than with a reasonable share of labour they would have occasion for, and have, therefore, no reason to complain if other nations, more industrious, and too closely confined, come to take possession of a part of those lands. Thus, though the conquest of the civilized empires of Peru and Mexico was a notorious usurpation, the establishment of many colonies on the continent of North America might, on their confining themselves within just bounds, be extremely lawful. The people of those extensive tracts rather ranged through, than inhabited them.' And again, he says,

'It is asked if a nation may lawfully take possession of a part of a vast country in which there are none but erratic nations whose scanty population is incapable of occupying the whole? We have already observed, in establishing the obligation to cultivate the earth, that those nations cannot exclusively appropriate to themselves more land than they have occasion for, or more than they are to settle and cultivate. Their removing their habitations through these immense regions cannot be accounted true and legal possession; and the people of Europe, too closely pent up at home, finding land of which savages stood in no particular need, and of which they made no actual and constant use, were lawfully entitled to take possession of it, and settle it with colonies. The earth, as we have already said, belongs to mankind in general, and was designed to furnish them with subsistence: if each nation had from the beginning resolved to appropriate to itself a vast country, that the people might live only by hunting and fishing and wild fruits, our globe would not be sufficient to maintain a tenth part of its present inhabitants. We do not, therefore, deviate from the views of nature in confining the Indians within narrower limits.'

Colonial Apologists

Debate about the land question has been part of Australian history since 1788. From the 1820s onwards settlers wrote to the newspapers defending the moral and legal rights of the Europeans to settle in Australia.

LETTER TO EDITOR OF *SYDNEY GAZETTE* FROM 'AMICITIA', 19 AUGUST 1824.

Any doubt, therefore, as to the lawfulness of our assuming the possession of this Island, must arise from the opinion that it was the *property* of the original inhabitants. Such opinion, however, would be incorrect; for the very notion of property, as applicable to territorial possession, did not exist among them. They had no civil polity, no regular organized frame of society, on the regulations of which the distinction of landed property depends. Which tribe, or which individual, could with propriety be considered as the proper owner of any particular district? Each tribe wandered about wheresoever inclination prompted, without ever supposing that any one place belonged to it more than to another. They were the *inhabitants*, but not the *proprietors* of the land. The country then was to be regarded as an unappropriated remnant of common property; and, in taking possession of it, we did not invade another's right, for we only claimed that which before was unclaimed by any.

We shall do no act of injustice to the aboriginal inhabitants, providing we suffer their condition to be as good in every respect now, as it was before our settlement among them. They were then the inhabitants of the land;—they still continue to be so; we have not driven them from it, nor should we be justified in doing it. They subsisted on the natural productions of the rivers and the forests:—a great part of these productions they still have the liberty to procure; and, if our occupation has diminished their means of subsistence, justice requires us to supply the deficiency. We have certainly deprived them, in some measure, of the unlimited range of their native wilds; but there is still sufficient space left for the full indulgence of their wandering habits. If, however, we have taken anything from their comfort in this respect, we are bound to make up the loss in another form. On the whole, the state of the black natives is, in general, as good at least as it was before the establishment of our Colony; we have left them all that they enjoyed before, or have supplied the deficiency; and we have only taken that which they never possessed.

* * * * * *

The argument was also pursued in the editorial columns of colonial papers.

SOUTHERN AUSTRALIAN, 8 MAY 1839.

As we have already intimated . . . we assert the *right* of the white man to locate himself in South Australia.

In our opinion, we have exactly the same right to be here, that the older inhabitants have. They at a remote, as we at a later period, were guided here by enterprize or accident. From the moment they arrived, until the present, they have not sought, and therefore not acquired as tribes a property in the soil—nor, as individuals, the ownership of things which grow or roam upon its surface. They have neither erected habitations upon it, nor pierced its bosom to make it minister to their support and comfort. Generation after generation, their thinly scattered tribes have wandered homeless over its fertile districts, unconscious or heedless of the treasures within them . . . We found the country in the state in which ages before the black people had found it—its resources undeveloped, unappropriated! In landing here, we exercised a right which we possessed in common with them. In locating ourselves on, and cultivating particular spots, we exercised one which they might previously have exercised, but which they did not.

* * * * * *

THE SYDNEY HERALD, 5 DECEMBER 1838.

The claims to compensation from the white inhabitants of this Colony, on behalf of the aboriginal natives, are founded upon the assumption that land has been taken from them to which they possessed an exclusive right. If, indeed, this really were the true state of the case, there can be little doubt that the claim would be irresistable . . . The question under discussion . . . is whether civilized man has not a right to occupy waste lands merely because they are roamed over by scattered tribes of wild men—whether, for instance, it could have been the design of the Creator that this vast territory . . . should remain for ever under the dominion of wild men and wild animals? It is admitted that to take possession of, stock, and cultivate, uninhabited countries, is to keep strictly within the limits of the law of nature. Then, we would ask, what is the difference, so far as the object is concerned, between taking possession of a desert country without inhabitants, and taking possession of a country of which a comparatively few wandering inhabitants make no use? Such a country is, a *desert* for every purpose involved in this question, and may be justly occupied by civilized man.

Growing Awareness of Land Rights

Two beliefs stood in the way of acceptance of Aboriginal land rights—the initial view that the interior of Australia was uninhabited and the more enduring argument that the Aborigines were aimless wanderers with no sense of property at all. The idea that the interior was uninhabited was overturned in the early years of settlement. Experience of Aboriginal society convinced many settlers that the various tribes lived within specific localities with known boundaries.

THE LAND QUESTION

D. COLLINS, *AN ACCOUNT OF THE ENGLISH COLONY IN NEW SOUTH WALES*, 2 VOLS., REED, SYDNEY, 1975, 1, P. 497; FIRST PUBLISHED 1802.

But, strange as it may appear, they have also their real estates. Bennilong, both before he went to England and since his return often assured me, that the island of Me-mel (called by us Goat Island) close by Sydney Cove was his own property; that it was his father's, and that he should give it to By-gone, his particular friend and companion. To this little spot he appeared much attached; and we have often seen him and his wife Ba-rangaroo feasting and enjoying themselves on it. He told us of other people who possessed this kind of hereditary property, which they retained undisturbed.

* * * * * *

Twenty years later one of Australia's first missionaries commented on Aboriginal attitudes to land.

W. WALKER TO R. WATSON, 5 DECEMBER 1821; BONWICK TRANSCRIPTS, 52, ML.

The Aborigines are brought up to wandering pursuits from their infancy, and to speak of making them stationary is to pierce them through with many swords. They possess some tract of country which they call their own but, even on this, although it may afford them animals and fish, they will not be permanent. Yet they are so senselessly bigotted to this particular spot, that when you would persuade them to settle in any place, they will not understand you, no more than if you discoursed with them in Latin or Greek.

* * * * * *

The prominent clergyman J.D. Lang wrote a letter to friends in England in 1839 in answer to their enquiry as to whether the Aborigines had 'any idea of property in land'.

PAPERS AND PROCEEDINGS OF THE ABORIGINES PROTECTION SOCIETY, V, 1839, PP. 140—44.

It is well known that these Aborigines in no instance cultivate the soil, but subsist entirely by hunting and fishing, and on the wild roots they find in certain localities (especially the common fern), with occasionally a little wild honey; indigenous fruits being exceedingly rare. The whole race is divided into tribes, more or less numerous, according to circumstances, and designated from the localities they inhabit; for although universally a wandering race, with respect to places of habitation, their wanderings are circumscribed by certain well-defined limits, beyond which they seldom pass, except for purposes of war or of festivity. In short, every tribe has its own district, the boundaries of which are well known to the natives generally; and within that district all the wild animals are considered as much the property of the tribe inhabiting, or rather ranging on, its whole extent, as the flocks of sheep and herds of cattle that have been introduced into the country by adventurous Europeans, are held by European law and usage the property of their respective owners. In fact, as the country is occupied chiefly for pastoral purposes, the difference between the Aboriginal and the European ideas of property in the soil is more imaginary than real, the native grass affording subsistence to the kangaroos of the natives, as well as to the wild cattle of the Europeans, and the only difference indeed being, that the former are not branded with a particular mark like the latter, and are somewhat wilder and more difficult to catch. Nay, as the European regards the intrusion of any other white man upon the *cattle-run*, of which European law and usage have made him the possessor, and gets it punished as a trespass, the Aborigines of the particular tribe inhabiting a particular district, regard the intrusion of any other tribe of Aborigines upon that district, for the purposes of kangaroo hunting, &c. as an intrusion, to be resisted and punished by force of arms. In short, this is the frequent cause of Aboriginal, as it is of European wars; man, in his natural state, being very much alike in all conditions—jealous of his rights and exceedingly pugnacious. It is true, the European intruders pay no respect to these Aboriginal divisions of the territory, the black native being often hunted off his own ground, or destroyed by European violence, dissipation, or disease, just as his kangaroos are driven off that ground by the European's black cattle; but this surely does not alter the case as to the right of the Aborigines.

But particular districts are not merely the property of particular tribes; particular sections or portions of these districts are universally recognised by the natives as the property of individual members of these tribes: and when the owner of such a section or portion of territory (as I ascertained was the case at King George's Island) has determined on burning off the grass on his land, which is done for the double purpose of enabling the natives to take the older animals more easily, and to provide a new crop of sweeter grass for the rising generation of the forest, not only all the other individuals of his own tribe, but whole tribes from other districts, are invited to the hunting party and the feast and dance, or corrobory that ensue; the wild animals on the ground being all considered the property of the owner of the land. I have often heard natives myself tell me, in answer to my own questions on the subject, who were the Aboriginal owners of particular tracts of land now held by

THE LAND QUESTION

Europeans; and indeed this idea of property in the soil, *for hunting purposes*, is universal among the Aborigines.

* * * * * *

The Polish-born explorer Strzelecki appreciated the importance of land to Aboriginal society.

P. DE STRZELECKI, *PHYSICAL DESCRIPTION OF NEW SOUTH WALES*, ETC., LONDON 1845, P. 340.

The foundation of their social edifice may, like that of civilized nations, be said to rest on an inherent sense of the rights of property. As strongly

An artist's impression of Batman's treaty with Port Phillip Aborigines in 1836 for the purchase of 600 000 acres of land. Though Batman's treaty was in many respects a confidence trick it did reflect the growing conviction in the 1830s that the Aborigines were the prior possessors of the land. The New South Wales Government refused to accept the treaty, but not, as many assume, because the Aborigines had no rights at all. The legal principle in question related to the long established practice that individual colonists could not deal with the indigenous people for land. Only the Crown could extinguish the native title. A. Garren (ed.), *Picturesque Atlas of Australasia*, 2 vols, Picturesque Atlas Publishing Co., Sydney, 1886, Vol. 1, p. 161.

attached to that property, and to the rights which it involves, as any European political body, the tribes of Australia resort to precisely similar measures for protecting it, and seek redress and revenge for its violated laws through the same means as a European nation would, if similarly situated.

The Reality of Dispossession

If the Aborigines lived in clearly defined areas and had a strong sense of property the implications were clear—the settlers had dispossessed them and had incurred deep moral obligations to the victims of their hunger for land. By the 1830s and 1840s a minority of humanitarian settlers were expressing deep concern about the development of Australian colonization. Their attitudes reflected the success of the Anti-Slavery movement in Britain and of the establishment of a House of Commons Select Committee to investigate the position of native people in the Empire. If Australia wasn't settled by occupation of waste land then the nature of local colonization was open to question.

G.C. MUNDY, *OUR ANTIPODES*, LONDON, 1857, P. 48.

We hold [Australia] neither by inheritance, by purchase, nor by conquest, but by a sort of gradual eviction. As our flocks and herds and population increase, our corresponding increase of space is required, the natural owners of the soil are thrust back without treaty, bargain or apology.

* * * * * *

While the visitor Mundy was able to look objectively at the situation, some settlers thought the taking of Aboriginal land was morally objectionable.

REV J. SAUNDERS REPORTED IN *THE COLONIST*, 19 OCTOBER 1838.

It is not just to say that the natives have no notion of property, and therefore we could not rob them of that which they did not possess; for accurate information shows that each tribe had its distinct locality ... from these their hunting grounds they have been individually and collectively dispossessed.

* * * * * *

The missionary Lancelot Threlkeld was even more outspoken on the issue.

L. THRELKELD, ANNUAL REPORT FOR 1838, P. 4, THRELKELD PAPERS, ML.

As a nation *we* have placed *ourselves* in a position that has compelled the Aborigines to become *our neighbours* and we have worked ill towards our neighbours, because we, the many, dispossess the few Blacks of their rights of birth, which convey to them a certain district in which they seek and obtain their means of subsistence. Our might deprives them of this right, without remuneration: and Immigration, so beneficial to us as a Colony, in increasing our population, decreases in an incalculable ratio, our neighbours as a people, by taking away the common hereditary privileges which they have possessed from time immemorial. The place of their birth is sold to the highest bidder. They are excluded from the soil, being found generally prejudicial to the pecuniary interests of the purchaser, and that exclusion works their death.

* * * * * *

Doubt about the nature of settlement was even heard in colonial courts. In a Supreme Court of New South Wales in 1836 during the trial of an Aboriginal, Jack Congo Murrell, for murder of another black the defence counsel S. Stephen argued that, as the victims of the process of colonisation, the Aborigines were in a very special position as regards the law.

J. LEGGE, (ED.), *A SELECTION OF SUPREME COURT CASES*, 2 VOLS., SYDNEY, 1896, 1, P. 72.

This country was not originally desert, or peopled from the mother country, having had a population far more numerous than those that have since arrived from the mother country. Neither can it be called a conquered country, as Great Britain was never at war with the natives, nor a ceded country either; it, in fact, comes within neither of these, but was a country having a population which had manners and customs of their own, and we have come to reside among them; therefore in point of strictness and analogy to our law, we are bound to obey their laws, not they to obey ours. The reason why subjects of Great Britain are bound by the laws of their country is, that they are protected by them; the natives are not protected by those laws, they are not admitted as witnesses in Courts of Justice, they cannot claim any civil rights, they cannot obtain recovery of, or compensation for, those lands which have been torn from them, and which they have probably held for centuries.

Land Rights Recognized

During the 1830s there was a growing belief in both Britain and Australia that something was very wrong with the path of development in New South Wales, Tasmania and Western Australia. There had been serious conflict with the Aborigines in each colony and there was little prospect that things would improve in the future. Prominent officials in Australia discussed the possibility of a treaty with the Aborigines. Humanitarian reformers in Britain focused their attention on the lack of any recognition of land rights, or native title, as it was known at the time. In North America treaties had been negotiated with the Indians and land purchased from them throughout the 18th century. It was Australia which was markedly out of step with accepted colonial practice and colonial law. Concern about Australia came to a head in 1835 when a new government came to power in England and reformers took control of the Colonial Office. These developments coincided with final preparations for the establishment of a new colony in South Australia promoted by a Colonization Commission. Prior to granting their final approval—and the issue of the so called Letters Patent—the Secretary of State for the Colonies, Lord Glenelg, informed the head of the Colonization Commission that the would-be colonists would have to make arrangements to buy the land from the Aborigines. The Imperial Government's commitment to native title in Australia was evident in one clause of the Letters Patent.

DRAFT OF LETTERS PATENT, COLONIAL OFFICE, RECORDS, SERIES 13/3.

Provided always that nothing in these our Letters Patent contained shall affect or be construed to affect the rights of any aboriginal natives of the said Province to the actual occupation or enjoyment in their own Persons or in the Persons of their Descendants of any lands therein now actually occupied or enjoyed by such Natives.

* * * * * *

The Commissioners were forced to draw up plans which paid at least token respect to Aboriginal rights.

FIRST REPORT OF THE COMMISSIONERS ON COLONIZATION OF SOUTH AUSTRALIA, *BPP*, 1836, 39, 426, PP. 8—9.

In considering the subject . . . [of the Aborigines] the following objects should be aimed at: to guard them against personal outrage and

MITCHELL LIBRARY, STATE LIBRARY OF NSW. W.A. Cawthorne. *Natives...being driven [to] the Police Court...1847* Pencil. If, as many colonists argued, the Aborigines had no claim on the land at all they could be driven off their territory by the pioneer Europeans. This was often accompanied by violence or by using the power of the state to treat them as trespassers.

violence; to protect them in the undisturbed enjoyment of their proprietary right to the soil, wherever such right may be found to exist; to make it an invariable and cardinal condition in all bargains and treaties made with the natives for the cession of lands possessed by them, in occupation or enjoyment, that permanent subsistence shall be supplied to them from some other source.

* * * * * *

The same principles were embodied in instructions sent from London to the Commission's officers in South Australia.

THIRD ANNUAL REPORT OF THE COLONIZATION COMMISSIONERS OF SOUTH AUSTRALIA, *BPP*, 1839, 225, 17.

You will see that no lands which the natives may possess in occupation or enjoyment be offered for sale until previously ceded by the natives to the Commissioners, and which cession you are hereby authorized to accept. You will furnish the Protector of Aborigines with evidence of the faithful fulfilment of the bargains or treaties which you may effect with the Aborigines for the cession of lands, and you will take care that the Aborigines are not disturbed in the enjoyment of the lands over which they possess proprietary rights, and of which they are not disposed to make a voluntary transfer.

* * * * * *

Despite all the fine words it is doubtful if the Commissioners ever really intended to respect Aboriginal land rights. From the very beginning they argued that the Aborigines were not in actual occupation of the land and therefore there was nothing to negotiate about, or to give compensation for. Not everyone was happy with this situation. Humanitarians in both Britain and South Australia felt betrayed.

LETTER TO THE EDITOR FROM 'A LOVER OF JUSTICE', *SOUTHERN AUSTRALIAN*, 28 JULY 1838.

The first Annual Report of the Colonisation Commissioners speaks of lands being reserved for the benefit of the natives. Have such reserves been made? *One* acre of land has been reserved for the tribes in this vicinity. Princely donation! Well may the native South Australians rejoice in their munificient Christian neighbours—reserve *one* and take *one hundred thousand.* But ought such things to be? The rights of the Original possessors are not at all affected by Acts of Parliament or Commissioner's Instructions: their right rests upon principles of justice. It is impossible to deny the right which the natives have to the land on which they were born, from which age after age they have derived support and nourishment, and which has received their ashes. We must give them compensation for that which we deprive them of. Let us, therefore, as honest men, do justice to the Aborigines of our adopted land . . .

* * * * * *

Robert Cock, a Quaker settler, took more practical action to show his displeasure with the failure of the Commissioners to honour their promises.

'A TENANT' TO THE PROTECTOR OF THE ABORIGINES, ADELAIDE, 7 SEPTEMBER 1838; ABORIGINES PROTECTION SOCIETY PAPERS & PROCEEDINGS, 5, LONDON, 1839, P. 137.

Sir,—Please to receive herewith the sum of £3 16s. 6d. being the interest, at the rate of 10 per cent., on one-fifth of the purchase-money of the town land, purchased by me, on the 27th March, 1837.

This sum, in accordance with the pledge given by the Colonisation Commissioners for this province, and in accordance with the principle therein signified in their first annual report, wherein it is stated they were to receive one-fifth of the lands to constitute a permanent fund for the support and advancement of the natives; I beg leave to pay the above sum for that purpose, seeing the Commissioners as yet have neither fulfilled their pledge in this respect to the public, or carried out the moral principle signified. Under these circumstances it is impossible to let the question rest; and until that be done, I feel it my duty to pay to the proper authorities for the use of the natives this yearly rent—the above sum being one and a half year's rent; viz. from 27th March, 1837 to 27th instant.

I disclaim this to be either donation, grant, or gift; but a just claim the natives of this district have on me as an occupier of those lands.

Reserves for the Natives

South Australia's second Governor, George Gawler, attempted to find a way to respect Aboriginal native title in the existing colonial conditions. He developed the idea of creating reserves for the local tribes by way of providing compensation for land occupied by the Europeans. In co-operation with his Land Commissioner Charles Sturt he explained to a group of prominent and disgruntled settlers why the Aborigines should be given the prior right to select land to be set aside for reserves.

CHARLES STURT TO D. MCLAREN AND OTHERS, 11 JULY 1840, *THE SOUTH AUSTRALIAN REGISTER*, 1 AUGUST 1840.

Gentlemen, I am desired by his Excellency to say, in reply, that it is to him a matter of deep surprise that persons of intelligence, like yourselves, who also . . . are well acquainted with the history of the establishment of the colony, should consider any rights which any European possesses to the lands of the province, as preliminary to those of the aboriginal inhabitants.

Those natural indefeasible rights which, as his Excellency conceives, are vested in them as their birthright, have been confirmed to them by the Royal Instructions to the Governor, and by the Commissioner's instructions to the Resident Commissioner.

The Royal Instructions command that they shall be protected in the free enjoyment of their possessions; ... and the Commissioner's instructions direct that they shall not be disturbed in the enjoyment of lands over which they may possess proprietary rights, and of which they are not disposed to make a voluntary transfer.

That this colony was publicly known to have been founded on principles of the strictest regard to the original rights of the aboriginal inhabitants, his Excellency need only refer you to a document with which you are well acquainted—the First Annual Report of the Colonization Commissioners [see above].

It is scarcely necessary for the Governor to mention, that, prior to the landing of the first British settlers, the natives possessed well understood and distinctly defined proprietary rights over the whole of the available land in the Province.

In the degree of knowledge to which they have attained, it would, however, have been to their great disadvantage to have entered into general treaties with them for the cession of lands, inasmuch such lands would certainly have been obtained for the most insignificant, ill-defined, and unsubstantial terms.

The course which the Governor and Resident Commissioner has preferred to take, is that of directing the Protector of the Aborigines to select such land for the natives, in moderation, as he may deem likely to be necessary for their future use, support and advancement in civilization.

* * * * * *

CHARLES STURT TO S. MCLAREN AND OTHERS, 17 JULY 1840, *THE SOUTH AUSTRALIAN REGISTER*, 1 AUGUST 1840.

The aboriginal inhabitants of this province have an absolute right of selection prior to all Europeans who have settled in it during the last four years, of reasonable positions of the choicest land, for their especial use and benefit, out of the very extensive districts over which, from time immemorial, these aborigines have exercised distinct, defined and absolute rights of proprietary and hereditary possession.

The invasion of those ancient rights by surveys and land appropriations of any kind, is justifiable only on the ground that we should, at the same time, reserve for the natives an ample sufficiency for their present and future use and comfort under the new state of things into which they are thrown—a state in which we hope they will be led to live in greater comfort on a smaller space than they enjoyed before it occurred on their extensive original possessions ...

Such spots of course must be within the native district of the tribe for whom they may be selected. If, in the proposition, you have intended to recommend that the native tribes shall be removed out of the haunts and districts, from time immemorial their own, the Governor cannot for a moment countenance a scheme which he is convinced would be practicable only by the severest coercion, and extremely harsh towards men who, by their general conduct, merit a very different treatment.

Compensation

Reserves were created for Aborigines in all parts of Australia during the second half of the 19th and the first part of the 20th century. However they were usually regarded as gifts bestowed rather than compensation provided for lost land. During the middle years of the 19th century it was common for settlers to talk of the need to provide compensation—or an 'equivalent' as it was called—for the Aborigines. The Imperial government provided for the expenditure of up to 15 per cent of revenue from land sales and rentals to be spent on Aboriginal welfare and education. But it never made such expenditure obligatory and no colonial government ever spent more than a fraction of the proposed amount. When Western Australia was granted self-government in 1890 the necessary Imperial legislation spelt out the expenditure which was to go to the Aborigines. However the clause was soon repealed and amounts spent on Aborigines were far below those projected by the British authorities.

THE CONSTITUTION ACT, 52 VIC., NO. 23, 1889; SECTION 70, PART 4.

There shall be payable to Her Majesty in every year, out of the Consolidated Revenue Fund the sum of Five thousand pounds . . . to be appropriated to the welfare of the Aboriginal Natives, and expended in providing them with food and clothing when they would otherwise be destitute, in promoting the education of Aboriginal children (including half-castes), and in assisting generally to promote the preservation and well-being of the Aborigines. The said annual sum shall be issued to the Aborigines Protection Board by the Treasurer on warrants under the hand of the Governor, and may be expended by the said Board at their discretion, under the sole control of the Governor, anything in 'The Aborigines Protection Act, 1886,' to the contrary not withstanding. Provided always, that if and when the gross revenue of the Colony shall exceed Five hundred thousand pounds in any financial year, an amount equal to one per centum on such gross revenue shall, for the purposes of this section, be substituted for the said sum of Five thousand pounds in and for the financial year next ensuing.

If in any year the whole of the said annual sum shall not be expended, the unexpended balance thereof shall be retained by the said Board, and expended in the manner and for the purposes aforesaid in any subsequent year.

Black Politics

During the 19th and early 20th centuries Aboriginal groups began to use the European political system to achieve their objectives. Two themes run through black politics—the desire for full civil rights and the demand for land and compensation in recognition of prior ownership. It is possible to trace the desire for land back to the earliest days of settlement. Francis Tuckfield, the pioneer Methodist missionary, watched the dispossession of Victorian Aborigines by the squatters in the late 1830s and early 1840s.

THE JOURNAL OF FRANCIS TUCKFIELD, LA TROBE LIBRARY, MSS. 655, P. 176.

They seem to be acquainted with the relative possessions of the Black and White populations—they are conscious of what is going on—they are driven from this favoured haunt and from their other favoured haunt and threatened if they do not leave immediately they will be lodged in gaol or shot. It is to the Missionaries they come with their tales of woe and their language is—'Will you now select for us also a position of land? My country all you gone. The white men have stolen it.'

* * * * * *

The desire for land became even more urgent as settlement spread and all over the country Aboriginal groups became landless fringe dwellers. In a book of reminiscences a New South Wales policeman recalled that local Aborigines approached him on the question of land.

M. BRENNAN, *REMINISCENCES OF THE GOLD FIELDS*, W. BROOKS, SYDNEY, 1907, P. 213.

In December, 1872, a large corroboree was held on the Braidwood gold fields, at which representatives from Bronlee, Shoalhaven, and coastal districts attended. When the festival was over, sixty two blacks called upon me. Jack Bawn and Alik were the leaders of the deputation. I asked

Jack what they wanted. He replied, 'We have come to you to intercede for us in getting the Government to do something for us. Araluen Billy, our king, is old, and cannot live long; my wife Kitty and self are old, too. I have assisted the police for many years, and we want to get some land which we can call our own in reality, where we can settle down, and which the old people can call their home. Everyone objects to our hunting on his land, and we think the blacks are entitled to live in their own country.

* * * * * *

There was a significant upsurge of Aboriginal political activity in the years before the second world war. But the emphasis was mainly on achieving full civil and political equality. The issue of land rights re-emerged during the 1960s and 1970s. In 1963 the Yirrkala people of the Gove Peninsula in Arnhem Land sent a bark petition to federal Parliament seeking to overturn a decision to excise their traditional lands from the Aboriginal reserve in order to make way for bauxite mining.

IDENTITY, JULY 1971, P. 9.

The Humble Petition of the undersigned Aboriginal people of Yirrkala, being members of the Balamumu, Narrkala, Gapiny and Miliwurrwurr people and Djapu, Mangalili, Madarrpa, Magarrwanalinirri, Gumaitj, Djambarrpuynu, Marrakulu, Galpu, Dhaluayu, Wangurri, Warramirri, Maymil, Rirritjinu tribes, respectfully sheweth—
  1. That nearly 500 people of the above tribes are residents of the land excised from the Aboriginal Reserve in Arnhem Land.
  2. That the procedures of the excision of this land and the fate of the people on it were never explained to them beforehand, and were kept secret from them.
  3. That when Welfare Officers and Government officials came to inform them of decisions taken without them and against them, they did not undertake to convey to the Government in Canberra the views and feelings of the Yirrkala Aboriginal people.
  4. That the land in question has been hunting and food gathering land for the Yirrkala tribes from time immemorial; we were all born here.
  5. That places sacred to the Yirrkala people, as well as vital to their livelihood, are in the excised land, especially Melville Bay.
  6. That the people of this area fear that their needs and interests will be completely ignored as they have been ignored in the past, and they fear that the fate which has overtaken the Larrakeah tribe will overtake them.

7. And they humbly pray that the Honourable the House of Representatives will appoint a Committee, accompanied by competent interpreters, to hear the views of the Yirrkala people before permitting the excision of this land.
They humbly pray that no arrangements be entered into with any company which will destroy the livelihood and independence of the Yirrkala people.

* * * * * *

A second petition was sent to the Prime Minister in May 1971, a few days after the Northern Territory Supreme Court had determined that the Yirrkala people had no legal rights to their traditional land.

IDENTITY, JULY 1971, P. 9.

The people of Yirrkala have asked us to speak to you on their behalf. They are deeply shocked at the result of the recent Court case. We cannot be satisfied with anything less than ownership of the land. The land and law, the sacred places, songs, dances and language were given to our ancestors by spirits Djangkawu and Barama. We are worried that without the land future generations could not maintain our culture. We have the right to say to anybody not to come to our country. We gave permission for one mining company but we did not give away the land. The Australian law has said that the land is not ours. This is not so. It might be right legally but morally it's wrong. The law must be changed. The place does not belong to white man. They only want it for the money they can make. They will destroy plants, animal life and the culture of the people.

The people of Yirrkala want:
1. Title to our land.
2. A direct share of all royalties paid by Nabalco.
3. Royalties from all other businesses on the Aboriginal Reserves.
4. No other industries to be started without consent of the Yirrkala Council.
5. Land to be included in our title after mining is finished.

* * * * * *

The land rights movement developed rapidly among urban Aborigines during the late 1960s and early 1970s. They also began to direct their appeal outside Australia. In 1970 the Aborigines Advancement League addressed a petition to the Secretary-General of the United Nations.

THE LAND QUESTION

ORIGIN, 30 OCTOBER 1970, P. 9.

Dear Sir,

This is an urgent plea of several hundred thousand so-called 'Aborigines' of Australia that the United Nations use its legal and moral powers for the vindication of our rights to the lands which we have traditionally occupied.

We make this plea under Item 55 of the General Assembly, which deals with the elimination of all racial discrimination for it is only racial discrimination which can explain the refusal of the Government of Australia to grant us, and us alone, our rights.

In support of our plea we call attention to Part II, Article II of Convention 107 of the International Labor Conference, to which conference the Government of Australia is a party: 'The right of ownership, collective or individually, or the members of the populations concerned over the lands which these populations traditionally occupied shall be recognized'.

And we call further attention to Article 12 of that convention, which provides that if traditional populations are removed without their free consent from their lands, they must be fully compensated.

By Aboriginal law in Australia generally, land was traditionally inalienable. Moreover, the only known time in Australian history when the invading white exploiters made so much as a pretence of negotiating for the purchase of land in Australia from the indigenous people was in March 1835, when one John Batman signed the Batman Treaty with eight Aboriginal Elders for the 'purchase' of 100,000 acres of land in the vicinity of Port Phillip, in exchange for smaller quantities of trade goods.

Even this supposed 'purchase' was never recognised by the governor in Victoria, Governor Bourke, when he stated that only the Crown had power to make treaties or contract for the acquisition of land.

We must emphasise: FROM THE TIME OF THE FIRST SETTLEMENT IN 1788 TO DATE, THE CROWN HAS NEVER USED EVEN ITS CLAIMED POWER TO TAKE OUR LAND, EITHER BY TREATY OR BY PURCHASE. THE CROWN HAS BLATANTLY TAKEN OUR LAND WITHOUT TREATY, WITHOUT PURCHASE, AND WITHOUT COMPENSATION OF ANY KIND.

We, the Aborigines of Australia whom the invaders have not yet succeeded in wiping off the face of the earth, are the owners of the land of Australia in equity, in the eyes of any system of civilised law and in justice and yet we have no share in the great mineral, agricultural and pastoral wealth of our country.

We are sent to reservations which are described as Crown Lands, and the Government has complete control over these lands. When we ask for certain lands in our tribal areas, we are told that the Government has leased them, sometimes at the rate of 50 cents (US) per square mile for periods of 99 years, but we never are consulted as to these unlawful leases.

To favor Bauxite miners, the lands of the Yirrkala people on the Gove Peninsula in the Northern Territory have been stolen from them and their special sacred areas desecrated.

The Gurindji people at Wattie Creek demanded remuneration of its claims to 500 square miles of their tribal lands, and also they were promised a meager 8½ square miles. They in fact have received nothing whatever on the pretext that the Government cannot reclaim the land from those to whom it has given it.

When bauxite was discovered at Weipa on the Western coast of Cape York Peninsula, the Aboriginal people living there were forcibly ousted so that the area could be mined. It was possible for the Government to make land available for the construction of a mining town for whites, but the Aborigines claims to their tribal lands were ignored.

We could recite case after case, but these three instances are enough to show that the rights of the Aboriginal peoples of Australia have been systematically taken from them.

* * * * * * *

The National Aboriginal Conference prepared a pamphlet on land rights which included a chapter on 'Aboriginal Ideology and Philosophy of the Land'.

NATIONAL ABORIGINES CONFERENCE, *LAND RIGHTS: ABORIGINAL LAND RIGHTS AND THE NEED FOR A NATIONAL POLICY*, NAC, CANBERRA, NO DATE.

In a time before, after the Dreaming, the world was ordered in things that made it up: the land, the sea, and all the living things. All these things were of two kinds, Dhua and Yirritja and these two things were in balance. Now the balance has changed.

The indigenous people of Australia are in the same situation as most of the other fourth world peoples of the world. They find themselves embedded in a society of people from other places who also live in their land. For Aboriginals as with others, in that situation, the most important characteristic, which distinguishes them from other people of the world, is that they have refused to surrender identity.

It is this identity based on indigenousness, which has built the Aboriginal ideology for living, and indeed for survival. They have survived active destruction of their society. They have seen the land changed and altered, in such a way that few of the people can still follow a lifestyle based on the economic system as it was before.

These survivors of the traditional form, bear witness to the order and perfection of Aboriginal society. And it is from them and only from them that Aboriginals properly learn the past—the way they are, and from whence they came.

Traditionally Aboriginal society is based on three major principles. The first of these is a powerful all encompassing religion. They believe that Aboriginal children are born of women but conceived of a spiritual source whose fonte is the land. And to them the land has two kinds of landscapes—one is physical, which all human beings can view. The other is spiritual, which only they can see. For Aboriginal people there is only one way to own land and that is to be conceived of it. Land is a parent. This very important principle prevents any kind of land aggrandisement which has been the scourge of the rest of the world.

The land, for Aboriginal people, is a vibrant spiritual landscape. It is peopled in spirit form by ancestors who originated in the dreaming, the creative period of time immemorial. The ancestors travelled the country, engaging in adventures which created the people, the natural features of the land and established the code of life, which is today called 'the dreaming' or 'the law'. The law has been passed on through countless generations of people through remembrance and celebration of sites which were the scenes of the ancestral exploits. Song, dance, body, rock and sand painting, special languages and the oral explanations of the myths encoded in these essentially religious art forms have been the media of the Law to the present day.

The way in which Aboriginals say they are related to each other is an intricate part of the people's relationship to the land. It is estimated that before the white invasion, there were 300,000 people in Australia speaking 500 languages. This great language diversity is the manifestation of each group's identification with 'country' and thus an expression of its difference from another group whose 'country' represents different travels and adventures of the ancestors. Despite the linguistic and, to a lesser extent, cultural diversity, it seems that there was a continent-wide philosophy—now called the Law or Dreaming. For at least 40,000 years prior to the British invasion, the Aboriginal economic mode was one of hunting and gathering according to a seasonal calendar largely within defined clan territories. The social organisation of people into clans did not result in discrete units, such as the case in tribal Africa, but rather these clans were interlocking units by virtue of the marital, economic, political and religious relations between them. Each clan consisted at its core of patrilineal and matrilineal descendants of a common ancestor who were the central characters around which the affairs of the clan revolved. It was primarily through marriage that political bonding of clans was achieved, because wives of clan members remained members of their own different clans and remained co-owners of their clan estates. Thus, kinship networks were abstracted to extreme exoteric extent, so that people over large areas were related through cultural and religious precepts.

The ancient and enduring ideology and philosophy of the Dreaming is today challenged by the insidious encroachment of white ideology which permeates all the institutions which are regarded in Australia as sole mentors of values, morals and law enforcement.

These two systems co-exist (although until recently the white system did not recognise this) and the two systems are fundamentally incompatible; the Aboriginal system of law being based on descent from ancestral heroes who laid down a blue print for the Aboriginal existence on this continent and the Aboriginal relationship to land and therefore to other people, and the white system being based on property relations, personal aggrandisement and monopolisation of resources by the few.

Aboriginal social existence and conflict with white society, nationally and internationally through the unacceptable relation of multi-national mining companies to Aboriginal communities, is based on the unrelinquished will of Aboriginal people to maintain identity, relationship to land and refusal to accept the interference of white institutions in their lives at national and community level.

This describes the present situation and it can best be summarised by saying that whites draw on myths of superiority to secure power and to rule in the land.

My people believe that the government has determined which values should prevail over Aboriginal communities and thus, the conflict between Aboriginals and white Australian [sic] ensues. It is the opinion of the National Aboriginal Conference that there is no common factor between white Australians and the Aboriginal people that could be used to develop mutual respect.

The differences between the two peoples are clearly defined in that the origins of white Australia are materially based, as opposed to Aboriginal society which has no concept of materialism and which is spiritually based.

Aboriginals believe that human beings are a synthesis of mortal and spiritual parts. Unlike many of the world's religions, they believe that personality is a product of this synthesis and not contained in any one part. At death the spirit persists and returns to the land.

The principle order is that of social organisation. When a child is born into the world he is related to every other human being that lives. He finds himself in a constellation of belonging. Aboriginals have one of the world's most extensive kinship organisations which interconnects, through religion, with all the world of living and inanimate things. Death cannot deprive a child of a mother or father or an uncle or an aunt or a brother or sister. Even today when Aboriginal people use the term brother or sister, it means far more than political brotherhood.

THE LAND QUESTION

The next principle in the society is that of our economic system. All human beings practice some form of exchange of materials and other things and Aboriginal society is no exception. It is the nature of the traditional Australian exchange system which is extraordinary.

Aboriginal people have often been described as a non-materialistic people. This is true, and the characteristics of our traditional economic system made it impossible for them to be anything else. They practice an almost exclusively, non-equittable debt system and the nearest other societies get to this is gift giving. The currency of exchange of beholdness, Materials, services, responsibility, bestowal of wives, all of these things can be exchanged and become part of this system, a 'merbok', (an event of exchange) as something passed from one hand to another, an unseen currency passed in reverse, the receiver beholden to the giver, and the debt which incurred can never be acquitted. It can be transferred and is regulated and ordered.

Because there is no acquittal on the exchange, the debt is eternal, and therefore all things within the system have a common value. The acquisition of material goods means nothing. But as somebody in modern non-Aboriginal Australian society may acquire wealth and, own a great deal of money, so Aboriginal people may also acquire wealth. What they acquire however is a great many people beholden to them and vice versa. So it is that the wealthiest of people may have the least possessions, and yet like all human beings of wealth and substance they have great status in the world.

These three principles form together a highly ordered and sophisticated society. The elements involved in the Aboriginal system are land, human beings and all other things that dwell with them. This system is in harmony and balance, and this is perfection.

The problem is that if any element of the system is destroyed, this circle of perfection is broken. 194 years ago this circle was broken, and in the Southern areas of the continent our society was all but destroyed.

The balance and harmony was lost but the strength of it lived within the survivors, and it gave rise to the identity that Aboriginals will carry with them into the 21st century and beyond. It is this identity which distinguishes them from anyone else who lives in their place. It is this identity that makes them what they are.

'We are Aboriginals, we are the desert winds, we are the sunlit plains, we are the bright waters, we are Australia. This land is our birthright. In this new world, in our new society, we have but a single principle. We are our brothers' keepers.'

As far as the rest of the world is concerned Aboriginals have the right to what they are, the right to independence, to self-determination, to their own destiny, the right to be. We are not mendicants. We seek only what is ours, and the land is ours. We live on the planet earth and are citizens of that planet. We do no wish to make refugees of those descendants of the invaders or those who will come to live here. We will walk beside them in friendship and in goodwill, but we will not be subjugated nor will we allow this land to be subjugated to alien demands or greed. This is our world. We are prepared to share it, but not to give it away.

The Makarrata

The land rights movement has always included both white and black Australians. While Aboriginal organizations pursued the issue a group of prominent white Australians established an Aboriginal Treaty Committee which called on the Australian Government to negotiate a treaty with the Aborigines. They launched their cause in an advertisement in the press in 1979.

J. WRIGHT, *WE CALL FOR A TREATY*, COLLINS, SYDNEY, 1985, PP. 318−20.

We the undersigned Australians, of European descent, believe that experience since 1788 has demonstrated the need for the status and rights of Aboriginal Australians and Torres Strait Islanders to be established in a Treaty, Covenant or Convention freely negotiated with the Commonwealth Government by their representatives. Australia is the only former British colony not to recognize native title to land. From this first wrong two centuries of injustice have followed. It is time to strike away the past and make a just settlement together. We believe this would be a signal to the world that we are indeed one Australian people, at last.

In New Zealand, at the Treaty of Waitangi in 1840, the Maori chiefs were guaranteed by their conquerors 'full, exclusive and undisturbed possession of their lands . . . so long as it is their wish and desire to retain the same', and most of these lands were later bought. In North America, Indian tribes negotiated treaties with their conquerors, who recognized the principle of purchase or compensation for the loss of their lands. The colonial authorities were directed by the government in London to deal with the tribes as 'foreign nations'. In Papua, in 1884, the conquerors assured the people 'your lands will be preserved unto you', again until they decided to sell. But in Australia there was no recognition of Aboriginal land ownership, no compensation for dispossession, no treaty, despite the resistance of the Aboriginal tribes to their conquerors.

Indeed, the absence of a settlement leads many Aborigines to conclude even today that their resistance is not yet over. It is a sad conclusion, for all of us, after so many generations of living together in this country. We believe there is a deep and wide concern among

Australians of European descent that our ownership of this land, as defined in the imported European law, should still be based solely upon force, without any documentary recognition of the quality and courage of those who were conquered. It is time to right this wrong.

In 1979, the National Aboriginal Conference asked unanimously for a Treaty to be negotiated. We call upon the Commonwealth Government to respond and we urge the Commonwealth Parliament to resolve that the Government should:

(a) enable the National Aboriginal Conference to summon a convention of representatives nominated by Aboriginal communities and associations to choose negotiators, who would propose the bases of negotiation and how any settlement should be confirmed;

(b) organise the negotiations;

(c) submit any Treaty, Covenant or Convention to Parliament for ratification.

We believe that any Treaty, Covenant or Convention should include provisions relating to the following matters:

i) The protection of Aboriginal identity, languages, law and culture.

ii) The recognition and restoration of rights to land by applying throughout Australia, the recommendations of the Woodward Commission.

iii) The conditions governing mining and exploitation of other natural resources on Aboriginal land.

iv) Compensation to Aboriginal Australians for the loss of traditional lands and for damage to those lands and to their traditional way of life.

v) The right of Aboriginal Australians to control their own affairs and to establish their own associations for this purpose.

The Question of Sovereignty

It is not always appreciated that when the British claimed possession of Australia there were two quite distinct issues involved—*sovereignty*, or the right to exercise political power over Australia, and *property*, or the actual ownership of the land. The second question has been much more open to debate than the first. But in recent years Aborigines have not only talked of their rights to land but also to their sovereignty. The issue was raised in a case brought by Aboriginal lawyer Paul Coe before the High Court in 1979. Coe's arguments were summarized by Mr Justice Gibbs.

COE V. COMMONWEALTH OF AUSTRALIA, *AUSTRALIAN LAW JOURNAL*, 53, 1979, PP. 407—8.

The following appear to be the main facts and circumstances asserted as the foundation of the appellant's claims:
  (a) There is an aboriginal nation which, before European settlement, enjoyed exclusive sovereignty over the whole of Australia, and which still has sovereignty.
  (b) Captain Cook wrongly proclaimed sovereignty and dominion over the east coast of Australia, and Captain Phillip wrongly claimed possession and occupation thereof, on behalf of His Majesty King George III, and the defendants are the successors in title, in Australia and the United Kingdom respectively, of that monarch; the Commonwealth now claims, and 'has purported to exercise' sovereignty over Australia.
  (c) Before European settlement, individual members, and tribes, of the aboriginal people had proprietary and possessory rights in land, subject to usufructuary rights in others, but the whole of Australia was held by the aboriginal nation for the benefit of all its members.
  (d) Australia was acquired by the British Crown by conquest, after which the aboriginal people and nation retained their rights in respect of their lands.
  (e) The Commonwealth has enacted legislation which interfered with the free exercise of the religion of the plaintiff and of the aboriginal community and nation, inter alia, by allowing parts of lands of religious significance to be mined and by permitting the mining and export of uranium.
  (f) The plaintiff and the aboriginal people are entitled at common law to the proprietary and possessory rights which they had prior to 1770, unless those rights were taken away by 'bilateral treaty, lawful compensation and/or lawful international intervention'.
  (g) Since 1788 certain of the aboriginal people have been unlawfully dispossessed of their lands by Captain Phillip and other persons including servants and agents of the defendants.

[In his judgement Mr. Justice Gibbs responded to the major claims advanced by Coe.]

It is clear that the allegations whose effect I have briefly stated . . . could not form the basis of any cause of action. The annexation of the east coast of Australia by Captain Cook in 1770, and the subsequent acts by which the whole of the Australian continent became part of the dominions of the Crown, were acts of state whose validity cannot be challenged. If the amended statement of claim intends to suggest either that the legal foundation of the Commonwealth is insecure, or that the powers of the Parliament are more limited than is provided in the Constitution, or that there is an aboriginal nation which has sovereignty over Australia, it cannot be supported. In fact, we were told in argument, it is intended to claim that there is an aboriginal nation which has sovereignty over its own people, notwithstanding that they remain citizens of the Commonwealth... The aboriginal people are subject to the laws of the Commonwealth and of the States or Territories in which they respectively reside. They have no legislative, executive or judicial organs by which sovereignty might be exercised. If such organs existed, they would have no powers, except such as the laws of the Commonwealth, or of a State or Territory, might confer upon them. The contention that there is in Australia an aboriginal nation exercising sovereignty, even of a limited kind, is quite impossible in law to maintain.

4

THE IMAGE OF THE ABORIGINES: BLACK BROTHERS OR DEGRADED SAVAGES?

The relations of settlers and Aborigines represent just one part of the much larger history of relations between Europeans and the non-European world. During that history Europeans developed a concept of savagery—a term applied to hunter-gatherers and village dwelling agriculturalists in Africa, the Americas and the Pacific. However there was never any agreement about the nature of savages. Theories abounded; the image changed over time. Sometimes the savages were noble, more often they were base and degraded. All these ideas came to Australia with the settlers and were applied willy-nilly to the indigenous people who in the early days were often called Indians, or negroes, as well as Aborigines.

> *Racial attitudes hardened during the first century of Australian settlement, reflecting both changes in European thought and local experience. Behaviour towards the Aborigines, public and private, was intimately connected with the images of the Aborigines embedded in European thought.*

Savages: Noble Or Not?

The status of 'savages' fluctuated in European thought. In the 17th century the common view was that of Thomas Hobbes who believed that the life of the 'savage' was 'solitary, poor, nasty, brutish and short'. A hundred years later educated Europeans had visions of noble savages wholly uncorrupted by the vices of civilization. Both views were brought to Australia as part of the cultural baggage of the colonists. Both were apparent in the 19th century, although the concept of the noble savage declined in popularity as the century advanced and experience of frontier life hardened racial attitudes. The differing perceptions of the Aborigines can be seen in the writing of the first two British visitors to Australia—Dampier in 1688 and Cook a century later.

W. DAMPIER, *A NEW VOYAGE ROUND THE WORLD*, THE ARGONAUT PRESS, LONDON, 1927, PP. 312—13.

The Inhabitants of this Country are the miserablest People in the World... [They] have no Houses, and skin Garments, Sheep, Poultry, and Fruits of the Earth... and setting aside their Humane Shape, they differ but little from Brutes. They are tall, strait-bodied, and thin, with small long Limbs. They have great Heads, round Foreheads, and great Brows. Their Eye-lids are always half closed, to keep the Flies out of their Eyes; they being so troublesome here, that no fanning will keep them from coming to one's Face; and without the Assistance of both Hands to keep them off, they will creep into ones Nostrils, and Mouth too, if the Lips are not shut very close; so that from their Infancy being thus annoyed with these Insects, they do never open their Eyes as other People: And therefore they cannot see far, unless they hold up their Heads, as if they were looking at somewhat over them.

They have great Bottle-Noses, pretty full Lips, and wide Mouths. The two Fore-teeth of their Upper-jaw are wanting in all of them. Men and Women, old and young; whether they draw them out, I know not: Neither have they any Beards. They are long-visaged, and of a very unpleasing Aspect, having no one graceful Feature in their Faces. Their Hair is black, short and curl'd, like that of the Negroes; and not long and lank like the common *Indians*. The Colour of their Skins, both of their Faces and the rest of their Body, is Coal-black, like that of the Negroes of *Guinea*.

They have no sort of Cloaths, but a piece of the Rind of a Tree tied like a Girdle about their Waists, and a handful of long Grass, or three or four small green Boughs full of Leaves, thrust under their Girdle, to cover their Nakedness.

They have no Houses, but lie in the open Air without any covering; the Earth being their Bed, and the Heaven their Canopy. Whether they cohabit one Man to one Woman, or promiscuously, I know not; but they do live in Companies, 20 or 30 Men, Women, and Children together . . .

* * * * * *

J. COOK, *JOURNAL OF THE 'ENDEAVOUR', 1768–1771*, FACSIMILE EDITION, SOUTH AUSTRALIAN LIBRARIES EDITION, ADELAIDE, 1968, P. 323.

From what I have seen in the Natives of New Holland they may appear to some to be the most wretched People upon Earth; but in reality they are far more happier than we Europeans, being wholly unacquainted not only with the superfluous, but with the necessary Conveniences so much sought after in Europe; they are happy in not knowing the use of them. They live in a Tranquility which is not disturbed by the inequality of Condition. The Earth and Sea of their own accord furnishes them with all things necessary for Life. They covet not Magnificent Houses, Household stuff, etc; they live in a Warm and fine Climate, and enjoy every Wholesome Air, so that they seem to be fully sensible of [sic], for many to whom we gave Cloth, etc, left it carelessly upon the Sea Beach, and in the Woods, as a thing they had no manner of use for; in short, they seemed to set no Value upon anything of their own nor any one Article we could offer them. This in my opinion Argues, that they think themselves provided with all the necessarys of Life, and that they have no Superfluities.

* * * * * *

The Baudin expedition, which was in Australian waters in 1802, was the most scientifically oriented of all early voyages. The zoologist Peron wrote an interesting account of the Tasmanian Aborigines. After his first friendly contact with the local clans he explained his enthusiasm about the meeting, believing that the Tasmanians were 'natural' men totally untouched by civilization.

N.J.B. PLOMLEY, (ED.), *THE BAUDIN EXPEDITION AND THE TASMANIAN ABORIGINES, 1802*, BLUBBER HEAD PRESS, HOBART, 1983, PP. 23, 82, 83.

Thus ended our first meeting with the inhabitants of Van Diemen's Land . . . and there is no doubt it would have been difficult not to succumb to the fond emotions which such relations had prompted. This happy trust of the inhabitants in us, the affectionate display of benevolence they lavished on us, the sincereity of their behaviour towards us and the frankness of their manners, the touching ingenuousness of their caresses, everything seemed to combine to form in us feelings of the most tender interest. The general relationships between the different individuals in the family and the sort of patriarchal life we had witnessed, had moved us deeply. With inexpressible delight I had come to realize in them those brilliant descriptions of happiness and simplicity of the state of nature of which I had savoured the seducting charm many times in my reading.

[A few days later Peron reflected on the philosophic importance of the study he was engaged in, heading his comments 'Interesting characteristics of man in these countries'.]

The study of man as he is around us, deserves an equal hold upon our attention and our thoughts in twenty different ways. Almost a stranger still to all principles of social organization, without arts, without laws, without chiefs properly speaking, without clothing, without culture, without fixed habitation, he presents himself to us with that valuable combination of characters which constitute Natural Man. Never perhaps has so immense a quarry been opened up for philosophy. Everything is curious in such a being, everything interesting: his antiquity, his origin, the changes in his affairs and his traditions in this regard, his customs, his language, his feelings, his ideas, his physical constitution, his increase in numbers, his infirmities, his longevity, his relationship to climate etc. etc. One must consider everything in order to study, analyse and meditate deeply upon each of these different questions. This is the story of Nature and of all mankind. Faithful trustee for the fundamental rights of the human species, he preserves them intact in their basic completeness. It is among these people, then, that we are able to rediscover those precious rights which we have lost following the upheavals among peoples and the progress of civilization. We see it here, and also in the virtues of savage man and his vices. We will look into here both the resources he receives from Nature and the obligations to which Nature necessarily subjects him. From the careful comparison of these resources and needs, we know we cannot fail to obtain precious information as to the extent of his pleasures and enjoyments, as well as his privations and sufferings.

A portrait of Ouriaga of Bruny Island, painted by a member of the Baudin expedition, which clearly displays the ideas about noble savages expressed by Peron in his writing. *Source*: Reproduced from the published accounts of the expedition in the book *The Baudin Expedition and the Tasmanian Aborigines, 1802*, edited by N.J.B. Plomley, Blubber-Head Press, Hobart, 1983.

The connection between means and resources should therefore show us the connection between the benefits and disabilities attached to this state of man, who is as close to the zero point of civilization. We can then try to find out what useful modifications and what harmful changes the progress of civilization has been able to bring successively to this primitive state, and by a long succession of accurate observations . . . we can perhaps reach the correct solution of this enquiry, one which is so difficult and so subtle that again today it divides all the moralists and philosophies. We can decide, perhaps, if, when man is entirely left on his own, brought up not to fear the promptings of his senses and the fire of his natural passions, he is truly as good and as perfect as he is happy, particularly in the way several philosophers have recently suggested him to be. Again, we can decide if this state of nature, so celebrated today, is truly one of innocence, virtue and happiness.

First Impressions

In the early years of settlement opinion about the Aborigines varied widely, reflecting both the growing body of local experience and the current state of European thinking on the subject. The two extracts that follow reflect the range of such opinions.

J. TURNBULL, *A VOYAGE ROUND THE WORLD* ETC., 2ND ED., LONDON, 1813, PP. 87–90.

These aboriginal inhabitants of this distant region are indeed beyond comparison the most barbarous on the surface of the globe . . .

The residence of Europeans has been wholly ineffectual, the natives are still in the same state as at our first settlement. Every day are men and women to be seen in the streets of Sydney and Parramatta, naked as the moment of their birth. In vain have the more humane of the officers of the colony endeavoured to improve their condition, but still they persist in the enjoyment of their ease and liberty in their own way, and turn a deaf ear to any advice on the subject . . .

They are still as unprotected as ever against the inclemencies of weather, and the vicissitudes of plenty and absolute famine . . . In their persons they are meagre to a proverb, their skins are scarified in every part, and their faces besmeared with shell lime and red gum, their hair is matted like a moss, and ornamental with shark's teeth; and a piece of wood, like a skewer, is fixed in the cartilages of the nose. In a word, they compose altogether the most loathsome and disgusting tribe on the surface of the globe . . . To me, indeed, they appeared altogether the most stupid and insensible race of men I have ever seen.

* * * * * *

W. TENCH, *SYDNEY'S FIRST FOUR YEARS*, EDITED BY L.F. FITZHARDINGE, ANGUS AND ROBERTSON, SYDNEY, 1961, PP. 281, 282, 293, 294.

To appreciate their general powers of mind is difficult. Ignorance, prejudice, the force of habit, continually interfere to prevent

Illustration which appeared in a published account of Governor Phillip's voyage to Australia. The Aborigines have the proportions and even adopt the poses to be found in renaissance painting and classical sculpture. A. Phillip: *The Voyage of Governor Phillip to Botany Bay*, London, 1789; facsimile edition, South Australian Libraries Board, 1968, p. 82.

---

dispassionate judgement. I have heard men so unreasonable, as to exclaim at the stupidity of these people, for not comprehending what a small share of reflection would have taught them they ought not to have expected. And others again I have heard so sanguine in their admiration, as to extol proofs of elevated genius what the commonest abilities were capable of executing.

If they be considered as a nation, whose general advancement and acquisitions are to be weighted, they certainly rank very low, even in the scale of savages. They may perhaps dispute the right of precedency with the Hottentots, or the shivering tribes who inhabit the shores of Magellan. But how inferior do they show when compared with the subtle African; the patient watchful American; or the elegant timid islander of the South Seas. Though suffering from the vicissitudes of their climate,— strangers to cloathing [sic]: tho' feeling the sharpness of hunger, and knowing the precariousness of supply from that element on whose stores they principally depend, ignorant of cultivating the earth,—a less enlightened state we shall exclaim can hardly exist.

THE IMAGE OF THE ABORIGINES

NATIONAL LIBRARY OF AUSTRALIA, REX NAN KIVELL COLLECTION. Charles Rodius, (1802–1860) *Scene in Sydney Street*. Lithograph. A very different view of the Aborigines. The product of two developments—the growth of scientific racism and the social breakdown witnessed by the settlers in fringe-dwelling Aboriginal communities.

But if from general view we descend to particular inspection, and examine individually the persons who compose this community, they will certainly rise in estimation . . .

To offer my own opinion on the subject, I do not hesitate to declare, that the natives of New South Wales possess a considerable portion of that acumen, or sharpness of intellect, which bespeaks genius. All savages hate toil, and place happiness in inaction: and neither the arts of civilized life can be practiced, or the advantages of it felt, without application and labour. Hence they resist knowledge, and the adoption of manners and customs, differing from their own . . . The tranquil indifference, and unenquiring eye, with which they surveyed our works of art, have often in my hearing, been stigmatized as proofs of stupidity, and want of reflection. But surely we should discriminate between ignorance and defect of understanding. The truth was, they often neither comprehended the design, nor conceived the utility of such works: but on subjects in any degree familiarized to their ideas, they generally testified not only acuteness of discernment, but a large portion of good sense. I have always thought that the distinctions they showed in their estimate of us, on first entering into our society, strongly displayed the latter quality:—when they were led into our respective houses, at once to be astonished and awed by our superiority, their attention was directly turned to objects with which they were acquainted. They passed without rapture or emotion, our numerous artifices and contrivances: but when they saw a collection of weapons of war, or of the skins of animals and birds, they never failed to exclaim, and to confer with each other on the subject. The master of that house became the object of their regard, as they concluded he must be either a renowned warrior, or an expert hunter...

To conclude the history of a people for whom I cannot but feel some share of affection: let those who have been born in more favoured lands, and who have profited by more enlightened systems, compassionate, [feel compassion for] but not despise, their destitute and obscure situation. Children of the same omniscient paternal care, let them recollect, that by the fortuitous advantage of birth alone, they possess superiority; that untaught, unaccommodated man, is the same in Pall Mall, as in the wilderness of New South Wales.

The Enlightenment at the Antipodes

Tench's observations embodied the major elements of the ideas about the nature of man contained in the work of the philosophers of the enlightenment. There was a belief in the universality of reason, and therefore of equality, and a conviction that human difference was to be explained by the influence of the environment rather than by innate characteristics. This being so there was optimism about the possibility of changing social customs and, in the Australian context, of 'civilizing' the Aborigines. Governor Macquarie's attitude to the tribes around Sydney reflected these views.

MACQUARIE TO LORD BATHURST, 8 OCTOBER 1814, *HRA*, SERIES 1, VOL. VIII, PP. 368–9.

Scarcely Emerged from the remotest State of rude and Uncivilized Nature, these People appear to possess some Qualities, which, if properly Cultivated and Encouraged, Might render them not only less wretched and destitute by Reason of their Wild wandering and Unsettled Habits, but progressively Useful to the Country. According to their Capabilities either as Labourers in Agricultural Employ or among the lower Class of Mechanics.

Those Natives, Who resort to the Cultivated Districts of this Settlement, Altho' prone like other Savages to great Indolence and Indifference as to their future Means of Subsistence, Yet in General, are of free open and favourable Dispositions, honestly Inclined, and perfectly devoid of that designing Trick and Treachery, Which Characterize the Natives of New Zealand and those of the Generality of the Islands in the South Seas. The Natives of New South Wales have never been Cannibals. In fact they seem to have as great an Abhorrence of practices of that kind as if they had been reared in a Civilized State. The Principal part of their Lives is Wasted in Wandering thro' their Native Woods, in Small Tribes of between 20 and 50, in Quest of the immediate Means of Subsistence Making Opossums, Kangaroos, Grub Worms, and such Animals and Fish, as the Country and its Coast Afford, the Objects of their Fare.

The Introduction of Herds and Flocks has not even Yet tempted them to Alter their Mode of living, Which is a Circumstance to be Calculated on as peculiarly fortunate; since, had they been Inclined to Make prey of them, it would have been a Matter of the Greatest Difficulty, if not altogether Impossible in the early state of the Colony, to have guarded against their Depredations, and the Consequence would have been that Instead of the Numerous and promising Herds and Flocks, which now extend over the face of the Country, very few would have been preserved, and the Supplies of Animal Food would not have been in any Degree equal to our Wants.

Those Natives, who dwell Near Sydney or the other principal Settlements, live in a State of perfect Peace, Friendliness, and Sociality With the Settlers, and even Shew a Willingness to Assist them Occasionally in their Labours; and it seems only to require the fostering Hand of Time, gentle Means and Conciliatory Manners, to bring these poor Un-enlightened People into an important Degree of Civilization, and to Instil into their Minds, as they Gradually open to Reason and Reflection, A Sense of the Duties they owe their fellow Kindred and Society in general (to Which they Will then become United), and taught to reckon upon that Sense of Duty as the first and happiest Advance to a State of Comfort and Security.

From Whatever Motives or Causes Some of these Natives have been induced to Commit Acts of Hostility against the Settlers, it seems to bear a reasonable Inference that Provocation or Aggression from some Undiscovered or Unacknowledged Cause may have given Rise to them, Under an Impression of temporary Revenge; but when once Induced to forego this Vindictive Spirit, which Kindness and Encouragement and Social Intercourses together Would Sooner or later bring about, their next Step towards Civilization would be rapid and easy, and they Would learn to Appreciate that Degree of Importance to Which they had thus progressively Attained.

From Considerations of this kind, Which in a great Measure have been Guided and Strengthened by My own personal Knowledge and

Observation, I have determined to make an Experiment towards the Civilization of these Natives.

* * * * * *

The importance of the environment was underlined in the observations of the surgeon Peter Cunningham.

P. CUNNINGHAM, *TWO YEARS IN NEW SOUTH WALES*, EDITED D.S. MACMILLAN, ANGUS AND ROBERTSON, SYDNEY, 1966, PP. 202–4.

We may, I think, in a great measure impute their present low state of civilization, and deficiency in the mechanical arts, to the nature of the country they inhabit, the kind of life they lead, and the mode of government they live under.

Civilisation depends more upon the circumstances under which man is placed than upon any innate impulse of his own, the natural inclinations of man tending toward the savage state, or that in which food is procured with the least possible effort; there being something so irresistibly captivating in a wild, roaming life of this description, that few who have made the trial ever relish civilised society thoroughly again. It is only necessity that urges mankind to congregate in fixed habitations, and raise their food by the sweat of their brow; for if it could still be procured in as easy a way by civilized Europeans as by our uncultivated tribes, the European woods would soon abound with creatures nearly as rude and idle as our natives.

Here, though game and other articles of sustenance in the interior woods be tolerably abundant, yet they are so scattered that the natives must be constantly on the move from place to place to obtain them, so that fixed residences would be impracticable; while, from this constant shifting, the lighter their baggage is the more expeditiously can they move along, and consequently only the most common and most useful utensils are carried with them.

The New Zealander is obliged to form a fixed residence, cultivate yams and sweet potatoes, and breed hogs for his support, because the woods do not afford him sufficient game wherewith to maintain life; he ornaments his huts with carved cups and other useful appendages, to amuse his leisure hours and serve, as objects of pride, to look at. Our Australian tribes, however, find sufficient amusement in the constant shifting of scene in pursuit of their necessary food, while by means of their perpetual wars and the practices of spear-throwing, child-murder, and concubinage, they keep down population, obtaining their livelihood thus easily through their diminutive numbers by roaming through the woods. They are never driven to the necessity of congregating, and supplying their wants by artificial means, like the natives of most of our southern islands.

It is, I repeat, the necessity springing from overgrown population, and difficulty in obtaining food, except by artificial means, that first drives man into taking up a fixed abode; but here neither of these causes operates; those natives at all approaching to the character of 'livers under roofs' being the inhabitants of some portions of the sea-coast, where fish and oysters so abound as to afford them a constant supply of food for the greater portion of the year, admitting them thus to remain for a considerable period at one spot, and inducing them to construct habitations for that period to shelter themselves in.

The mode of their government, however, is I think by far the most insuperable bar to their civilization; and I know of no savages living in the same state, who have as yet readily been exalted above the debased condition in which they were originally found. The first symptom of advancement in a savage body is the establishment of chiefs, either elected or heredeitary [sic], to whom all pay submission, and to whose protection they trust their persons and properties. But here no such institution exists; might alone constitutes right; and as, consequently, the weak and industrious have no protection for their property against the strong and lawless, they have no inducement to accumulate that which may draw down violence upon their persons.

Phrenology: 'Scientific Racism'

But while some European thinkers were talking of human equality others were developing ideas of innate differences and of racial hierarchy. The Great Chain of Being was one of the most influential concepts at the time of the first settlement and early development of Australia. It was a way of arranging all living matter on a great chain from the simplest organisms at the bottom to man at the top. By the late 18th century it was increasingly common to place the various 'races' in hierarchical order with northern Europeans taking up the number one position. This led to a search for demonstrable differences between the 'races'. Anatomy provided what appeared to be the surest way of achieving a science of race. Scientists took an increasing interest in such matters and turned their attention to the shape, size, volume and configuration of skulls which were avidly collected and minutely studied. Phrenology was probably the most influential of these 'sciences' and was widely discussed in the Australian colonies from the 1820's onwards. It was based on two linked beliefs—that skills and traits of character were located in specific areas of the brain and that the configuration of the skull reflected the shape of the brain underneath. Thus the trained phrenologist could determine the character and ability of a person by feeling the bumps on the skull. Phrenologists frequently provided 'readings' of Aboriginal skulls.

'ANEAS' IN THE *COLONIAL LITERARY JOURNAL*, 29 AUGUST, 5 SEPTEMBER 1844.

The Aboriginal cranium appears to be large, although in reality the brain is not so. The uncommon thickness of the skull and in the integuments surrounding it, accounts for this; and the strength of the Aboriginal head-piece in resisting the most powerful blows of their waddy is well known. This, indeed, seems to be their invulnerable part, and a stroke upon it, has as little influence as upon a block of wood. Proverbial expressions have had their origin in common sense, and the epithets *thick-head, block-head,* have been bestowed with a considerable degree of point and shrewdness.

The great proponderancy of brain in the New Hollander, as in all savage nations, lies in the posterior parts of the head—the seat of the passions, and inferior sentiments; the moral and intellectual portions, with few exceptions, are very deficient. One of the most striking instances in which the development of the brain of the Aborigines harmonizes with their actual character, is in the deficiency of the organ of Constructiveness. The locality of this organ, on the temple, almost invariably presents a contracted and hollow appearance. It is principally to the want of constructive ingenuity, and mechanical genius in the Aborigines, that their inferiority as a people, and their degraded character (more so indeed than is just), are owing. The most barbarous and uncivilized people ever known, far surpass them in this respect. We are all acquainted with their wretched substitute for a habitation—a gunyah composed of three forked sticks about the height of a man, stuck into the ground at short distances, and with their pronged extremities interlocking at the top, covered over in the most careless way with the pliant bark of the tea-tree!

It is a very common error, to suppose that they have well-developed foreheads—the contrary, however, is undeniably the case, though an inexperienced person would be very apt to make such a mistake. An instance of this error occurred some time ago at a debate in the hall of the School of Arts, upon the question, 'Whether the doctrine of Phrenology is true or not?' In reply to some observations made by one of the debaters, contrasting the development of the head of the Aborigines with their character, a gentleman rose up and stated that he had been struck with what he considered their exceedingly well-developed foreheads. The fallacy of this is easily shown. The forehead consists of two divisions, the upper and lower—the upper including the reflective faculties, and the lower the perceptive. The latter are in truth very largely developed in the Aboriginal skull, which I hope to be able to show is in perfect conformity with their character; but the former are deficient, the forehead receding rapidly. The prominency of the organs, immediately over the eyes, will be remembered by those who have taken notice of their forehead; and in particular, we shall notice the prominence of the organ of Locality, with Individuality. A large development of the former will give the talent of remembering places, also of enabling its possessor to track his way through localities to which he is a partial and even entire stranger. The skill of the Aborigines in this respect is well known, and it is an instance of the wise dispensation of Providence, that they should be endowed with a faculty, a high degree of which is indispensably necessary to them in their peculiar mode of life. A great development of Locality also inspires the love of roaming from one place to another, and an aversion to any fixed place of residence. How remarkably does this agree with the character of the New Hollander! It is one of their greatest failings that they possess so much of this locomotive propensity; there is no consideration which can induce them to remain any length of time in one place, and this has actually become a passion with them, so much so indeed, that the Australian tribes make periodical migrations to different localities. There is no doubt that this arose at first from necessity, being compelled to shift their habitations in search of food; but that their passion for roaming exists, independently of any extraneous influence, is undeniable, for, when individual natives have been placed in situations where their wants were supplied, and themselves in possession of comforts to which they had been strangers, they have invariably deserted all these enjoyments and returned to their savage brethren, again to chase the nimble-footed kangaroo over the flower-enamelled plains of their country. We mentioned that their organ of Individuality was large—hence their surprising talent for observation. The accuracy with which they follow the track of any object has surprised many, and is usually ascribed to their excellent eyesight; but this is very superficial inference, the real cause lies in their large development of the faculty of Individuality, brought to great perfection by constant exercise. Time is much more largely developed in their forehead than Tune— hence their comparative skill in the modulations of time displayed in their grotesque dances and corroborries, and the almost total want of any thing like melody in the discordant noises which form their national music.

* * * * * *

Professional phrenologists engaged in lecture tours through the colonies. One addressed a Brisbane meeting in 1851.

MORETON BAY COURIER, 1 NOVEMBER 1851.

But we have only to look at the degraded condition of our own black fellows to assure us of the truth of what I have been advancing. The Cape Caffre and the New Zealander possessing superior phrenological development to our aborigines, have each cost the British nation much blood and treasure to subjugate, while the dim twilight intellect of a New Hollander yields his country a bloodless conquest.

The smallness of the aboriginal brain is the cause of his miserable manifestations of mind. I have examined the skulls of many 'blackfellows' in different parts of the colony, and invariably found that these were about double the thickness of a white fellow. Consequently, even if the external measurement of such a skull was equal to that of a European, the measure of brain or thinking power would be much superior [in the European].

* * * * * *

But not everyone was convinced by the phrenologists. Opponents saw through the intellectual 'sleight of hand' and were also aware of the dangerous implications of scientific 'confirmation' of the opinion that the Aborigines were fundamentally inferior to the settlers.

L. THRELKELD, ANNUAL REPORT FOR 1838, THRELKELD PAPERS, ML, PP. 5–6.

The fashionable philosophy of the day, speculating on the intellectual powers of the Aborigines, as manifested in the Bumps of the Brain, is a splendid specious fallacy leading away the mind from the hope of the influence of God's holy spirit regenerating the heart . . . and instead of depending as christians, on the promised divine secret influence of the Holy Spirit, this specious science, contemplates only the quantity of accumulation of matter in the formation of the brain, the depositions of bone in the various corresponding concavities and convexities of the skull . . . to assume an hypothesis, amusing in theory, but dangerous in practice.

This miserable attempt to deduce from such a science, falsely so called, that these Black human beings 'have an innate deficiency of intellect rendering them incapable of instruction', would arrive at the natural conclusion that it would be useless to attempt it, and consequently the Blacks being but a part and parcel of the brute creation, being deficient of intellect, there can be no responsibility attached to their destruction, more than there is to the extirpation of any other animal whose presence is obnoxious to the possessor of the soil.

It is to be lamented that such sentiments have most likely had their influence on men of corrupt minds, who gladly avail themselves of any specious argument to enable them to gratify their love of cruelty, which has ended in blood ... Nor, have some, it is to be feared, who are termed well educated minds, escaped the contagion of the mental poison, which insidiously perverts the judgement, and has led to the adoption of means and arguments alike discreditable to Christian honor ...

Christian Philanthropy

The rise of phrenology coincided with an upsurge of Christian philanthropy which was instrumental in bringing slavery to an end in the British Empire in 1833 and dispatching missionaries to many parts of the world including the Australian colonies. The Christian philanthropists argued strongly in favour of racial equality based on the doctrines embodied in the bible.

In a sermon delivered in Sydney in 1838 the Rev John Saunders hit back at those who argued that the Aborigines were not men at all.

VERBATIM REPORT IN WILLIAM THOMAS, DIARY, 1839, WILLIAM THOMAS PAPERS, ML.

If you converse with him you will find he only wants cultivation to make him like ourselves, by his joy, by his susceptibility to grief, by his powers of speech ... by his knowledge of brotherhood and by his acknowledgement of a Supreme being, we discover such a difference between the Aborigines and the low animals. Does it seem strange to speak of the Majesty of the New Hollander? Wilt though despise the Saviour of the world then despise not him who sprang out of the same stock, despise not him for whom Christ died, the Saviour died as much for him as he did for you. Now by every sentiment of humanity and love you are bound to love him, to admit him into your fraternity and to treat him as a fellow man ... The New Hollander is a man and a brother.

* * * * * *

Thirty years later a West Australian clergyman wrote to the local press calling for more missionary work among the Aborigines.

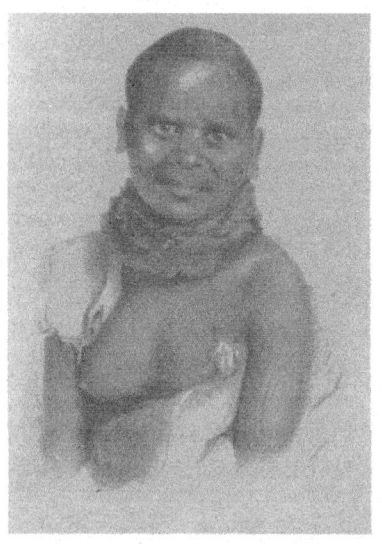

TASMANIAN MUSEUM AND ART GALLERY; MITCHELL LIBRARY, STATE LIBRARY OF NSW.
These three pictures can be very usefully compared. They are all of Tasmanian Aborigines painted at about the same time by two convict artists Thomas Bock and William Buelow Gould. Bock's painting of two individuals, 'Jinny' and 'Manalargenna' are sympathetic portraits of real people

JAMES M. INNESS, 'THE ABORIGINES OF WESTERN AUSTRALIA', *THE INQUIRER*, 25 DECEMBER 1867.

We commend to the compassionate regards of our fellow christians, these poor and perishing natives of the colony—men who, though so fearfully sunk, are yet partakers of the same human nature as that which the Son of God took upon him. With all their debasement, they are 'brethren according to the flesh'. Though differing in complexion, in features, and in language from us, they and we are descended from a common stock. The highest authority states that God 'hath made of one blood all nations of men'—a passage which conclusively proves that all the families of mankind have descended from the same curator; and that one and all are to be regarded and treated as brethren.

* * * * * *

But given the range of opinion in society at large it is not surprising that clergymen themselves should adopt widely differing views of the Aborigines. The following extracts are from two clergymen writing at much the same time in different parts of the continent.

REV C. EIPPER, *STATEMENT OF THE ORIGIN, CONDITION AND PROSPECTS, OF THE GERMAN MISSION TO THE ABORIGINES AT MORETON BAY*, SYDNEY, 1841, P. 9.

Whether the physical or the moral condition of these children of the forest is considered, the picture they present is one of gross darkness and misery. Their God is their belly; their will, or rather their passions, are their law, as long as they are able through violence and cruelty to maintain their point, and the testimony of the Scripture, that 'the dark places of the earth, are full of the habitations of cruelty' finds in their case an awful verification.

LETTER OF REV R.W. NEWLAND, ENCOUNTER BAY, 8 DECEMBER 1840, ANTI-SLAVERY PAPERS, RHODES HOUSE, OXFORD.

The Natives here are a shamefully calumniated Race—I am utterly astonished how any person however prejudiced can propagate the doctrine that either in Intellect or form they are a connecting link

---

with character and intelligence. Gould's is of a group of unnamed Aborigines. Their faces are distorted in a way that reflected contemporary scientific thinking—they have receding foreheads and projecting jaws. They are totally unlike Bock's handsome subjects. It would appear that racial dogma has prevented Gould from seeing his subjects as they really were. Thomas Bock (1790–1855) *Jinny* and *Manalargenna*. William Gould *A Group of Aborigines, Van Diemen's Land* Watercolour

between the Baboon and the Human Race—I will boldly affirm any where any time that finer formed men and more brilliant Intellects are not to be found than some among the Natives around us—Some there are of an opposite class and so there are in England and elsewhere.

* * * * * *

The 'friends of the blacks' lost the intellectual argument. Opinion hardened against the Aborigines as the century progressed. Belief in racial equality faltered. In 1845 James Dredge, Assistant-Protector of the Aborigines at Port Phillip, bemoaned the course being taken by popular opinion.

J. DREDGE, *BRIEF NOTES OF THE ABORIGINES OF NEW SOUTH WALES*, GEELONG, 1845, P. 9.

In almost every reference to the moral condition of the Aborigines of Australia which has obtained publicity, they are represented as a race of beings either entirely destitute of rational mind, and thus ranging only at the head of the order of inferior animals; or, if allowed to be men at all, are described as possessing such diminished mental capabilities, and exhibit such a humiliating specimen of the degradation of which human nature is susceptible, as to indicate their position at the very lowest point in the scale of rationality.

Social Darwinism

During the second half of the 19th century and the first third of the 20th, thinking about the Aborigines was dominated by social darwinism. In the first half of the 19th century Aborigines were seen by many as being a lower link of a static chain of being. Social darwinists regarded them as an earlier, less evolved people, a relic of the childhood of the race preserved by Australia's isolation. They were, as a result, doomed to die out. They could not compete in the struggle for existence with the higher white race. Humanitarian concern might ease the passing but nothing could bend the iron laws of evolution.

D. MACALLISTER, 'THE AUSTRALIAN ABORIGINES', *MELBOURNE REVIEW*, 3, 1878, PP. 153–58.

The Australians surely demonstrate, by their evident doom, that races below the level where self-prompted progress exists are unable to adapt themselves to the conditions forced upon them by civilization, and that, therefore, they must perish when brought into contact with it. The same great fact is being exemplified in every land where savagery has been brought into sudden conflict with a high civilization. Even among the less rude of savage peoples, as the Maoris, the Fijians, or some of the American Indians, although they may hold their own, and bravely too, for some time, yet all sink in the struggle, because of their inability to keep step with the forward movement, or to adapt themselves to the new conditions constantly brought to bear upon them by the civilization by which they are surrounded.

As to the future of these people, there is scarcely room for two opinions: the *fiat* of Fate has gone forth, and nothing seems capable of staying the progress of their extinction. The introduction of civilization and the civilized European has done its work, by introducing to the natives numbers of diseases before unknown to them; these, including alcohol, tobacco, and syphilis, combined with the physical changes effected by the axe, the plough, and the cattle of the white man, in their country and on their climate, tell a sad tale of havoc and death among their continually lessening numbers.

The total extinction, however, of these people, which seems, and is so certain, is not without an important significance to those who are conversant with the theory of 'Evolution', or who have kept abreast of 'The Drift of Modern Thought', for being admittedly on the very lowest link of the long chain embraced by mankind, we cannot fail to recognize in their extinction a decided widening of the chasm by which mankind is now cut off from its animal pregenitors. Not only is the chasm thus widened, but the difficulty of its ever being bridged over becomes greater, and the chances less—and how know we but that the fate which is now so rapidly overtaking this race, in its competition with the higher white races, may not have removed races of beings still lower in the scale of civilization and humanity than the Australian Aborigines? For rude and unprogressive even as they were, it is possible they may have trampled out of existence races of creatures far their inferiors in the characteristics of humanity, although, perchance, as high proportionally to the civilization before which succumbed, as the Australians now are to that of Europe.

Thus, then, we see a double process at work, by which is being effected the extinction of all traces of the unity of the organic chain. One, the dying out of the lowest races of men; the other, the steady forward movement of those races which are able to hold their own in their internal struggles and against natural changes.

* * * * * *

JOHN OXLEY LIBRARY, BRISBANE. Europeans had a number of quite distinct images of the 'dying race' as these two pictures show. There was the sentimental view of the blacks as representing the natural world fast being replaced by civilization. Aborigines were therefore dressed in 'tribal' garb, given traditional weapons to hold and pictured with native animals and reptiles against painted studio backdrops. c. 1875.

NATIONAL LIBRARY OF AUSTRALIA. 'King Mickey Johnson, c. 1896 Illawarra' By the 1890s, almost every district in the settled parts of Australia recognised some old person as the 'last of the full bloods', giving them brass plates to prove it. Micky Johnson, 'King' of Illawarra, was clearly a man of immense dignity and presence.

'SAVAGES AND CIVILIZED MEN', UNSIGNED ARTICLE IN *SCIENCE OF MAN*, II, NO. 6, 21 MARCH 1903, P. 34.

The idea that all men are equal is one of those errors that will soon be corrected by a residence and observations in Australia, for on the one hand will be seen the savage aboriginals, and on the other the civilized white people. These two varieties of peoples differ from each other in all essential particulars. One of them is from a black race, the others from white ones. The blacks have been for thousands of years roaming over the plains and forest lands of Australia, and have died without leaving any buildings, gardens, farms or erections of a permanent character. The whites have only been here for little more than one century and have everywhere given evidence of their presence by what they produced of houses and other buildings, or farms, orchards, gardens, with all that pertained thereto. From Sydney to Bathurst, or Bowral, or other parts of the country districts, railroads well planned, constructed and worked convey passengers and goods in a few hours from the shipping from all countries into Port Jackson, etc., to the various parts of the country and the residents therein. While the whites have brought all this about, the blacks during all the centuries of their undisturbed wanderings over the wilderness have never even thought of constructing a road, highway, bridge, or street through their camp, or attempted to make a farm, garden, house or manufactury of any kind; instead, it seems ridiculous to expect such savages as the blacks to make any such improvements. From the commencement of the Christian era the whites have in all countries been improving all the time, but during all these generations the blacks have made no improvements or advancements of themselves, what they were then they are still, without any fresh inventions or progress made towards civilized culture or home comfort, but instead of progress they die off by the circumstances the whites have introduced. The blacks domesticated none of the animals they found here, nor did they cultivate any food plants of any sorts. But the whites, from their first entry into this country, began the cultivation of the soil and the breeding of domesticated animals for food, pleasure or profit. Both physically and mentally the blacks and the whites were in all things unalike, and it is not possible for observing people to believe that they both were offsprings from one stock or race originally. The white man or woman is always inventing new or improving upon old methods to build and furnish an enjoyable home, to lay out, plant, and cultivate flowers, fruits, trees and other things for their beauty or pleasure; but the blacks can neither appreciate nor understand why any such things are done, and would never of their own volition attempt to do anything similar. Even if the black boys and girls are taught to live and practise the modes of life in a white man's house, as soon as they have grown up they abandon all and return to the savagery of living in the rude camps of the wild blacks. Since the whites have resided here the blacks have ceased to practise their Bora rites and ceremonies, and their ancestral laws and customs, and instead of advancing they have retrograded to a still lower degree of savagery. The examples of buildings, farms, orchards, vegetable gardens, have grown up under the blacks' sight, but they have never tried to imitate them for their own benefit but have continued to sink lower all the time. With the single exception of the dingo, which their ancestors brought to Australia with them as their hunting dog, they have no domesticated animal, although the emu, the kangaroo and other creatures could have been easily tamed and trained to live with them; all of which shows how much lower the blacks are than the whites. What the blacks' ancestors brought with them to this country, as the boomerang, their spear thrower and fishing utensils, these things they have kept, but through all the thousands of years of their sojourn here have invented no others. They have only been able to count up to two or three, and then to repeat these terms for any beyond these numbers. Their matriarchal relationships and their androgamous marriages prove how widely they differ from the whites in the families, the tribes, and in the race peculiarities. The young blacks from infancy to youth learn any lessons as quickly as the whites, but then the sutures of the cranium are ossified, and the power to learn and keep pace with the whites is then lost. Instead of the blacks understanding—as the whites do—that disease and deaths come from natural causes, they believe that they arise from witchcraft or sorcery from one who is an enemy in another tribe. Both anthropometrically and psychometrically the blacks differ from the whites to so great an extent that it is quite impossible that the ancestors could have been the same in both these people. The blacks *never* by their own unaided inventions or efforts rise into civilized conditions, and are not often able to adopt and follow the examples presented to them by the whites.

Race in the Twentieth Century

Many of the ideas which emerged last century continued to influence Australian thinking well into the 20th century. The belief that the Aborigines were a 'primitive' and inferior race proved very resilient and still survives. During the 1920s and 1930s psychological testing bolstered conventional racial ideas. 'Intelligence' was measured in place of the skulls and brains of the nineteenth century scientists.

A.P. ELKIN, REVIEW OF THE BOOK BY S.D. PORTEUS, *THE PSYCHOLOGY OF A PRIMITIVE PEOPLE*, LONGMAN, LONDON, 1931 IN *OCEANIA*, III, 1, SEPTEMBER 1932, P. 111.

Professor Porteus finds that the [psychological tests] ...support the conclusion which he based on psychological examination of the Aboriginal social order, namely, that while the intelligence of the natives is not characterized by an all round inferiority, yet they are in many respects unadaptable to our civilization. This is the general opinion. The smaller brain capacity of the Aborigine as compared with that of the bearers of the new culture suggests at least a handicap. And the experience of the last 145 years offers little hope that the Aborigines will adapt themselves to the new human and cultural environment which has come upon them. We are almost forced to realize the possibility that the Aboriginal race may have been so completely adapted biologically as well as mentally to its own cultural environment that it cannot adapt itself to a culture of a different type, or, in other words, it lacks the 'ethnic capacity' to become civilized.

* * * * * *

One of the first systematic attacks on racial orthodoxy was launched by the anthropologist Ashley-Montagu in 1938.

M.F. ASHLEY-MONTAGU, 'THE FUTURE OF THE AUSTRALIAN ABORIGINES', *OCEANIA*, 8, 3, PP. 344—80.

... in considering the future of the Aborigine it is essential to inquire into the degree of his educability. Is he an individual whose mind is capable of a degree of cultivation or education which, assuming for the moment that the obstacles of white prejudice and resulting lack of opportunity were overcome, would enable him to assume a position equal or nearly equal to that which any white man could occupy in the great Commonwealth of Australia?—such, for example, as many Maoris have assumed in New Zealand, American Indians and Negroes in North America, Hawaiians, Filipinos and other peoples have done in our own day. I am fairly convinced that there exists no reason to believe that the Australian Aborigine could not attain such a level of intellectual and social development. I am fairly convinced that were he afforded the proper opportunities he could attain such a degree of development, and become in time a useful and desirable citizen of any State. What evidence that would bear a moment's critical examination has ever been produced to the contrary? None whatsoever. Prejudice and ignorance, assisted by a scarcely disguised feeling of superiority, have combined to condemn the Aborigine here, as elsewhere, without fair trial. The

THE IMAGE OF THE ABORIGINES 121

Aborigine, it has been said, is 'bestial', 'low', 'mentally inferior', 'better dead than alive', for his future 'a speedy extinction' has been wished, and so most painfully on.

It has sometimes been stated that the evidences of the Aborigine's mental inferiority to the white are to be found in the structure, weight and conformation of his brain. Such statements have no foundation whatsoever. Upon this basis it would be possible to argue that Neanderthal and Piltdown men were mentally superior, or potentially so, to modern man because their brains were appreciably larger and weighed more. The fact is that in the development of modern man there has been a gradual reduction in the size of the brain since palaeolithic times, and further, that differences in brain size, weight, convolutional pattern, and form are factors which have no demonstrable relation to intelligence or to mental capacity. The so-called 'marks of inferiority' of the Aboriginal brain are strangely enough encountered with a suspiciously high frequency in the brains of men of outstandingly high intellectual achievements . . .

It cannot be too frequently reiterated that the gross form, size or weight of the brain is not related to an individual's mental abilities. It is rather the complexity of the cellular organization of his cerebral tissues, not the cortex alone, which is related to his mental abilities, and this, I repeat, has nothing whatsoever to do with the gross characters of the brain, whether of size, weight or form.

No one has yet been successful in demonstrating a deficiency in the cellular organization of the aboriginal brain, nor do I think it likely that anyone ever will. If such differences were to be found it would still not prove a biologically determined mental inferiority. Only one thing remains certain, and that is that there exists no good reason to believe that the Aborigine is in any way mentally inferior to any other people; on the contrary, there are many reasons which would lead to the belief, or at least the working hypothesis, that given an adequate chance he is capable of attaining to a place as an equal among the peoples of the earth.

* * * * * *

After a century, thinking about the Aborigines had returned to the point that had been abandoned in the 1830s and 1840s. Racial ideas were further discredited by events in Nazi Germany and occupied Europe. The anti-colonial revolution of the post-war era further eroded the base on which belief in white supremacy had been built. Yet the past survived. Racism continued to run like an undercurrent through Australian society. It had been submerged but had not disappeared. Older people often clung to the discredited doctrines of the past.

R. CILENTO & C. LACK, *TRIUMPH IN THE TROPICS*, SMITH AND PATERSON, BRISBANE, 1959, P. 179.

It is usual to assess the Aboriginals . . . by comparison with mature or, indeed primitive civilizations . . . (but) . . . they must be considered as nomads of the jungle or savannah or desert, comparable with the animal groups that inhabited those areas, for which they felt . . . an affinity. If their reactions are estimated along those lines, they become logical and understandable. Like other nomadic food gatherers . . . the Aboriginal ignored what he did not comprehend or showed indifference, rather than astonishment, when faced by something he failed to classify among his schedules of experience. Like his own half-wild dogs, he could be frozen into shivering immobility or put to frenzied flight by people or things that provoked impressions of terror . . . Like his dogs, too, he could be cowed by direct and confident stare into a wary armed truce, but would probably attack with fury if an opponent showed signs of fear . . . These are primitive reactions common to many feral jungle creatures, and not uncommon to higher races.

5

ABORIGINES IN WHITE SOCIETY: CITIZENS OR OUTCASTS?

A large part of Aboriginal history of the last 200 years is the story of their relations with Europeans either as protagonists in frontier skirmishing, guides and troopers assisting the outflow of settlement, as labourers, lovers or fringe dwellers. The story has two sides. The European one deals with the development of policy towards the Aborigines and the question of whether to assimilate or exclude them from white society, with the attempt to turn Aborigines into wage labourers or industrious peasant farmers. The black part of the story tells of the 'coming in' to white society, of the exploration of, and attempt to comprehend a strange new world and to learn a new language, new customs, skills and patterns of life.

Coming In

As European settlement expanded more and more Aboriginal tribes were brought within the reach of the new society. Everywhere Aborigines eventually 'came in' to become fringe dwellers on the outskirts of pioneer towns or to provide a source of cheap labour for a variety of rural industries. In many cases settler violence had forced the amalgamation. But on other occasions the coming in was voluntary, more particularly in the early 20th century when white brutality had been partially curbed. Edward Curr summed up the typical 19th century situation, where frontier conflict forced beleaguered Aboriginal clans to accept any situation forced on them.

E. CURR, *THE AUSTRALIAN RACE*, 3 VOLS., MELBOURNE, 1886, I, P. 106.

A considerable portion of the males of a tribe having been shot down, the Black learns the uselessness of his resistance and sues for peace. When the White man is of opinion that the tribe has been so weakened and subdued that his small party has no longer anything to fear if moderate precautions are taken, peace is granted, and the tribe is allowed to 'come in', as it is termed; that is, to make its home at some appointed place at or near the establishment of the station-holder. From this epoch, a few of the men of the tribe receive occasional employment on the station, for which they are paid in food. The refuse of animals slaughtered for station use is also generally given over to the tribe. Food is also received by the Blacks from some of the men in payment for the prostitution of their wives and daughters.

* * * * * *

The anthropologist W.E.H. Stanner described a different situation in the more remote parts of Australia in the 20th century.

W.E.H. STANNER, 'CONTINUITY AND CHANGE AMONG THE ABORIGINES', *AUSTRALIAN JOURNAL OF SCIENCE*, 21, 1958—59, PP. 100—2.

I have come not long since from a part of Australia, the Fitzmaurice River in the Northern Territory, which is entirely empty of its former inhabitants. To the best of my belief, the aborigines began to drift away from it as recently as the turn of the century, perhaps a little earlier. Some went east, south and south-west to cattle stations or to Wyndham, others north and east to stations, settlements or towns on the north–south road, even as far afield as Darwin itself. The original population

NATIONAL LIBRARY OF AUSTRALIA, REX NAN KIVELL COLLECTION. **Augustus Earle** (1793–1838) *A native family of New South Wales sitting down on an English settler's farm, c. 1826* Watercolour. This painting is a clear illustration of the relationship between the settlers—represented by the figure on the verandah—and the Aborigines who had 'come in' to white society.

---

must have been very substantial. The life-supporting power of the country is high by aboriginal standards, although I found it somewhat inhospitable, and topographically too broken to have much attraction from a European's point of view. There is no evidence of any kind that the exodus was other than entirely voluntary. Expropriation or foreclosure of land did not occur. There was no forced labour. Conflict with settlers and police took place some distance away, but did not directly concern the riverine clans. The whole tract was—and still is—beyond the margin of European settlement and development. Now and then, one or two restricted localities on the southern bank may be visited by stock parties for the few days needed to round up wandering cattle. More rarely still, a prospector, dingo-scalper or crocodile hunter may go there briefly. At longer intervals again a police party may pass through one of the routes by which the river may be forded. Otherwise, it is quite deserted. Had it not been for the shelters I found, each with many splendid paintings testifying to the fact that men had been there who lived a life of high imagination, I should have no physical proof that it had ever been anything but the wilderness it is now.

The evidence, and discussions with natives who lived there as children, satisfied me that the aboriginal explanation is correct. They say that their appetites for tobacco and to a lesser extent for tea became so intense that neither man nor woman could bear to be without. Jealousy, ill-will and violence arose over the division of the small amounts which came by gift and trade. The stimulants, if I may call them such, were of course not the only, or first, European goods to reach them; probably iron goods were the first, but it was the stimulants that precipitated the exodus. Individuals, families and parties of friends simply went away to places where the avidly desired things could be obtained. The movement had phases and fluctuations, but it was always a one-way movement.

Now I think voluntary movements of this kind occurred widely in Australia. I will not say universally, but I have seen the process in several regions. There is a task here for historical anthropology. But even if our information is imperfect we must look all over again at what we suppose to have been the conditions of collapse of aboriginal life. If we make a full allowance for what Andrew Lang called 'the ferocity and almost equally fatal goodwill' of Europeans, and for the spread of disease, the range and rapidity of collapse seem far too great for the known causes. We have been prone to argue, too directly, and probably far too simply, from half-known cases to unknown cases. Our models of explanation have been based either on the dramatic secondary causes—violence, disease, neglect, prejudice—or on the structure of aboriginal society, or both. The structure has been depicted as so rigid and delicate, with everything so interdependent, that to interfere with any part of it—say by fencing off the hunting territories, or by prohibiting ceremonies—is to topple the whole in rationale, design and structure. But there is at least some evidence which allows one to say that here were a people exploring a potential of their structure, a people taking advantage of its flexibility. For one of the enabling causes of the exodus I have described was a circumstance which certainly existed over all Australia. The so-called tribes were not self-sufficing entities but were interdependent in many important ways. Interconnexions by marriage, economy, trade, friendship, ceremonial intercourse and patterned conflict were fundamental features of life . . .

The arrival of Europeans here and there in the region of which I speak—a vast region, never fully explored or occupied by the newcomers—was sufficient to unsettle aborigines still long distances away. The repercussions spread, evidently with great rapidity, along the network of structural interconnexions. Eventually, for every aborigine who, so to speak, had Europeans thrust upon him, at least one other had sought them out. More would have gone to European centres sooner had it not been that their way was often barred by hostile aborigines. As late as the early 1930s I was able to see for myself the battles between the encroaching myalls and weakening, now-sedentary groups who had monopolized European sources of supply and work.

The encroachers used every claim of right they had—kinship, affinity, friendship, namesake-relationship, trade partnership—to get and keep a toehold.

I will say something later of how this compares with the present time, but, fundamentally, little has changed. The drive and vitality are still there. So is the external structure of the somewhat different groups into which the aborigines have re-sorted themselves. And so, too, are many of the internal structures of thought and activity, or others derived from them.

A disintegration following on a voluntary and banded migration is a very different kind of problem from the kind we usually picture—that of the ruin of a helpless people, overwhelmed by circumstances, and by something like the mechanical collapse of their social structure. Whatever the secondary causes of the subsequent disintegration in this region, it was a voluntary movement which began it.

The primacy of that fact is important. It continues in the self-will and vitality of the aborigines. These things are still very visible of those observers who are not blinded either by interest or preconception. They underlie what I represent as the modern struggle in parts where any considerable numbers remain.

The search for stimulants by these particular people must have been to them something like the spice-trade to the mediaevals. The new things gave a tang and zest to life which their own dietary lacked. In becoming their own voyagers, the aborigines claimed, coaxed and fought an opening into an incomprehensible new world. Many died, and many others were ruined, those who survived found they could not go back; and it does not seem that many even wanted to.

'This Repugnance to Regular Work'

In the first half of the 19th century colonial officials showed a strong desire to absorb Aborigines into the new society. They had both economic and social objectives. Aboriginal labour would be a useful addition to the workforce and regular employment would be the easiest way to impose order and discipline on people who had until recently followed their own—and quite different—patterns of life in the bush. Official reports bristle with plans to induce the Aborigines to 'settle', to 'locate', and with complaints about the difficulty of bringing the various schemes to fruition. The Governors of Australian colonies discussed the problem with their superiors in England.

GOVERNOR HUTT (WESTERN AUSTRALIA) TO LORD STANLEY, 8 APRIL 1842, ABORIGINES, AUSTRALIAN COLONIES, *BPP*, 1844, P. 412.

They cannot be persuaded to give up their roaming propensities, and to associate together in a self supporting community, they dislike regular habits, and, above all, they are averse to continued toil and industry—and the question of civilization or non-civilization can only be satisfactorily replied to by discovering some method of overcoming this repugnance to regular work.

* * * * * *

The frustrating thing was that anyone who was free of prejudice could see that the Aborigines were able to quickly adapt to new circumstances and to learn most of the skills used in various labouring jobs. A South Australian official explained the situation in 1843.

A clear contrast between the shepherds who were willing to work for the Europeans and the man lying down who saw no reason why he should. A. W. Stanley, *The Never Never Land*, London, Sampson Low, 1884, p. 224.

REPORT OF M. MOORHOUSE, PROTECTOR OF ABORIGINES, 20 FEBRUARY 1841, *BPP RELATING TO SOUTH AUSTRALIA*, 1843, P. 326.

That they are able to acquire dexterity enough for the ordinary purposes of farming and building is now proved beyond a doubt. At the location they have built one house, with but little help from Europeans, if the doors and windows be excepted; they have made lime floors in the school and hospital and plastered the whole outside, so as to protect the *pisé* work from the action of the weather; they have also fenced in their location with posts, rails and narrow palings, an area consisting of about thirteen acres of ground. Their powers of acquiring are not so limited as those of the New Hollander have generally been represented; but these powers are united so intimately with unconquerable indolence that the ingenuity they possess cannot be satisfactorily brought into operation; hence the received opinion—utter incapacity.

* * * * * *

The Crown Lands Commissioner at Moreton Bay had similar complaints.

S. SIMPSON, ANNUAL REPORT FOR 1849, COLONIAL OFFICE FILES, CO/201/430.

I myself have made repeated trials with boys of every age and have invariably found the same result viz. an insuperable aversion to submit to the habits of civilized life neither food, clothing, or even pecuniary recompense which they much value will induce them to settle down for more than a few days at a time, every species of labour seems to be irksome to them unless perhaps the tracking of cattle and the occasional acting of shepherd.

* * * * * *

On the other side of the continent a West Australian official drew up a detailed plan for an institution which would inculcate habits of labour.

PETER BROWN TO COLONIAL SECRETARY, 20 JULY 1840, WEST AUSTRALIA COLONIAL SECRETARIES OFFICE, CSO 1840/89.

Few places in the colony could afford as good a prospect of success in the work of civilization [as Albany] where an establishment might be formed to which Aboriginal children should be induced—and even compelled—to come, and enter upon a field of action which would gradually wean them from their present erratic habits . . . the children should first be trained to walking to and fro, for a limited distance, *in*

Gangs merely to form a *habit*. The next stop would be to make each boy bring any loose wood, that might be laying about, to the establishment for cooking purposes, and Fire.

Next to this they might be made to carry with them an axe *to cut wood*, thus bringing them on *by steps* to a *habit of labour*.

A Problem of Culture

The more perceptive settlers came to realize that there was little incentive for Aborigines to commit themselves to regular work, that such a life had little appeal and that when they did work it was often done as a favour to the European in question.

A LADY, (PSEUD.), *MY EXPERIENCES IN AUSTRALIA*, LONDON, 1860. EXTRACT IN I. MCBRIDE, ED., *RECORDS OF TIME PAST*, AIAS, CANBERRA, 1978, PP. 248–49.

They seem to hold the opinion that the *dolce far niente* [sweet idleness] constitutes the summit of earthly happiness, and that nothing can really repay them for performing any labour beyond that necessary to procure them enough game to enable them to exist from day to day. They know quite well that there is no station in the interior where their services would not be acceptable and amply remunerated in clothes, food, and money, yet it is very rarely they can be induced to work at all steadily, though when an occasional industrious fit seizes them they make good shepherds and stock keepers.

For some months during our residence in the bush my husband had three or four of his flocks tended by blacks, another as a sort of groom; while others, who were too idle to undertake any fixed employment, would come and work occasionally in the garden or vineyard, expecting merely food for their services.

But they all looked on working for us as a personal favour, and gave us to understand as much, for it was only when my husband was unable to get European servants that he could induce them to shepherd for him; even then they always stipulated that in a certain number of days, weeks, or at the outside, 'moons', he could get 'white-fellow' to relieve them of their uncongenial occupation.

* * * * * *

C.J. GRIFFITH, J.P. IN EVIDENCE TO THE SELECT COMMITTEE ON THE ABORIGINES AND THE PROTECTORATE, *NSWLCV&P*, 2, 1849, P. 17.

The main obstacle which has hitherto presented itself to all attempts at civilizing the Aborigines has been the difficulty of finding some inducement sufficiently powerful to excite them to continuous exertion. They do not court a life of labour—that of our shepherds and hut keepers—our splitters or bullock drivers—appears to them one of unmeaning toil, and they would by no means consent to exchange their free unhoused condition for the monotonous drudgery of such a dreary existence. If you wish them to labor, you must hold out a brighter prospect and supply a stronger motive... The position of an European settler is too entirely beyond their power of attainment to excite their ambition, and that of the European labourer, too unsuitable to their tastes to be an object of desire...

* * * * * *

The difficulties involved in transforming hunter-gatherers into agricultural labourers was discussed by Jack McLaren, who attempted to establish a coconut plantation on Cape York in the early years of the 20th century.

J. MCLAREN, *MY CROWDED SOLITUDE*, SUN BOOKS, MELBOURNE, 1966, PP. 37–40.

As the time went on, the difficulties of my task increased. It was, for instance, no easy matter to persuade the natives to work on succeeding days. We worked yesterday and are tired and would rest, they would say, adding pointedly that in their habitual mode of life they worked not at all, and hunted only when need for food was on them. Whereupon I would point out that in their wild life they had no tobacco, or flour, or coloured cloth, or tinned meats or tinned fish, or any other of the luxuries they coveted, and that the only way to obtain them was by working all day and every day; and it would be only after further and more elaborate argument of the kind that they would take up again the hated tools of labour.

Then, they took an exceedingly long time over their meals. Even when they rose early in the morning, they so dawdled over breakfast as to be late for work. They ate with remarkable slowness, consuming the food in small pieces, and masticating it most thoroughly... The midday meal was an even lengthier affair, it being the principal meal of the day, and after it, it was their wont immediately to go to sleep—and sleep away the whole afternoon had I not gone to the camp and awakened them. A lunchtime visit to the camp was one of my daily duties—and a most irksome one, there being few things I disliked more than the lengthy and provoking business of awaking sleeping natives. It was such a dreadfully thankless task.

Again, their labours were often interrupted by the fact that it was their age-old habit never to pass by food. Should a man in the course of his cutting away the undergrowth come across the thin trailing vine of a wild yam, he would at once abandon his attack on the undergrowth in favour of digging the tuber, a matter which might occupy an hour or more. Should a tree when it was felled prove to have in it a wild bees' nest, the men who found it would do no more felling till the nest was cut out. Should they disturb a wallaby or other animal, all hands would immediately set off in pursuit, abandoning their axes for the spears they kept always by them, streaming off through the timber, calling directions one to another regarding flanking the quarry and heading it off, and returning not for an hour, or several hours maybe. To my remonstrances concerning these interruptions they paid little heed, save to remark that the wasting of food was not their fashion, and that because they worked for me was no reason why they should no longer dig yams, dig out bees or hunt wallabies.

Further, those of the labourers who were married were in the habit of going off to the camp every now and then to see that all was well with their wives. These people had a most absolute distrust of their women. They believed no woman should be out of her husband's sight for long. There was always some other man who desired her, I was told, and as often as not the woman desired the man. It was quite an easy matter to lose a woman, and the only thing for a husband to do was to keep alert.

There was also need for constant supervision while they worked, for if I left them at any time they would immediately sit down and smoke or go to sleep—if they didn't chase wallabies or go spying on their wives. They had an astounding facility for going to sleep at an instant's notice at any time or in any place. Often in those early days did I return from a brief absence to find the whole of the labourers stretched like black shadows on the ground. I tried upbraiding them. It was no use. I tried ridiculing them—saying scornfully that they worked like women or children, that they had neither strength nor endurance. That was of no use either; they had none of that acute sense of shame I had noted among the Papuans and Solomon Islanders and others. There were, in fact, no means by which I could persuade them into sudden acceptance of a daily routine of toil; and at last I saw that my only chance lay in gradually accustoming them to it.

* * * * * *

When they were in a position to choose Aborigines worked for Europeans in order to survive and to afford such things as tobacco, tea, guns and alcohol, but continued to preserve as much of their own ways as possible, to the concern of well-meaning whites who looked forward to the complete assimilation of the indigenous people.

HALF-YEAR REPORTS OF THE GUARDIAN OF ABORIGINES (VICTORIA), 15 JANUARY 1853, 17 JANUARY 1854, W. THOMAS PAPERS, ML.

The condition of the Aborigines in these counties are materially improving, their erratic habits have at length given way to European employment, it may be safely asserted that their nationality is weakened if not totally broken up, and tho [sic] they have imbibed deeply European vices especially drunkenness, yet are as hirelings working for their support and know well the value of money and receive not as formerly merely a good feed and tobacco for payment but hard cash very little below the European standard. The diversity of labour required in a bush life has added in no small degree to their advancement and general usefulness, consisting of breaking in horses, mustering cattle, shepherding, sheep washing (at which they excel Europeans *in care* which has been testified to me by highly respectable Sheep Farmers) reaping even to tying up and will do as fair a days work as a day laborer.

As a natural result attending labour their erratic movements are merely shifting from one locality to another as they finish their work not as formerly when . . . their subsistence was the vegetable and animal productions of the forest . . . but [they] haven't forgotten bush tucker and get it when they can.

All efforts however so far to improve their condition have been without avail. I have pressed, the farmers and others have urged they become as us not merely in work and diet but to stop in a house . . . comfortably clad and stretched is what they'll hear nought of [sic], the hook, axe or bridle down and all further of civilization for the day is over, off goes apparel and they bask under the canopy of heaven as in their primitive wildness evidently enjoying their freedom from encumberance . . . nor have they any desire to be meddled with further, such is their wandering propensities, that all the kindness entreaty or persuasion can not secure them one day beyond their determination and latterly they have been particularly cautious how they make bargains for labour on this account.

'Such Extraordinary Terrorism'

But in other parts of Australia Aborigines experienced far worse conditions. In the outback there was little choice of employer. Cattle stations were often as large as the home territories of resident clans. The tradition of violence lived on with vigour in areas remote from government or urban public opinion. A Queensland official toured the pastoral country of the south-west in 1900 and wrote a report for the government about the conditions of local Aborigines.

H. MESTON, ABORIGINALS WEST OF THE WARREGO, QUEENSLAND COLONIAL SECRETARY, COL/144, 1900.

In reporting on the Western blacks of the present day it is necessary to remember the influence of tradition and custom . . . We meet there with people who still regard the aboriginal as no more value in the scale of being than a horse or a bullock, an inheritance from those who shot him like a kangaroo, abducted his women and sent his children away to distant friends with as much indifference as if they were pet squirrels or tame galahs . . . A few stations are remarkable for the fairness with which they treat their blacks and others have an unenviable notoriety for ill-usage of the men and the disgraceful treatment of the women. Never before had I seen aboriginal men living under such extraordinary terrorism, many of them fine athletic fellows who could in case of a row have settled with their terrorisers in a very summary fashion. But many of them had long been treated as the dogs are treated and were scared into a belief that their employers wielded the power of life and death.

They also knew that among most of the stations there was a mutual understanding that any run-away black would be hunted and brought back, and as they had no one to whom they could appeal and nowhere to go they finally regarded their doom as inevitable and bore their wrongs in silence.

The aboriginal men who work on the stations are frequently as competent as any white man and yet they receive usually only their feed and clothing, the food being of the roughest description and the clothing of the cheapest kind.

On each station I was informed that the blacks received wages varying from 5/- to 20/- per week but in nearly every case it appears to have been balanced by the store account, as none of them seemed to have a shilling . . . In only two cases did I find during the whole of my tour, any women or girls receiving any wages at all. And yet several mistresses admitted to me that their aboriginal women did work for which they would have to pay a white woman 15/- or 20/- per week . . .

The men's most serious grievances related to the treatment of their women. It is a grievance as old as settlement. On many Western stations there are no white women at all. On these the aboriginal women are usually at the mercy of any body, from the proprietor or Manager to the stockmen, cook, rouseabout and jackaroo . . .

If they have Aboriginal husbands, who are likely to object, those

MITCHELL LIBRARY, STATE LIBRARY OF NSW. ORIGINAL IN CLARENCE RIVER HISTORICAL SOCIETY. An enigmatic picture entitled 'Going on the Land'. Two young men have apparently recently selected a property and have built a small hut. A group of Aborigines accompany them, including two figures who have apparently been told to strike poses with their weapons. The two figures in the foreground are intriguing. The white man stands slightly behind and to one side of the young woman but he has a hand on her shoulder. It is not a stance suggestive of affection but of possession.

---

husbands are either employed on distant parts of the run or are sent away altogether. Husbands and wives, mothers and daughters are frequently separated for years, sometimes for ever. Frequently the women do all the housework and are locked up at night to keep them from their own people. I found this done even where the manager's wife was living on the station.

The Aboriginal Contribution

Australian historians have frequently overlooked the contribution of Aborigines to the pioneering and development of the country. As guides, trackers, police troopers, stock-men and women, domestic servants and pearl divers they were of crucial importance to frontier

JOHN OXLEY LIBRARY, BRISBANE. An afternoon tea party at the station homestead with two Aboriginal servants in attendance, dressed in spotless white uniforms. The contrast between the boys at opposite ends of the group is most interesting. They are about the same age and could well be playmates. But look at their stances. The Aboriginal boy stands a little removed from the group. He stands to attention with his hands behind his back. His white counterpart already exhibits all the self-assured ease of his race and class. c. 1890.

industries: because there was no other labour available, because they were poorly paid or not paid at all, and because they brought into white society invaluable skills and knowledge of the country. In 1903 Queensland's Northern Protector of Aborigines canvassed opinion about Aboriginal stockmen from Gulf country squatters.

REPORT OF THE NORTHERN PROTECTOR OF ABORIGINES FOR 1903, QPP, 1, 1904, P. 847.

Value of Aboriginal Labour. During the course of certain inquiries made by Protector Galbraith, the following expressions of opinion as to the comparison of white with aboriginal labour were obtained from some of the leading pastoralists in the Gulf country: 'As stock-riders, better than ordinary pick-up hands' (W. Ormsby Wiley, Milgarra); 'Better than the class walking about in the Gulf' (John Epworth, Delta Downs); 'They suit the purpose just as well as white labour' (W. Wright, Wallabadah); 'As good and, in a great many instances, better' (G.A. Bristow, Miranda Downs); 'Have proved more reliable than the general class of white stockmen in this district' (Thos. A. Simpson, late manager Carpentaria

Cheshunt Station, c. 1920. Aboriginal stockmen were the mainstay of the northern cattle industry because of the traditional skills brought into the white economy and new ones, like horsemanship, gained in the industry. Source: *North Queensland Register*, 28 February, 1921.

Downs, Forest Home, and Magowra stations); 'Better than the general run of pick-up white men. They know the country better, and are more biddable' (A.H. Underwood, Midlothian); 'Better than the average white' (Daniel Thorn, drover and station manager since 1872); 'As stock-riders and bushmen in many cases superior to the general station hands' (Reginald Hillcoat, Bonnarra); 'They are preferable and far more reliable than white labour among cattle, always sober, and more biddable' (John T. Roberts, Pastoral Inspector for the Bank of New South Wales); 'As good' (J.V. Milson, manager, Forest Home); 'Compare favourable with the ordinary class of white stockman' (Ross Maclean, manager, Magowra); 'Compare better, with the ordinary run of white labour' (Robt. Currie, Marine Plains). 'In the Longreach area,' says Protector Dillon, 'aboriginal labour is much in demand on the cattle-stations on the Lower Thomson and Cooper districts; on one station alone there are eight employed . . . They are giving every satisfaction.'

* * * * * *

Aboriginal labour was also important in pioneer townships for performing the essential tasks of gathering and cutting firewood and carrying water.

R.B. MITCHELL, REMINISCENCES, 1855–66, P. 104, ML.

Gladstone would suffer much from want of labour, if the despised black was not to be found, for a small piece of tobacco or a handful of flour . . . ever willing to render any service required of them, many a time have I noticed a Native groaning under a heavy load of bark, that he was carrying on his naked back to some white that would perhaps swear at him, not give him the promised tobacco or flour, and if he hung about his dwelling, bring out a pistol [and] threaten to shoot if he did not move off.

* * * * * *

In his reminiscences a West Australian pioneer provided a detailed account of the value of Aboriginal labour in that state.

J.H. HAMMOND, *WINJAN'S PEOPLE*, IMPERIAL PRINTING, PERTH, 1933, PP. 73–77.

In the pioneering days, the settlers who had sheep enough employed shepherds to look after them in the bush. Natives were sometimes employed, and made much better shepherds than white men for several reasons. The first was that a native never lost any sheep. If any were missing he could soon track them up. He also had his gin with him and that meant another pair of eyes for the work. A second reason was that native shepherds never knocked the sheep about or hurt them in any way. When they were given charge of a flock they soon got to like the sheep and had pets among them . . .

The natives were good rouseabouts at shearing time, but very few of them made shearers, as they were not fast enough. They were very gentle with the sheep and made a nice clean clip, but about 30 sheep a day would be a good day's work for a native . . .

As horsemen and stockmen natives were very useful. Several natives once worked with me continuously in this capacity for two years, and I found that they could do in the bush and on a horse what a white man could not do . . .

In the days of hand reaping and threshing with flails, some of the old settlers engaged native men and women at harvest. They made really good reapers. I well remember two black women who beat all other reapers in their section of the Pinjarra district . . . In that district, too, the black women often helped the settler's wives in carrying water and doing the heavy washing.

DIXSON LIBRARY, STATE LIBRARY OF NSW. S.T. Gill (1818–80), *The colonised*
A well known watercolour which illustrates the importance of Aboriginal labour in performing many of the more onerous household tasks and particularly the collecting of firewood and the delivery of water.

On the pearling grounds in the North-West quite a number of natives were used as divers in the early 'seventies before diving suits were needed. They did good work for their employers . . .

The natives also made good marksmen. I have never seen a white man do with the rifle in the bush what I have seen a native do. Seldom did a native miss. If he did not kill at the first shot, he would wound and track up his game and get it at the second shot. One great advantage that the native had over the white man was that he could creep much closer to the game than the white man could do. Having a keener eye and knowing more about the habits of the wild animals, the native could tell at once if the game were alarmed and, as soon as he saw that an animal was startled, not the slightest movement would he make until the animal seemed to think all was safe again. Then the native would take the first chance to shoot . . .

Perhaps the most striking ability that the blacks have and the way in which they have given greatest service to the whites is in tracking. The natives were employed as police trackers to my knowledge in the early 'sixties, and since then they must have saved the Police Department many thousands of pounds and been the means of bringing many lawbreakers to justice. Their ability to track over all sorts of country is wonderful. In this connection they also have a great deal to their credit for saving the lives of many white men, women and children who have been lost in the bush.

The natives also proved particularly useful to explorers, stockmen, and pioneers in teaching them the peculiarities of the country and in showing them where water could be found. In any sort of bush they were unbeatable. The late Lord Forrest had two natives with him on each of his three big exploring expeditions, and gave them the highest praise for their assistance, especially in finding water and tracking. In my own experience of work in the bush, progress would not have been half what it was if we had not had natives with us. Our trouble was that stock were breaking away from us in hard country, and we could never have tracked them up without the natives. They could sit on their horses and track the beasts as fast as the horse could walk, while in softer country they could track at the trot. When it came to finding water the native read and understood signs that the white man would never look for. On one occasion we were all in a bad way for the want of a drink, and it was getting towards sundown, and we did not know where to get any. An old native man who was with us noticed a pigeon flying. He watched it as far as he could, and then said, 'I find water'. He went about two miles in the direction the pigeon had flown and found water easily. He had been guided not so much by the direction but by the way the pigeon was flying, and he was able to check his observation by other tracks that a white man would never have noticed.

NATIONAL LIBRARY OF AUSTRALIA. Aboriginal trackers were a familiar figure in rural Australia. Their unerring ability to read the terrain made them invaluable to their 'masters' for tracking convicts, lost children or lost animals.

A Legacy of Violence

Aborigines suffered from a range of disadvantages. The tradition of violence born on the frontier lived on long after the shooting stopped. The law provided little protection nor did public opinion. Racial ideology was used to justify the brutality suffered by Aborigines in all parts of the continent. Settlers were quite open about their use of violence to 'chastise' their black servants and employees and to 'keep them in their place'.

A.H. PALMER (COLONIAL SECRETARY): *QPD*, XXXIII, 1880, PP. 1137-8.

The nature of the blacks was so treacherous that they were only guided by fear—in fact, it was only possible to rule a savage race, and the Australian aboriginal in particular, by brute force, and by showing him you are his master... They knew that the native black of Australia was essentially a treacherous animal—that they would spare neither man, woman, nor child, cattle, sheep, horses, nor pigs—that the only way to keep him down was by using a firm hand, and that the only way to ensure that firm hand was to show them that the whites were superior animals and could beat them down.

* * * * * *

D.W. CARNEGIE, *SPINIFEX AND SAND*, LONDON 1898, PP. 121—2.

Great tact is necessary in the education of the aboriginals. Neglect turns them into lazy, besotted brutes who are of no use to anybody; too kind treatment makes them insolent and cunning; too harsh treatment makes them treacherous; and yet without a certain amount of bullying they lose all respect for their master, and when they deserve a beating and do not get it, misconstrue tenderheartedness into fear. The 'happy medium' is the great thing; the most useful, contented and best behaved boys that I have seen are those that receive treatment similar to that a highly valued sporting dog gets from a just master...

* * * * * *

S. BURT (ATTORNEY GENERAL), *WAPD*, II, NEW SERIES, 1892, P. 398.

I have come to the conclusion myself, and have done so for years, that the only way of effectually dealing with all these coloured races, whether blackfellows, or Indians, or Chinamen, is to treat them like children. I have proved it—in my own small experience. You can only deal with them effectually, like you deal with naughty children—whip them. It is the only argument they recognize, brute force. It is no use talking to these blackfellows, and be kind to them, and expect them to take any notice; not the slightest use. It has no effect upon them. But give a blackfellow a little stick—if he deserves it, mind: I draw attention to that, for if you give it to them when they don't deserve it, it only makes them infinitely worse; but give them a little stick when they really deserve it, and it does them a power of good—far more good than any other punishment. If they deserve it, they never forget it. They rather delight in it, in fact; they will tell you so afterwards, and thank you for it.

Kidnapping

Frontier settlers often took young children away from their families to be 'bred up to stock-work' or to be used as household servants. Although some people disapproved, the common view was that the children would be better off living in a 'civilized' environment.

PROTECTOR GALBRAITH, NORMANTON, QUOTED IN THE ANNUAL REPORT OF THE NORTHERN PROTECTOR OF ABORIGINALS FOR 1903, *QVP*, 1904 SESSION I, P. 871.

A large number of individuals have an idea that they can trade an aboriginal as they would a horse or bullock. Some of these people are good church-goers. One lady informed me that an aboriginal had been left to her by will. She did not, however, mention if probate had been granted.

REPORT OF THE NORTHERN PROTECTOR OF ABORIGINES FOR 1902, *QVP*, II, 1903, P. 461.

It is known that in past years a most obnoxious practice grew up of the police supplying their friends *etc* with aboriginal children ... This 'trucking' in children is still going on. 'Settlers in outside districts'—I am quoting Protector Galbraith—'who have plenty of myalls about their country are often importuned by town residents and others to bring them in a boy or a girl. In due time the child arrives. How the children are separated from their parents is a subject of conjecture and surmise. Most people will tell you that the child is better off with Europeans: in my opinion the contention is absurd. Most of the children will bolt (if old enough, and the distance not too great), and then they are termed ungrateful by *their owners*. This practice has been going on for years, and, with the exception of one or two cases personally known to me, without good results to the children: they change masters and mistresses, prostitution and disease follow, they can only speak pidgin English, and finally become pariahs amongst both whites and blacks.

* * * * * *

Women were also taken away by white men and sometimes never saw their families again.

CONSTABLE R.C. THORPE, CAMMOOWEAL, 5 MARCH 1898 SUBMITTED TO SELECT COMMITTEE ON THE ABORIGINES BILL, *SAPP*, 1897, NO. 77, PP. 113–14.

I feel sure that if half the young lubras now being detained (I won't call it kept, for I know most of them would clear away if they could) were approached on the subject, they would say that they were run down by station blackguards on horseback, and taken to the stations for licentious purposes, and there kept more like slaves than anything else. I have heard it said that these same lubras have been locked up for weeks at a time—anyway whilst their heartless persecutors have been mustering cattle on their respective runs. Some, I have heard, take these lubras with them, but take the precaution to tie them up securely for the night to prevent them escaping. Of course, sirs, these allegations are, as you know, very difficult to prove against any individual persons, still I am positive these acts of cruelty are being performed, and I think still worse.

The Caste Barrier

Despite the professed wish to 'civilize' the Aborigines, to make use of their labour and engage the women in sexual relations there was always a 'caste barrier' which prevented the movement into white society. Two observers discussed the situation in the 1840s—the explorer and colonial governor George Grey and the editor of the Adelaide *Examiner*, Richard Penny.

G. GREY, *JOURNALS OF TWO EXPEDITIONS OF DISCOVERY IN NORTH-WEST AND WESTERN AUSTRALIA*, 2 VOLS. LONDON, 1841, II, PP. 367−8.

If we enquire into the causes which tend to retain them in their present depressed condition, we shall find that the chief one is—'prejudice'. The Australians have been most unfairly represented as a very inferior race, in fact as one occupying a scale in the creation which nearly places them on a level with the brutes, and some years must elapse, ere a prejudice so firmly rooted as this can be altogether eradicated, but certainly a more unfounded one never had possession of the public mind.

Amongst the evils which the natives suffer in their present position, one is an uncertain and irregular demand for their labour, that is to say, they may one day have plenty of means for exerting their industry afforded them by the settlers, and the next their services are not required; so that they are necessarily compelled to have recourse to their former irregular and wandering habits.

Another is the very insufficient reward for the services they render. As an example of this kind, I will state the instance of a man who worked during the whole season, as hard and as well as any white man, at getting in the harvest for some settlers, and who only received bread, and sixpence a day, whilst the ordinary labourers would earn at least fifteen shillings. In many instances, they only receive a scanty allowance of food, so much so, that some settlers have told me that the natives left them because they had not enough to eat.

* * * * * *

THE EXAMINER, 3 DECEMBER 1841.

All the efforts for civilizing the native, have been with the object of his becoming a portion of our labouring, civilized, population, and forming

NATIONAL LIBRARY OF AUSTRALIA. We don't know anything about these children. We can assume they lived with a European family and may well have been kidnapped. They look anxious and miserable. The girl looks resigned, the boy has a hint of future rebellion.

an integral part of it; and it has been this, that has caused all such attempts to end in failure. The two races can never amalgamate—the white labourer, and the native, (be he ever so useful) can not be brought to work together on equal terms. We could never succeed in incorporating the native with the mass of the labouring population, for there is always enough of that antipathy of races existing, to induce the settler to place the native, however deserving, in an inferior position to his white servants, and to give him the more menial offices to perform; but if the settler, being a friend of the aboriginal cause, were not disposed to make any distinction, but that of merit, the servants themselves would not perform those offices, whilst they could shift it on that of the blacks; therefore, if the native were to accept the terms of civilization that we offer him, everything would conduce to keep him in the lowest scale of society; he would be constantly subject to all sorts of oppression, and would make a bad exchange for his native independence.

* * * * * *

The sharp inequality between white and black was clearly shown in sexual relations. European men pursued Aboriginal women but were rarely willing to publicly admit their liaisons or to accept responsibility for their half-caste children. Aboriginal men were rarely, if ever, accepted as sexual partners by European women. Numerous writers commented on this question.

W. SHELLEY TO GOVERNOR MACQUARIE, 8 APRIL 1814, HRA, 1, VIII, PP. 370–1.

Notwithstanding the prejudices that many have against the probability of success in Civilizing the Natives of New South Wales, yet, if we consider that human nature is the same in every Clime, allowing for the difference of manners and Customs and variety of Circumstances in which they are placed, I think this opinion supported neither by theory or experience. I know it has been alleged that men have been Carried to England, lived in civilized Society during a long space, and on their return relapsed into their former habits and Society; but it must be acknowledged that they learned no means of supporting themselves in their improved habits, nor Could they make themselves respectable in their new Society. They were generally despised, especially by *European females*; thus all attachment to their new Society was precluded; they learned neither mechanical arts, nor manual labour, so as to make them pleasant or useful to them; long Contracted habits recurred with greater force on this account. Where is the human being, who would be pleased to live at a Gentleman's table, and wear his Clothes, without having any prospect in view but food and

Clothes, while he remained useless and despised in the Society in which he lived? Young Men live in a prospect of Marriage, and have ambition and pride to be respectable in their own Society. No European Woman would marry a *Native*, unless some abandoned profligate. The same may be said of Native Women received for a time among Europeans. A Solitary individual, either Woman or Man, educated from infancy, even well, among Europeans, would in general, when they grew up, be rejected by the other Sex of Europeans, and must go into the Bush for a Companion; Or, if educated among drunken or thievish Servants, must become Still worse.

EVIDENCE OF J. GREEN, ROYAL COMMISSION ON THE ABORIGINES, *VPP*, III, 1877−8, NO. 76, P. 532.

I have known several cases where aboriginal and half-caste children have been kept in European families and educated as same as one of the family. All would go well until they came to an age that they would like to make love. As soon as this was known by mamma or papa, there must be something done to stop it, so the white daughter or son is told they must not make so free with the darky; they must remember that, although he or she has been educated in the family, it would be degrading to make love with them. So the cold shoulder is soon turned on the darky; they very soon feel it, and a change is seen in the darky; instead of one of the most cheerful they will mope about until they can find a chance to join their old friends the aborigines. Now say the wise ones, 'Did I not tell you what would be the end of all that kindness to these darkies? There is that J– R–, who was sent to college, he is gone back to the camp and has married an aboriginal.' The wise ones forgetting that it was mainly ourselves that was the cause of the poor fellow's downfall by raising him too high and not providing those supports that are so beneficial to keep young men from falling viz. the prospect of getting married with someone they love.

EVIDENCE OF MRS. J. MATTHEWS, ROYAL COMMISSION ON THE ABORIGINES, *SAPP*, II, 1915, NO. 26, P. 58.

So much unhappiness comes from them mixing with white people. I know of a family . . . who had a very nice half-caste girl in their service, and as soon as she grew up one of the sons wanted to marry her. The mother sent her off to Point McLeay and the attachment was broken off. I saw the girl afterwards living with her native people in the camp. It would not be wise to encourage such a union, and it would have brought a great deal of trouble to that family. I know of a case where a white gardener took a native girl and lived with her, but he could not mix with white society afterwards.

NATIONAL LIBRARY OF AUSTRALIA. 'Aboriginal family outside their house'. Not all Aborigines lived in poverty. By the late 19th century many were regularly employed on the land or had actually taken up selections. This picture is very similar to contemporaneous ones of white selector families. The bark hut is of standard design and construction, there are casement windows, neat curtains, a post and rail fence and a family horse. Their standard of living was apparently no worse than that of most small selectors. c. 1900.

Casualties

From the time of the first settlement there have been Aborigines who have endeavoured to win acceptance in white society. They invariably suffered frustration and rejection. Four examples are cited below.

W. RIDLEY, SELECT COMMITTEE ON THE NATIVE MOUNTED POLICE; *QVP*, 1861, P. 116.

Many a blackfellow brought up among civilized men has been tractable and quick at learning up to a certain time, when he has suddenly thrown aside the garb and habits of civilization. And looking on such instances good people exclaim that their supposed improvement is but superficial, that their nature is incorrigible. But is it reasonable to expect that they should lose their attachment to their kindred and the customs of their fathers?—that a solitary black, among people who look upon him as an alien in blood, will be content to remain a stranger to his own people also?

Bungaree, who after taking prizes in Sydney College, speaking good Latin, and behaving as a gentleman in elegant society, returned to the bush, and then entered the black police, once said in a melancholy tone to Lieutenant Fulford (who repeated the remark to me at Surat, on the Condamine) 'I wish I had never been taken out of the bush, and educated as I have been, for I *cannot be a white man*, they will never look on me as one of themselves; and I *cannot be a blackfellow*, I am disgusted with their way of living.'

* * * * * *

Bishop Matthew Hale referred to the fate of an Aboriginal girl called Maria who lived as a servant in Government House, Adelaide, during the 1840s. The following material is from his book, *The Aborigines of Australia*, London, c. 1889, pp. 24–5.

Maria, the black girl at Government House, was known by repute to almost every one in Adelaide. The fact of her being an inmate of Government House, and the further fact of the remarkable progress which she had made towards civilizaton, combined to give her this general notoriety . . . As I have already implied, Maria was a person much talked about, and many little incidents were repeated to illustrate her advancement towards civilization, and to show that she attached considerable importance to her attainments. For example, it was said that some young man once spoke to her in that jargon in which the uncultivated natives are usually spoken to. Whereupon Maria drew herself up and said, 'Why do you talk to me like that? I can speak English as well as you can.'

Maria came to us in October 1850, probably about two years and a half after the writing of the Bishop's letter. She had unhappily, in the meantime, fallen into disreputable habits of life. But, as she was willing to join us, I was quite willing to receive her, hoping that she might retrieve her character, and become a respectable woman. She brought with her a little half-caste son about seven months old; and partly on the child's account, and partly on her own account, she remained at first chiefly in our own house. But, we found after a time, that it was impossible to keep her. She conducted herself in such a way that it was quite certain that she was not trying to reform her own habits; and that she would, necessarily, do much harm as an inmate of the Institution. I kept her only about four months, and was then obliged to send her away.

This case of Maria, being so very widely known, became a stock case

NATIONAL LIBRARY OF AUSTRALIA. Among the most tragic victims of all the last of the Tasmanian Aborigines—dressed up in formal wear to attend the Governor's Ball, the most important event on Hobart's social calendar, but the blacks seem unimpressed by the 'honour' bestowed on them.

in the mouths of all persons who wished to throw cold water upon efforts to civilize and Christianize the natives. 'Look at the case of Maria; think what was done for her! Think how everyone was led to suppose that she was going to be a truly respectable woman. See now what has become of her; she has taken to bad ways, and has altogether gone wrong.' Yes, but who led her into those bad ways? I have the authority of Mr. Moorhouse himself for stating that the person who first led her astray was the proprietor of a thriving store in one of the best streets of Adelaide. He systematically laid siege to the girl, gave her presents, flattered and fed her vanity, and set her going upon her downward path.

* * * * * *

The third case was provided by Sir George Grey who referred to the Aboriginal Miago in his book, *Journals of Two Expeditions etc., op. cit.*, Vol. II, pp. 370-1.

The officers of the 'Beagle' took away with them a native of the name of Miago, who remained absent with them for several months. I saw him on the North-west coast, on board the 'Beagle', apparently perfectly civilized; he waited at the gun-room mess, was temperate (never tasting spirits), attentive, cheerful, and remarkably clean in his person. The next time I saw him was at Swan River, where he had been left on the return of the 'Beagle'. He was then again a savage, almost naked, painted all over, and had been concerned in several murders. Several persons here told me,— 'you see the taste for a savage life was strong in him, and he took to the bush again directly.' Let us pause for a moment and consider.

Miago, when he was landed, had amongst the white people none who would be truly friends of his,—they would give him scraps from their table, but the very outcasts of the whites would not have treated him as an equal,—they have no sympathy with him,—he could not have married a white woman,—he had no certain means of subsistence open to him,—he never could have been either a husband or a father, if he had lived apart from his own people;—where, amongst the whites, was he to find one who would have filled for him the place of his black mother, whom he is much attached to?—what white man would have been his brother?—what white woman his sister? He had two courses left open to him—he could either have renounced all natural ties, and have led a hopeless, joyless life amongst the whites,—ever a servant,—ever an inferior being;—or he could renounce civilization, and return to the friends of his childhood, and to the habits of his youth. He chose the latter course, and I think that I should have done the same.

* * * * * *

The case of a Victorian boy who trained as a draughtsman was discussed in evidence given to a Royal Commission.

ROYAL COMMISSION ON THE ABORIGINES, *VPP*, III, 1877—8, NO. 76, P. 534.

As a rule Europeans of the middle class shun an aboriginal, they will not associate with them, and hence they are driven to associate with a lower grade, and the tendency thus is to degrade them by the company they have to keep. There was one boy I remember distinctly now who used to be in the Mining Office, apprenticed, and he was an excellent draughtsman; but at night, because the other officers would not associate with him, he went and associated with the lowest characters about town . . . He became unmanageable from his associations in the town; but he was an excellent draughtsman in the office, and did his work as well as possible.

You attribute the probability of their lapsing into bad habits to their being shunned by the ordinary white class, and thus being driven to low company?
Yes, that is principally it.
Then their physical appearance is of importance; with the quadroon or the octoroon, the less he is like a native the better the chances of success?
Yes.

Fringe-Dwellers

Some of the worst conditions were found in fringe-camps on the outskirts of country towns where Aborigines lived in makeshift camps. They were no longer able to live off the land. Casual work in town, begging and prostitution provided meagre and uncertain earnings. Disease and malnutrition were rife, mortality high and addiction to alcohol or opium was commonplace. While surveying the Aboriginal population in Western Queensland in 1897 the Southern Protector of Aborigines visited a number of town camps.

A. MESTON, THE WESTERN ABORIGINES, JUNE 1897, QUEENSLAND HOME SECRETARY, COL/144.

The 64 blacks I saw at Charleville are the remnant of one of the most powerful tribes in Australia. Their condition is too sad and deplorable for accurate description . . . The accursed opium habit, and the incidental starvation, neglect and exposure, had reduced them to a position of unspeakable degradation . . . they have not even energy enough to

ABORIGINES IN WHITE SOCIETY

JOHN OXLEY LIBRARY, BRISBANE. Three men in a Queensland fringe camp show unmistakable signs of severe deprivation. The man on the right holds out empty hands in supplication.

construct camps, either lying out in the open air, or in miserable ricketty structures of tin and rags, neither proof against wind nor rain. The majority were fairly healthy though showing the effects of continued defective nutrition . . . saddest of all was the condition of the women and children. Two women were blind, and three or four practically dying of that terrible disease which they owe solely to their intercourse with white men . . .

At the small township of Mitchell . . . I found a camp of blacks on the bank of the Maranoa River, three quarters of a mile from the town. There were 32 altogether, and among them were three half caste children, and one half caste woman. The frightful mortality at this camp from opium, disease and starvation, is sufficiently shown by the melancholy fact of nearly 20 deaths in six months, four having died in one week. These people were also camped in the open, on a bleak cold bare ridge exposed to wind and rain. Here also every penny is spent on opium, and the general condition is the same as that of the blacks at Charleville. They told me they were often two or three days without food, and related pitiful tales of hardship and misery of such a character that I was surprised any of them had survived . . . I arranged for a week's provisions for the camp, and saw the first lot delivered. They said it was the only satisfactory meal they had eaten for years, and there was no mistaking their hunger . . .

At Roma I mustered 28 men, 22 women, and 12 boys and girls . . . if possible they were nearly all in a more degraded condition than those at Charleville. They were camped on the Bunjel Creek about a mile from town . . . Their camps were no protection against rain or cold, their clothing was certainly not the kind required to keep them warm in a Roma winter, and they suffered frequently from periods of enforced starvation. They were nearly all dirty and ragged, and spiritless and miserable . . .

At Roma, Mitchell, and Charleville, there are so many of the men and women who go daily into town and receive food or a few shillings in return for household services, or work in the stables and gardens. In all three places, as elsewhere, there are a few kindly persons who give them gratuitously any food and clothing they can spare. The old people who remain in the camp, the sick, and the helpless opium smokers, are kept alive with food brought in by those who go out to work or forage. The women are everywhere the prey of white men and chinamen, frequently with disastrous results to all concerned. The white fathers of some of the half-caste children are men whose positions should be some guarantee of a higher code of morality.

In no case did I find that any aboriginal mother had ever received, on behalf of herself or half caste child, the slightest subsequent recognition of ordinary decent benevolence from the father.

6

MISSIONARIES: SAVIOURS OR DESTROYERS?

Christianity was a major aspect of the transplanted culture. It was even more important in the 19th century than it has been in more recent times and has played a central role in the history of white–Aboriginal relations. It continues to be a major influence in Aboriginal society.

Religion moved from the background to the foreground in Aboriginal experience of European culture with the arrival of missionaries in the 1820s when the tribes targeted for conversion were directly challenged by the doctrines and practices of the newcomers. Of all Europeans the missionaries must have seemed the most enigmatic. They didn't seek land, they were often, though not always, disinterested in black women. They were so unlike the majority of frontier settlers and while they expressed goodwill and concern for the Aborigines they were far more intrusive and interfering than other Europeans, often seeking to disrupt the ceremonies and beliefs that were at the heart of Aboriginal society. The following documents will provide some help in understanding the complex relations which developed between Aborigines and Christian missionaries.

Founding a Mission

J.B. Gribble was one of the most famous of 19th century missionaries who worked in New South Wales, Western Australia and Queensland. This account of the founding of Warangesda Mission contains many themes which ran through his turbulent career—deep, paternalistic concern for the Aborigines, a profound sense of mission, of doing God's work, a conviction that he was confronted with evil both in everyday life and in the spiritual world.

J.B. GRIBBLE, *BLACK BUT COMELY; ABORIGINAL LIFE IN AUSTRALIA*, LONDON 1884, PP. 34–47.

When in the order of God's providence I crossed the Murray, for the first time, between six and seven years ago, little did I think that such was the very first step towards a home and a work amongst the abandoned waifs and strays of the once teeming race of 'Murri'; but so it was. While travelling from station to station in the wilds of Riverina, scattering the incorruptible seed of the Word amongst the white settlers, I unexpectedly came in contact with the blacks. I found them in a condition most shocking to contemplate. I visited their camps! I entered their wretched bark and bough gunyahs. I went from place to place, and everywhere I met with the same wretchedness and woe. In some instances, on making a first visit to a camp, the children ran away from me terrified at my presence; whilst their mothers—some of them, alas! only children themselves—cowered in their little dens like so many wild beasts, doubtless wondering what brought me to such a place. In one camp I gleaned from the women that a tiny half-caste infant was concealed close at hand. I made a search, and by and by I discovered what I at first supposed to be a bundle of dirty rags stowed away under some bushes, but on raising it I found it contained a dear little infant girl. Oh! at that sight how my heart sickened and my blood warmed! Such helplessness, such woe, caused by the professedly Christian white man! And this case, I soon learned from good authority, and from personal observation, was, so to speak, but an index to a ponderous volume of iniquity existing throughout the colony in this very respect. One evening, after spending some time with the blacks, and having heard the poor young women say that they would like to have a home such as I described to them as existing in Victoria, I returned to — Station, where I was engaged to hold service. I told the lady of the house what I had heard and what I had seen. She replied: 'Mr. Gribble, I have often thought what a sin it must be for Christian ministers to pass through these parts and never to speak a word to the poor blacks. I can assure you that of all the clergymen who have called here, the Rev. A. Hardie, of Victoria, and yourself, are the only two who seem to care anything about them. If some earnest and kind-hearted minister would only take the matter up, something might be done to induce the Government to take steps to ameliorate their condition.' A long conversation followed, in which this lady (a resident of the Murrumbidgee for twenty years) drew a picture most sad to contemplate, which sent me to my room filled to overflowing with the wants and woes of this unhappy people. I threw myself upon my knees, and wept before God, and said: 'O Lord, show me Thy way; teach me Thy path; tell me what to do for these perishing aborigines.' The answer was: 'I will instruct thee, and teach thee in the way which thou shalt go.' I rose from my knees calmly resigned to the Divine will, and feeling confident that something would be done, but not even then for a moment thinking it was my duty to become a Missionary.

I subsequently removed several young women to my home at Jerilderie, where they were properly cared for. But all this time the conviction grew stronger and stronger that a Mission should be founded at once on the Murrumbidgee; therefore I wrote to Mr. Matthews, and asked him whether he would be willing to break up his small Mission school, and undertake the founding and management of a large concern elsewhere. After much thought and prayer he informed me that he could not leave his Murray blacks. What, then, was I to do for my own unfortunates? I saw very plainly that one of two things must be done— either I must abandon the idea of the new Mission, and remain at my regular work, or else relinquish my comfortable position and undertake the real work of the Mission myself. For six months a severe struggle was kept up between the flesh and spirit. The flesh said—'Stay where you are; why impoverish your wife and family, and isolate them from all society?' But the spirit said—'Go and rescue the perishing! Go and build them a home in the wilderness!' At length I said to my wife—'I cannot bear this any longer; I must bring the matter to some issue. I have just been praying about it, and I seem directed to leave the whole matter with you. If you say No, I will not go; but if you say Yes, I will go.' Her answer decided me. In her own quiet way she said—'If you think God is leading us amongst the blacks, go, and I will do what I can to help you; but if God is not leading us, don't go.'

I wrestled no longer with the flesh, but set about arranging matters for the establishment of the Mission. I resigned my charge, a very comfortable and profitable one, and early in March, 1880, to the utter amazement of our old friends, we left the town of Jerilderie with our little belongings.

As we passed through the town we must have made a singular procession, for everybody 'came out for to see'. Our household stuff was conveyed in two waggons; my wife, little ones, and several black girls followed in a waggonette, the rear being brought up by myself and the black lads driving the cattle and goats.

After three days and nights spent on the road we arrived at our destination—a rough log cabin in the wild forest, which I had secured from the owner as a temporary home for Mrs. Gribble and our children, and the few black girls we had brought from Jerilderie. After a day or two I drove down the river, with my four black men, in search of a suitable spot for our proposed Mission; and decided to commence operations on a reserve which I knew had but recently been revoked from lease. I hoped that I should thus escape all unpleasantness with the squatter, for I was led to understand that the establishment of a home for the blacks was not well received in the district. Here, then, on the south bank of the Murrumbidgee, three miles from Darlington Point, and twelve from our temporary home, we knelt down amidst the beautiful pine trees, and gave ourselves to God for the work. We then began in real earnest, cutting down the trees, and preparing timber for building. In about a month, two huts (the first for a married black couple, the other for my own family) were drawing near completion, when suddenly I received a letter from the Lands Department cautioning me not to proceed any further, and this notwithstanding a distinct promise made beforehand. I at once told the poor black fellows to leave off, and we returned with heavy hearts to our rough bush home to acquaint Mrs. Gribble and the black women with the circumstances of our seeming failure . . .

But although our work during the first two years was very hard, and our privations many, these trials did not affect us nearly as much as did the cruel conduct of those around us, who were professedly Christians. In different ways they sought to break up the Mission and to scatter the blacks. On one occasion a man, who passes for a gentleman, bought a case of gin during my absence, sent it to the women's camp, at some distance from the Mission, and made them all drunk. The scene which followed was indescribable.

On another occasion the keeper of a low bush hotel supplied the camp with drink, called in the white men around, and, as an eye-witness informed me, 'the scene was a little hell'. The following morning I visited the camp, and there I witnessed a most revolting sight—poor old women and quite young girls helplessly drunk. One poor young creature, with a half-caste babe upon her bosom, staggered towards me at my approach. I said: 'What have you been doing, Louisa?' 'I have been drinking,' she replied, 'Who gave you the drink?' 'Mr. D—,' referring to the publican; and then, with the big tears streaming down her black face, she cried:

'Oh, do take me away from this place. I don't want to be a bad girl. I did not want to take the drink, but they made me take it.' I said, 'If you will wait till tomorrow I will bring a buggy and take you away,' which, of course, I did, to the exceeding joy of the poor creature.

Even after the Mission home was founded, and we had gathered in a goodly number, wicked white men continued for a long time to cause us annoyance. One night the girls' cottage was broken into, and the poor things ran screaming to the Mission House for protection in the greatest alarm, and I was compelled to mount my horse and to go in pursuit of the offenders. At daybreak they were captured and conveyed by the police to Narandera, a distance of forty miles, where they were made to suffer for their misconduct.

One day an *employe* [sic] from a neighbouring station rode deliberately into the Mission square, and, after tearing off the stirrup-iron from his saddle and flourishing it over his head, swore that he would kill the first man, white or black, that ventured near him. After keeping everybody in a state of the utmost terror for about half an hour, he gave me a *fortnight's notice* to break up the Mission, saying that if I did not abandon it I should have to stand to the consequences. Thus in many ways was the good work opposed by those who should have regarded the movement with favour. Before our fences were erected our small reserve was daily flooded with neighbours' flocks driven there on purpose, and even when we were doing all in our power to protect ourselves peaceably they set fire to our fences, and would not desist until the law was brought to bear upon them.

Before the establishment of Warangesda, Darlington Point was, so to speak, the very *focus* of iniquity on the Murrumbidgee, so far as traffic in the blacks was concerned. Therefore when the carnal interests of men were interfered with by us they did all in their power to thwart our endeavours.

For the first two years of our Mission life the main difficulties we had to encounter were from the white man's horrible passions. But, thank God, stronger was He that was for us than all the powers of evil that were arrayed against us; and now, after four years' struggle, we see the same Darlington Point, once the standing horror and disgrace of the district, thoroughly reformed as regards the traffic in the bodies and souls of the poor blacks.

But all through our difficulties, both from without and from within, the work was never allowed to stand still. Believing that God had sent us to set up a place of refuge for those who were ready to perish, we continued building, fencing, and clearing, combined with preaching and teaching, feeling assured that we should in due time reap the promised harvest.

'Conflict with Heathenism'

Practically all 19th century missionaries saw their task as not only the conversion of their flock but also their 'civilization'. In practical terms that meant imposing all aspects of Western culture and at the same time suppressing Aboriginal customs and ceremonies. They were proud of their moral tyranny and wrote extensively of their triumph over 'savagery' and 'heathenism'. Marriage and funeral rites were often the sharpest point of conflict.

D. MATTHEWS, 'NATIVE TRIBES OF THE UPPER MURRAY,' *JOURNAL OF THE ROYAL GEOGRAPHICAL SOCIETY, SOUTH AUSTRALIA*, SESSIONS 1898–9 TO 1900–1, VOL. IV, PP. 48–9.

One of the first acts of reform I adopted in collecting and bringing them into the Government reserves and villages was to induce them to marry according to our British laws. This they objected to at first, telling me they had been 'married enough'. By judicious and firm action, I then locked the store door, refusing the food unless they obeyed. After a few days of conference and empty stomachs, a deputation waited upon me with the information that they were willing to get married. Through taking this stand I was enabled to put a stop to their illicit and unhappy relationships, and so brought in joy and contentment...

* * * * * *

In July 1895 the missionaries at Yarrabah recorded their triumph in imposing Christian burial rites on the body of the small daughter of 'John', one of their first converts, against the opposition of other members of the community.

MISSIONARY NOTES, 15 AUGUST 1895, P. 72.

John has just lost another little girl, three years of age, by death. When away last month at Port Douglas a little crippled daughter died, but owing to John's absence the old natives embalmed the body and went through all the revolting rites and ceremonies usual on such occasions. This little thing that we have just buried had been a fine healthy child up to a short time ago, when she began to suffer from eating sand, a habit common among children in these parts, and which generally proves fatal. I have known cases in Cairns among white children of this sand-eating propensity. Before death the body turns quite yellow in colour. On Sunday last I gave the little thing some medicine and spent some time applying external medicine, but all could see that the end was near. Early yesterday morning she died, and as soon as possible I went down to John's camp, for he had vacated his house as soon as the child died, and had taken the body with him. After speaking a few words of comfort to him, I asked him if he would have Christian burial, to which he answered in the affirmative, but stipulated that the burial should not take place till to-day, as he wished some natives (to whom they were then signalling with fires) across the bay to come in. Mother went down with my wife and laid out the poor little body, much to the surprise of the old women, who are considered very important persons in these cases by the natives. During the morning I was told that the old women had influenced John not to have the body buried but to have it embalmed and treated in the native fashion. I at once went down and found that the other natives had come in and were wailing most piteously beside the body, which had evidently been freely handled by them in their excessive grief. John assured me that he would, as he put it, '*set* her to-morrow.' During the afternoon Mr. Reeve made the coffin, and painted her name and age and date of death on tin, affixed to the lid.

Early this morning, Mr. Elwin, with the two lads Pompo and George, went to the cemetery and dug the grave, while Mr. Reeve and myself went to the camp and put the body into the coffin. After placing it in the coffin I waited some time before putting on the lid; one old woman stepped up and put an old garment and several pieces of bark into the coffin. Then I placed the lid on, and as soon as I did so the old women set up a most fearful din, and acted in a truly disgusting manner; rolling in the sand, throwing it at the coffin and over each other, and looked perfect fiends. They did not want the whites to have anything to do with the dead. John again assured me that he wished for Christian burial, and Mr. Reeve and myself carried the coffin into the School-Church and placed it near the communion rails across two forms. After breakfast the bell tolled, and the people being assembled, we had the first part of the Burial Service, commencing with a little children's hymn much liked by our children here. I spoke at some length to the people present, and also told them how glad I was that John had determined to have Christian burial, and had refused to allow the old natives to go through their disgusting rites. Forming into procession outside, all started for the burying ground about a mile distant. I led the way in surplice and stole, followed by Mr. Elwin and Mr. Reeve. Then came the coffin carried by four girls; after them came the girls and boys in twos, followed by the adults; in all we numbered forty-eight. At the grave I again spoke to those present, and then read the remainder of the service. After the grave had been filled in, all placed stones round it and planted some flowers on it. While the grave was being filled in, poor John walked off by himself; I went after him and spoke a few comforting words to him. He told me that he would soon be all right, but that he would feel sorry until next moon, as he was

MORTLOCK LIBRARY, ADELAIDE. Missionaries measured their success by the converts they made. All would have relished the experience of the earnest young Salvation Army couple surrounded by their followers, who were not only pious but respectable and respectful as well.

MISSIONARIES

'very much sorry yet.' Eva was the first black baby on the Yarra Bah Mission and was a nice little thing, and during a severe illness was baptised by myself—the first to be baptised on the place, and the first native child baptised by myself. The natives old and young were most attentive during the service, the old people being much interested in all the proceedings.

This has indeed been a triumph for us as Missionaries, a real triumph over heathen rites.

* * * * * *

The South Australian missionary George Taplin wrote an account of his successful defiance of the attempt by the Narrinyeri people to impose their own marriage laws.

G. TAPLIN, 'THE NARRINYERI', IN J.D. WOODS, ED., *THE NATIVE TRIBES OF SOUTH AUSTRALIA*, ADELAIDE, 1879, PP. 105–7.

The introduction of Christian marriage gave sanctity to the nuptial tie, and made it appear more indissoluble. The old heathen blacks saw this, and after the first two marriages they set to work to try if they could not undo them. Amongst the Aborigines it has been often the case that where a young woman has been given in marriage against the wishes of some of her relatives, they have tried to take her away from her husband and give her to somebody else. Laelinyeri had been legally married to Charlotte by the Rev. J. Gardner, as stated above; so a party of the old blacks pretended that they were offended at this, especially an old savage called Fisherman Jack. Soon after the marriage, down came the Lower Murray tribe to the station and encamped near. With their usual deceit they pretended to be quite friendly with the newly-married couple, so as to throw them off their guard. When they had accomplished this they suddenly seized Charlotte by force in the absence of her husband, and went off rapidly to an island called Towadjeri, on the Lower Lake, about ten miles from the station. There they defied her husband to get her, and declared he should never have her again, as they would give her to another man. Laelinyeri came to me and told his story in great grief, as was natural. I could see that a crisis had arisen, and sought, by the help of God, to be equal to the occasion. I got our farm overseer and a friend who was staying with him to go with us, and I and Laelinyeri got into the boat, and we four sailed off down the Lake to Towadjeri. When we got there we anchored, and while we were doing so somebody said, 'There is Charlotte on the shore, sitting under a bush.' I saw that the girl, suspecting that I was coming to fetch her, had slipped away from her captors, and was waiting for me; so I jumped into the dingey (it would only carry two), and bade Laelinyeri put me ashore. When I got there I saw all the Lower Murray tribe—about sixty men—drawn up in rank about 200 yards off with their fishing spears (ugly three-pronged weapons) in their hands, and trying to look as fierce and angry as they could; but I believed it was all bounce, and walked up the shore, sending Laelinyeri back to the boat for my two friends and my gun. Then I went up to Charlotte and told her to follow me. This she readily and joyfully did, and I led her to where the dingey was again approaching the shore. Just then old Fisherman sprang out of the ranks and began dancing about and swearing at me in native, and whirling his spear round his head, and calling on the other blacks to come and take the girl out of my hands; but not a man moved. Up came the dingey; my friends jumped ashore, in stepped Charlotte, and her husband took her on board the cutter. I now knew she was pretty safe; so we walked up amongst the blacks and began to talk in a friendly way to them, not alluding to the subject in dispute. One of the fellows pointed to my gun and said, 'What! you going to shoot blackfellow?' I said, 'No; I only want to shoot ducks.' We stayed half an hour, and then went off to the cutter and sailed for home. That put an end to all attempts to undo legal marriage; it has never been attempted since.

* * * * * *

Taplin described the conflict arising over the decision of a young man called Waukeri to defy the traditions of his people.

G. TAPLIN, *OP. CIT.*, PP. 77–79.

I had not been more than three months preaching the gospel to the natives before there appeared a token of God's grace in the decision of a young man named Waukeri to become a Christian. The decision was clear and unmistakable. It may not have been very enlightened, any more than that of many others who have made the same resolve, but it was a decision adhered to until death. Waukeri had been forcibly seized and compelled to go through the disgusting rites of making narumbe. Before this he had heard me preach and teach for about three months. So he began to refuse to conform to the native customs of the narumbar; he would eat with the women, he would not smear himself with red ochre and grease, and he would not go about in a state of nudity. So one night the old men of the tribe solemnly threatened to kill him for his disobedience. He then came away to our house and asked for my protection. This conduct led me to inquire the reason for his desire to give up native customs, and he declared his resolve to be a Christian; his expression was that he did not mean to serve the devil any longer, but would serve Jehovah. I warned him of the persecution which he might expect, then prayed with him, and commended him to the protection of Jehovah. Now I never specially noticed this young man Waukeri, nor offered him any inducement to take this step. He never went back from his decision. His profession of religion had many faults and inconsistencies, as might have been expected, but still it was maintained amidst difficulties and persecutions and discouragements to the last. When he first became a Christian he set to work to wash off the grease and red ochre with which he was bedaubed from head to foot. He succeeded pretty well with his body, but he could not get the mixture out of his really fine head of hair; so he came for assistance, and my dear wife and her servant-girl set to work and with a tub of hot water and soap gave his head a good scrubbing, and got all the red stuff out of his curls, and restored them to their original glossy black. Waukeri was a really handsome fellow; his face was by no means destitute of comeliness, and his form was of perfect symmetry. He was of a kindly, affectionate disposition, but yet with a great deal of firmness. I heard of several instances in which he showed even to ungodly white people that he was not ashamed of his profession. He died of pulmonary consumption in November 1864, as I shall hereinafter relate, and I trust found acceptance with Him who will not break the bruised reed nor quench the smoking flax. I felt this young man's decision at such an early period of my work was the voice of God bidding me go forward . . .

Taplin did not give any indication of Aboriginal opinion in his published work but in his journal he recorded the detail of a heated argument with Waukeri's brother.

THE JOURNAL OF GEORGE TAPLIN, MORTLOCK LIBRARY, ADELAIDE PR6 186/1/3, JANUARY, 1860, P. 58.

[The brother] had been with others persecuting [Waukeri] and compelling him to comply with their customs and I expostulated with him, at the same time telling him that I should help Waukeri to break their customs. He replied, 'What for you do that? You know God tells us to do these things.'

'O,' I said, 'Where in the Bible does God tell you to do them, for there is only one God, Jehovah, and only one Bible.'

'Well,' he answered, 'how do you know that Bible (is) Jehovah's book? Did he give it to you? Did he tell you it? Did not white fellow make it?'

'No, Jehovah gave it to my fathers long time ago.'

'Well, our God tell my father these customs long time ago, so we must do them.'

'Yes, but your God is a devil, he is not Jehovah. Jehovah only tells people to do things to make them live. White fellow do these things and they increase and get to be many in number, but your God only tells blackfellow to do things to make them do, because he wants to kill them. Where all Adelaide blackfellows? Dead, because he did what [his God] tell him. And you know that this blackfellow only a few now, to what they were a long time ago. So we know what your God is a devil.'

'No, No,' he answered, 'we must do what he tells us.'

I replied 'You do not believe what I say.'

'No,' he said, 'we dont.'

'Well then Jehovah tells me to tell you that if you will not believe, you will go to hell when you die.'

With this the conversation closed.

* * * * * *

The Anglican missionary James Gunther recorded an instance of the internal conflict experienced by the young men living on the mission stations—in this case Bungary and Cochrane.

JAMES GUNTHER LETTERS, 1840, CHURCH MISSIONARY SOCIETY RECORDS, AJCP.

I observed that Bungary had, at last, conformed to the practice of making incisions in the skin, to which he was long opposed. I reproved him for it and reminded him of his former opposition. It is not many months since, that he, significantly, pointed out to me a passage in the Bible prohibiting cuttings in the flesh. He was at a loss to reply but said at last, joined by Cochrane that the women thought those 'ugly fellows' who had no marks on their skin.

'Aha,' I replied, 'you wish to please the women.'

Bungary felt ashamed and wanted to deny it, but Cochrane, in his usual candour called out,

'Certainly we do.'

* * * * *

The Methodist missionary at Port Phillip, Frances Tuckfield, reported the case of Kam-kam, another young man who was attracted to the Christian message.

THE JOURNAL OF FRANCIS TUCKFIELD, P. 299, LA TROBE LIBRARY, MELBOURNE.

I have witnessed instances in which the natives have appeared to be under Divine influence and on these occasions they have expressed themselves in the most decided and encouraging manner about becoming settled and adopting the European mode of living in their habits and have made some very strenuous efforts to do so, but have been compelled by other natives to return to the bush. Kam-kam for instance went so far as to build himself a house and during the short time he lived in it and when urged to join his tribe in their wanderings and aggressions he would sometimes bring his instruments of war to the Missionaries that he might urge this as an excuse for not going.

* * * * * *

A missionary from Yarrabah in North Queensland provided an insight into his methods of preparing adult Aborigines for baptism.

C.J. FLETCHER, 'THE TEN COMMANDMENTS AT YARRABAH,' *NORTH QUEENSLAND NOTES*, OCTOBER 1930, PP. 1714—15.

A recent article in *North Queensland Notes* gave a revised table of the Ten Commandments as adapted for teaching Kanakas at the old Mission at Mackay. That even such a simplified version of the [commandments] is beyond the mental capacities of a certain grade of Australian aborigine was discovered by me when I was first confronted with the task of preparing a group of 'myall' natives at the Yarrabah Aboriginal Mission, in North Queensland, for the Sacrament of Holy Baptism. The group consisted of three men and five women. All were, of course, illiterate. One of the men and one of the women had worked on stations for white people, but all were almost totally devoid of any conception of the Christian religion. Enquiry revealed a strong belief in 'kootcha' or 'debil-debils' (malignant spirits)—a term which I learned was also applied to white men—and in some cases an idea of 'big fellow up top' with a strong faith in the ministrations of the native medicine men or witch doctors. Some of the [converts] knew very little English beyond 'tobacco', 'tucker', 'boss', etc., and the teaching had to be conveyed to them in a form of pidgin English, with the use of such native words as I could manage to pick up from more educated natives. The age of the candidates and the exigencies of the Mission made it very difficult to have them taught English first, so I decided to go ahead and do my best with their present intellectual equipment. Fortunately, one word, which was understood by the whole class was 'Rule', and on its associations I built my interpretation of the Ten Commandments. Starting with a brief comparison with the rules of the Mission, I proceeded to explain 'God's Rules' by the following method:

Illustrations from magazines were used in each case, accompanied by the use of the digits of both hands, and a great deal of pantomimic gesture. Let me give a few instances. In teaching the First

JOHN OXLEY LIBRARY, BRISBANE. ORIGINAL IN HISTORICAL SOCIETY OF CAIRNS. A photo taken at Yarrabah Aboriginal Mission, North Queensland, which may actually include C.J. Fletcher. The missionaries are surrounded by their flock, who look far from enchanted with proceedings.

Commandment, I used an advertisement for Eno's Fruit Salt, representing an Eastern sitting by the roadside and holding a lemon in his hand. After blackening the face in the picture to make it appear more like that of an aborigine, the cutting was shown to the class and introduced as the illustration of a medicine man—the lemon was misrepresented as a stone which the magician had just pretended to have extracted from the organs of a patient. (This, of course, is a common trick of the native witch doctor.) In association with this picture was learned by the class, 'Only one God—no more medicine man.'

For the Fourth Commandment was used a view of the interior of a Church, with the phrase, 'Go to Church on Sunday.'

The fingers were used to reinforce the illustrated teaching. For example, for the Seventh Commandment a finger was dipped in the dirt and used to dramatise, 'No think dirty, no speak dirty, no do dirty'; while the attractive properties of another digit smothered in glue were used to illustrate 'No steal'.

These very crude methods were successful, as was shown by the response given to questions asked on the production of the respective pictures, or the holding up of a finger. Thus, with the further help of Crucifix and pictures from the life of Our Blessed Lord, a simple instruction in the Christian faith was given to these people, who really seemed to apprehend it, and, after careful dealing with the class individually, I was convinced that the 'right disposition' was there, and the members were all baptized on Sunday 26 January last.

* * * * * *

The missionaries often found that the Aborigines were bored by their incessant preaching or incredulous about what they were saying. The German missionaries at Hope Vale in North Queensland had a much more realistic view of their impact because they learned the local Aboriginal language as a matter of priority.

MISSIONARY PFALZER IN *CHURCH NEWS*, VOL. 20, NOS. 3 & 9, 1888.

I have no sooner shown them the existence of a Creator of Heaven and earth, spoken to them of the Almighty, All-knowing God, than they feel they know enough and don't need to stay on here.

Even while they are here their interest is of a dubious kind. That is recognizable by the questions they ask. One of them interrupted me in the middle of a story with the call: 'Do we get rice or flour after this today?' and another wanted to know: 'Are we going to chop wood or dig ditches?' A third one cut in with 'When do we get trousers, shirts and blankets' and someone else suggested: 'We've heard enough today; lets stop.'

At the beginning I was being asked about points which proved a genuine interest in the subject. Lately I have had an audience of a more sluggish nature. They sit still enough and seem to listen, but when I ask something to make sure they understand me, then I am told by the young ones that I must ask the older men, and the old ones reply: 'You tell us! You always know everything best' . . . I usually start instructions with the message that there is a God, a being superior to all humans. Who was already when there was nothing on earth or in the heavens. They usually ask at this stage whether this God is a *bama*, i.e. a black man or a white one? So I repeat that He is not a man at all, but a *wau-u*, which means basically air, but also 'spirit' and 'ghost' . . .

Anyone who died has, according to them been killed by an enemy: by a black man of another tribe. The foe creeps up from behind and breaks his victims neck, by clashing it against a piece of wood or a stone.

I tried of course to teach them something nearer to the truth. But when I told them that after death the body would then turn to earth, but that it would come back to life later, when it would rejoin the soul; and at that time all good people would be gathered in a good place, called heaven; and at the same time all evil people would be sent to a bad place; when

I told them all that, they just laughed. 'No,' they said, 'it was not like that at all. They know better.'

Suffer Little Children

The missionaries and other philanthropic Europeans believed that the Aboriginal children were the key to success in their task of 'civilizing the natives'. If only they could be removed from tribal influences at a tender age they could be brought up in the ways of the white man. Such was their enthusiasm for this task that 'parsons' gained an evil reputation among Aborigines as people who stole children. On reserves and missions where it was possible to impose white authority children were taken from their parents and raised in single-sex dormitories. Such institutions still existed in the 1960s and 1970s. The view was that because the task was so difficult extremely rigid training was necessary to overcome the 'wildness' in the children.

REGULATIONS AND ARRANGEMENTS RELATIVE TO THE NATIVE CHILDREN WHO MAY BE PROVIDED WITH SITUATIONS IN THE HOUSES OF THE SETTLERS AND WHO ATTEND THE WESLEYAN MISSION SCHOOL AT PERTH, *BPP*: ABORIGINES-AUSTRALIAN COLONIES, 1844, PP. 387–88.

1. ... Each boy and girl is expected to attend two hours daily (Saturdays excepted) from one to three in the winter, and from two to four in the summer season.
2. After school, the children will return direct to their employers' home; any charge of loitering on the road, if reported, will be investigated.
3. The children are to be allowed to sleep at the house of Mr. Armstrong, the teacher, as it appears that being permitted to pass the evening with their little brothers and friends, and sleep in company, is the only present means of keeping them together, and preventing them from tiring of the white people. A separate sleeping apartment is provided for the boys.
4. On Sunday the children remain at Mr. Armstrong's house during the whole of the day, and attend the school and Divine service, morning and evening, at the Wesleyan chapel.
5. Should the children not suit their employers, or misconduct themselves, any complaint will be immediately looked into by the committee; and if, after being threatened and repeatedly punished, they appear to be incorrigible, they may be sent back, and others, if disengaged, will be provided in their stead.
6. Severe restrictions will be placed upon the children loitering on the

road and playing at marbles or other games, as there will be sufficient time for recreation on returning to Mr. Armstrong's house at sunset.

7. As many of the children have been for a considerable time at Mr. Armstrong's house previous to entering on their situations, and are under his daily care at school, and moreover have been especially placed by their parents under his protection, with strict injunctions for their safe keeping, Mr. Armstrong naturally feels much interested in the welfare of these poor children; and by the assistance of the committee and their employers, will consider it his duty to do all in his power for the improvement of their condition.

8. It is respectfully requested that the parties employing the children shall provide them with week-day garments, washing. &c.; the charge for those worn on Sundays will be borne on the general expenses of the establishment.

9. It is particularly requested that no child be sent away without such intention on the part of the employers being first communicated to the committee, in order that warning may be given to the child, as likely to produce a good effect, and cause a reformation of conduct.

10. Too much should not be expected from the children on first entering upon any situation, as several instances have occurred of parties having been on the point of dismissing children, who, upon further trial, and, with the exercise of some patience on the part of their employer, have proved themselves most useful.

11. The children are expected to wash themselves every morning.

12. Mr. Armstrong will occasionally call upon each employer, and learn in the presence of the children their general behaviour, thus showing them that there is some one interested in watching over their welfare and comfort.

13. It will be expected that in case any of the children are taken sick, that they may be sent to the house of Mr. Armstrong, where medical aid is provided by the Government, and that 1 $s.$ per day be allowed by their employers for their support during their sickness, if not exceeding one fortnight; beyond that period the committee will provide.

14. The children are to be allowed to have one day in every two months for a holiday, as recreation and encouragement.

15. These regulations by some may be considered too diffuse, but they have been suggested by an anxious wish to endeavour to surmount the many difficulties that occur in the first introduction of native children into the families of the colonists. Considerable success has hitherto attended these efforts for ameliorating the condition of the children, but in spite of every precaution, it cannot reasonably be expected that the same favourable result will invariably follow. The patience, therefore, and good feeling of the masters and mistresses are earnestly requested,

in bearing at first with the awkwardness and possible wayward habits of their little charges.

* * * * * *

Bible studies usually played a central part in the training of Aboriginal children. The instruction was usually in English and was often as not of the most mechanical kind with rote learning playing a major role. A good insight into methods common in the early 19th century can be gained from reports of the formal examination of Tasmanian Aboriginal children on Flinders Island in the 1830s. The children had been given the names of great men and women in European and classical history.

J. BONWICK, *THE LAST OF THE TASMANIANS*, LONDON, 1870, PP. 260—62.

Leonidas, the hero of the class, repeats the Lord's Prayer, the Collect, the names of the months and days of the week, in addition to counting up to one hundred. His theological knowledge was sounded. I copy a few of the questions and answers.
 Do you like the devil?—No
 Do you like God?—Yes
 Can you see God?—No
 What is the Devil?—The father of lies
 What did God do with Adam's rib?—Make a woman of it
 Who did God take the woman to?—To Adam
 Do you pray to God?—Yes
[Neptune was then interrogated.]
 What will God do to this world by and by?—Burn it
 What did God make us for?—His own purpose
 Who are in Heaven?—God, angels, good men, and Jesus Christ
 What sort of country is heaven?—A fine place
 What sort of place is hell?—A place of torment
 What do you mean by a 'place of torment'?—Burning for ever and ever

* * * * * *

The fear of hell played a central part in the work of the missionaries. It often had the desired effect, but not always so.

JOURNAL OF W. WATSON, 5 APRIL 1833, CHURCH MISSIONARY SOCIETY RECORDS, AJCP.

I asked one of our little boys Dickey Marshall this evening as we were walking in the bush, where wicked children go when they died?

He said, 'to that very bad place.'
I then asked him, 'who were wicked children?'
He replied, 'Those that are disobedient, say naughty words, play or bathe on a Sunday.'
He spoke this in so simple and artless a manner as made it very pleasing. Tears often run down his cheeks when we speak to him on religious subjects.

(*Ibid.*, September 21, 1834, reporting a conversation between Watson and a little girl called Yeenar.)

Watson: Where do wicked people go at death?
Yeenar: To very great fire I believe.
Watson: That is very bad, and is not to be trifled with.
Yeenar: Oh yes fire very good, very good.

* * * * * *

The German missionaries in North Queensland in the 1880s translated Bible stories into the local Aboriginal dialect. This created more interest but not always in the way the missionaries expected.

MISSIONARY POLAND WRITING IN *CHURCH NEWS*, 21, NO. 5, 1889, P. 33.

The children are behaving much better and several of them are writing of their own accord. Podaigo and Kakural are ahead of the others in this skill as they are in most. All of them are now reading well enough to enjoy it, and I am kept busy supplying them with reading matter. On the whole they are given the Old and New Testament stories which we have already translated . . . We keep revising the Bible stories and they must surely derive some benefit from them; but some of them get them terribly mixed up. Of course Podaigo and Kakural, in particular, is amazingly expert in the family relationships of the various biblical characters. For such connections seem most important to the blacks, who all claim to be some degree related to each and can always explain these complicated ties, when someone asks about them.

* * * * * *

Aboriginal pupils sometimes posed questions which the missionaries found difficult to answer. W. Watson reported the conversation which followed his assertion that an old Aboriginal man who had died some time before would not go to heaven because he had not been taught about God.

W. WATSON JOURNAL, 4 JULY 1834, *OP. CIT.*

One of the boys observed: 'I believe all children go to heaven.'
I said they are not baptised.
He then remarked: 'What for all pikininny go to fire, no good that.'
Another of the boys said: 'It is devil devil will not let them go to Heaven.'
They frequently asked questions which we do not think it prudent to answer.

Success or Failure?

Their intolerance and spiritual arrogance notwithstanding, the missionaries constantly examined their own performance and noted their success and failure. James Gunther reported on the failure of the Mission at Wellington Valley in New South Wales in 1843.

ANNUAL REPORT FOR 1842, *NSWLCV&P*, 1843, PP. 482–83.

Amongst all those young men, who, for years past, have been more or less attached to the Mission, there is only one who affords some satisfaction and encouragement. Deep religious impressions have been made on his mind, and we have reason to believe, he is undergoing a change of character. For more than two years, he has distinguished himself above the rest by a desire for improvement, inquiry, and reflection. He has gradually shaken off the yoke and dominion of the elderly men, and superstitious notions from his mind. But I am sorry to observe, that this young man is not likely to live much longer, so as to become useful among his countrymen; he having, for a considerable time, shown strong symptoms of a consumptive disease, and is, of late, quite unable to make any bodily exertions.

As regards the others, I can give no very favourable account of their conduct, during the past year. Several of those who used to stay at, or frequent the Mission, resorted to their old migratory habits, and one of them, I fear, in consequence of depriving himself of the advantages and comforts of civilized life, to which he for years has been accustomed, has died in a state of decline. Instances of the kind, I lament to say, frequently occur.

Even those few who may be considered as still attached to the Mission, only about four besides the one I have described, have, too frequently, during the year, made excursions into the bush, and when at home, they evinced not much desire for instruction and improvement. They have, however, often been very usefully employed in the general work of our establishment, particularly at building and fencing.

I very much regret, that on account of the smallness of their number and their frequent absence (during which time the work usually accumulates), they could, by no means, be regularly or daily instructed when here. I could rarely get more than one or two at the one time, to be instructed, which is very disheartening. Their thoughtlessness, a spirit of independence, ingratitude, and want of sincere straightforward dealing, often try us in the extreme.

* * * * * *

The South Australian Taplin confided his disillusionment in his journal.

JOURNAL OF GEORGE TAPLIN, *OP. CIT*, 5, 14 JUNE, 4 JULY, 5, 18 AUGUST 1861.

I cannot express the anxiety which I feel for the children who have attended the school but are now absent. O if none should be saved, what an awful disappointment. The thought of it fills my eyes with tears . . .

O how depressed I feel. There is no good done yet. No fruit yet . . . Alas! Alas! But cannot help thinking on and mourning over the state of these tribes. I cannot tell you how much I am cast down. I seem to have sorrow upon sorrow . . . There I am—my wife ill—myself weak in health, often far from well—without servant of any kind except natives . . . my children almost daily harrowing up my soul by showing they have picked up some abomination from the blacks . . . O Lord, help me to glory in tribulation.

* * * * * *

The Poonindie Mission near Port Lincoln in South Australia was widely regarded during the middle decades of the 19th century as the most successful Aboriginal settlement in the Australian colonies. It was frequently referred to as proof of the view that the Aborigines could be 'civilized'. What this meant can be seen by the enthusiastic reports written about Poonindie at the time.

REPORT IN THE *MELBOURNE MISSIONARY* PRINTED IN M. HALE, *THE ABORIGINES OF AUSTRALIA*, LONDON, 1889, P. 91.

'What a curious village! No public-house and no gaol or police-barracks! Here in this arcadia the little community men, women, and children,

AUSTRALIAN INSTITUTE OF ABORIGINAL STUDIES. This photograph of an Aboriginal mission in New South Wales illustrates the ideal for most missionaries—the patriarchal figure flanked by well-dressed members of his congregation.

JOHN OXLEY LIBRARY, BRISBANE. This photograph presents a bleak picture of the mission experience. Women, all in prison-like garb, hair cropped, look sullenly at the camera.

morning and evening, meet in church for prayer and praise. None of its members ever go to law; no drunkenness or crime is here found, and should any little dispute arise it is settled among themselves in a Christian manner, in accordance with St. Paul's instructions to the Corinthians. There is an educational establishment, where some of the pupils can show creditable specimens of penmanship, &c. Singing classes for practising sacred music are held in the church. Everybody looked fat, happy and clean. One of the laws is that every one must have a hot bath every Saturday evening, and a cold one as often as he or she likes. The curfew-bell tolls a little later than under the Norman rule, and when it rings lights are put out and all retire to rest. Every morning the men proceed to their rural avocations—some reaping, some shepherding, some building. Meantime the wives are washing and cooking, and the children learning and playing, and on the Sabbath they listen in their beloved church to their pastor, and chant their *glorias* and anthems and sing hymns in a beautiful manner. Now, who are those people living in such an orderly and exemplary manner? The despised aborigines of South Australia.'

* * * * * *

A 1921 account of Yarrabah provided further information on the type of settlement admired in missionary circles.

J.O. HARRIS, 'THE AUSTRALIAN ABORIGINES IN QUEENSLAND,' *NORTH QUEENSLAND NOTES*, JANUARY 1921, PP. 810–11.

In a clearing in the scrub (the tropical jungle) stand the Church and the Mission house, where the head of the settlement lives, and a dozen houses that constitute the native village. How far have the blacks got after twenty years? The Church was built by the men in their spare time, who have been taught by their missionary that they can thus show their love to their Master. In it from time to time the chaplain gives them their communion after gently dealing with the sins of little children, quarrelling, 'yarn carrying', lying, petty thieving, disobedience, or perhaps using the discipline of the early Church towards the graver sins of murder, adultery, or witchcraft that scandalize the community—public excommunication and public penance. Here they meet for their daily prayers, often led by the black 'layman', as they designate the office of reader.

The missionary, who is often a married man, lives with every detail of his home life open for them to read—a city set on a hill that cannot be hid. Morning by morning he rings the work bell, calls the roll, and starts the day's work with prayer. Then up to the plantation to plant potatoes, pick the cotton or clear new land. Sweet potatoes are the staple food.

NATIONAL LIBRARY OF AUSTRALIA, REX NAN KIVELL COLLECTION. J.M. Crossland (1800–1858), *Portrait of Samuel Kandwillen, a pupil of the natives' training institution, Poonindie, South Australia* Oil on canvas. This picture and the one that follows both capture the spirit of Poonindie, where the upper-class Englishman Matthew Hale sought to impose Christianity and British 'standards'. The portraits were probably painted to illustrate the success of the mission.

The older man, formally dressed, holds a book—presumably the Bible. The young man, in what today would be called smart-casual wear, holds his cricket bat aloft. Cricket was an institution at Poonindie. J.M. Crossland (1800–1858), *Portrait of Nannultera, a young Poonindie cricketer* Oil on canvas.

The aboriginals get no free rations beyond tea, sugar and tobacco. The plantation, worked on the company system, each man with equal shares, must supply their needs. Laziness now means to be short of food six months ahead and then extra work in playtime to make 'yucal' mats or collect cuttlefish to pay for the flour that must be bought. Hard work means a surplus of produce to sell to the head station, the industrial centre, credited to all equally, money that they can spend on clothes or meat or other comforts of life. To avoid the black's fatal propensity to gambling, no money passes hands. As the missionary works he remembers that it is not what he does himself, but what by example and precept he gets them to do that counts. He has to remind them continually that they work not for him but for themselves. The savage, who forgets so easily and sees only the present need, or immediate pleasure, must learn to think ahead. The keener spirits are encouraged, he must be careful to develop *esprit de corps*, he can spur them to greater activity by others' success. It is a constant effort, humdrum and not at all adventurous. Then, after the day's work is over, the individual interviews, the fights to disentangle, with each offender reasoned with and shown his fault. Sometimes sternness and discipline, fines of tobacco or Saturday punishment work, sometimes the appeal to the slowly developing conscience. This is the way for real character building, the opportunity of showing where Christ touches daily life. Sometimes it is the world of devils, and devils are very real here to both missionary and native. A spirit of opposition to overcome, a sinister influence to drag out into the light, one of Satan's mouthpieces to be publicly exposed and reproved. Sometimes a strike must be deliberately broken, and even the lever of actual starvation used to force home the fact that men's Christianity is no shield to save them from the consequences of their sins. Actually, while in the middle of it, it seems as if no progress is possible, but let us look at the results of past years. See those neat houses of mangrove posts, split palm floors and thatched grass roofs with ambitious verandas and much originality in architecture, built now, in total independence of white command, with home-made furniture and utensils bought by their own work. It took years of steady fostering to bring the builder of mia mias up to this standard, but it is the settled public spirit of the community that does it now. Then the women, with a pride in the neatness of their dress—not the naked savage—proper housewives, many of them dating their training back to the same patient teaching in school and girls' home.

Modern Reassessment

Since the second world war there has been a fundamental reassessment of missionary endeavour. In some cases churches have withdrawn from the field altogether turning missions over to the local people. Elsewhere contempt for Aboriginal culture, so apparent in the past, has been replaced by a realization that it must be preserved at all costs. Christianity itself has been 'decolonized', losing its close identification with European mores and customs. Indigenous churches have flourished in many parts of the world and the same spirit has emerged in Australia.

In 1981 a World Council of Churches team reported on the Aboriginal situation and considered the role of Christianity in the history of black Australia.

JUSTICE FOR ABORIGINAL AUSTRALIANS, AUSTRALIAN COUNCIL OF CHURCHES, SYDNEY, 1981, PP. 8−10.

The Church in some instances was an instrument which saved some groups from total extinction. On the 'reserves' or 'mission stations' it also preached the Gospel, even if this was sometimes done in a paternalistic form. There were some efforts on the part of the Church to prepare Aboriginal school teachers, church leaders and community workers, but it is also true that the Church took a part in the destruction of Aboriginal culture and institutions. Unfortunately, in the history of Australia, the Christian religion has been used as a means to help the settlers achieve their goals.

Racism is entrenched in every aspect of Australian society. It is tied up with historical, economic, political, cultural and religious interests . . .

For the children, racism is a sin against God and against fellow human beings. It is contrary to the justice and love of God revealed in Jesus Christ. It destroys the human dignity of both the racist and the victim. When practiced by Christians, it denies the very faith we profess and undoes the credibility of the Church and its witness to Jesus Christ . . .

To practice *racial discrimination* is to break the unity of the body of Christ, to fracture the Church. To face uniformity on a diversity of cultures, ethnic churches, Aboriginal churches, and force them to become part of and like the Anglo-Saxon church in this country is to fracture the Body of Christ, a witness to the Kingdom of God.

* * * * * *

DJINIYIHI GONDARRA, ABORIGINAL AND CHRISTIAN—DEVELOPING AN INDIGENOUS THEOLOGY, *NATIONAL OUTLOOK*, FEBRUARY, 1984, PP. 11−12.

To me as a black theologian, God is black as much as white. Why? Because God speaks our language, knows our culture, and made this land we now live in and enjoy.

If I am to have my true identity before God, you cannot lock me into white ways. You must give me freedom to be me. God has the same concern for the Aboriginal as for the white . . .

So spiritual revival among the Aboriginal people in Australia is a turning point. We no longer see God as a white man's God or a God that the missionaries brought to us, but as our God who has lived with us in history. God is living with us now in the person of the Holy Spirit who has given us the vision of the Aboriginal Church to think and theologise the gospel in the language and culture of the people . . .

I believe that the Aboriginal Church should not always be a branch of Western Churches. It must be a Church that organises itself in its own context of structure, tradition, style and with a theology which is our own.

When the Lord calls Aboriginal men and women out of this world to do His work, He does not take away their culture or language and their true identity as Aboriginal people. He blesses them and gives them His word of commission to go into the world and preach the gospel to all mankind. He makes them His disciples and baptises them in the name of the Father, the Son and the Holy Spirit, and also teaches them to obey every thing that He commands them to do. Jesus' last words were that He will always be with them. Christ uses all men to be His disciples and He wants His disciples to communicate His words, in the context of their own culture, so that people can understand and make their response to the gospel in their own understanding.

7

GOVERNMENT POLICY: ASSIMILATION OR SEGREGATION?

From the beginning of settlement, government has had a major impact on Aboriginal people, whether or not they have understood the source of policies which so greatly affected their lives. In 200 years, Aborigines have been both protected, and neglected, by an assortment of governments—British, Colonial and State, Australian—and by innumerable officials from an anthology of different departments and agencies. It is a large and complicated story, yet certain lines of development can be traced from the late 18th century to the late 20th century.

The King's Subjects

The constitutional and legal doctrine of the British Government held that the Aborigines became subjects of the monarch on the assumption of sovereignty at 1788, 1824 and 1829, even though they had no idea of their new status and may not have been Europeans until many years after the event. In practice the Aborigines were severely disadvantaged. No regard was paid to their possession of the land. They could not give evidence in court until late in the 19th century. The various governments did little to stop the bloodshed on the frontier. Some positively encouraged it. We should keep these things in mind when judging the benevolence expressed in formal government documents like the instructions given to the early governors.

INSTRUCTIONS GIVEN TO GOVERNOR PHILLIP, 23 APRIL 1787, *HISTORICAL RECORDS OF NEW SOUTH WALES*, SYDNEY, 1889, 1, P. 485.

You are to endeavour by every possible means to open an intercourse with the natives, and to conciliate their affections, enjoining all our subjects to live in amity and kindness with them. And if any of our subjects shall wantonly destroy them, or give them any unnecessary interruption in the exercise of their several occupations, it is our will and pleasure that you do cause such offenders to be brought to punishment according to the degree of the offence.

INSTRUCTIONS GIVEN TO GOVERNOR DARLING, 16 JULY 1825, *HRA*, 1, 22, P. 125.

And it is Our further Will and Pleasure that you do, to the utmost of your power, promote Religion and Education among the Native Inhabitants of Our said Colony, or of the Lands and Islands thereto adjoining; and that you do by all lawful means prevent and restrain all violence and injustice, which may in any manner be practised or attempted against them; and that you take such measures as may appear to you, with the advice of Our said Archdeacon, to be necessary for their conversion to the Christian Faith and for their advancement in Civilization.

Imperial Protection

The 1830s saw the climax of humanitarian concern for the 'coloured' subjects in the Empire. The Anti-Slavery movement mounted one of the most powerful popular crusades of the 19th century and succeeded in having slavery abolished in 1833. The reformers then turned their attention to the indigenous people spread throughout the Empire and founded the Aborigines Protection Society. The leading humanitarian T.F. Buxton chaired a House of Commons Select Committee on the Native Inhabitants of British Settlements in 1837 which foreshadowed a policy of trusteeship.

MITCHELL LIBRARY, STATE LIBRARY OF NSW. 'Proclamation to the Aborigines'. Unknown artist, oil on Huon Pine. Governor Arthur's pictorial proclamation has often been reproduced and just as often derided. However it does express the ideal of racial equality. It was a *radical* document at the time. The suggestion that intermarriage would take place, that white women would take black husbands or lovers would have been highly offensive to colonists later in the century. c. 1830.

SELECT COMMITTEE ON NATIVE INHABITANTS ETC., *BPP*, 1837, PP. 3—4.

The situation of Great Britain brings her beyond any other power into communication with the uncivilized nations of the earth. We are in contact with them in so many parts of the globe, that it has become of deep importance to ascertain the results of our relations with them, and to fix the rules of our conduct towards them. We are apt to class them under the sweeping term of savages, and perhaps, in so doing, to consider ourselves exempted from the obligations due to them as our fellow men. This assumption does not, however, it is obvious, alter our responsibility; and the question appears momentous, when we consider that the policy of Great Britain in this particular, as it has already affected the interests, and we fear we may add, sacrificed the lives, of many thousands, may yet, in all probability, influence the character and the destiny of millions of the human race.

The extent of the question will be best comprehended by taking a survey of the globe, and by observing over how much of its surface and intercourse with Britain may become the greatest blessing, or the heaviest scourge. It will scarcely be denied in word, that, as an enlightened and Christian people, we are at least bound to do to the inhabitants of other lands, whether enlightened or not, as we should in similar circumstances desire to be done by; but, beyond the obligations of common honesty, we are bound by two considerations with regard to the uncivilized: first, that of the ability which we possess to confer upon them the most important benefits; and, secondly, that of their inability to resist any encroachments, however unjust, however mischievous, which we may be disposed to make. The disparity of the parties, the strength of the one and the incapacity of the other, to enforce the observance of their rights, constitutes a new and irresistible appeal to our compassionate protection.

The duty of introducing into our relations with uncivilized nations the righteous and the profitable laws of justice is incontrovertible, and it has been repeatedly acknowledged in the abstract, but has, we fear, been rarely brought into practice: for as a nation, we have not hesitated to invade many of the rights which they hold most dear . . .

The British empire has been signally blessed by Providence, and her eminence, her strength, her wealth, her prosperity, her intellectual, her moral and her religious advantages, are so many reasons for peculiar obedience to the laws of Him who guides the destinies of nations. These were given for some higher purpose than commercial prosperity and military renown. 'It is not to be doubted that this country has been invested with wealth and power, with arts and knowledge, with the sway of distant lands, and the mastery of the restless waters, for some great and important purpose in the government of the world. Can we suppose otherwise than that it is our office to carry civilization and humanity, peace and good government, and, above all, the knowledge of the true God, to the uttermost ends of the earth?' He who has made Great Britain what she is, will inquire at our hands how we have employed the influence He has lent to us in our dealings with the untutored and defenceless savage; whether it has been engaged in seizing their lands, warring upon their people, and transplanting unknown disease, and deeper degradation, through the remote regions of the earth; or whether we have, as far as we have been able, informed their ignorance, and invited and afforded them the opportunity of becoming partakers of that civilization, that innocent commerce, that knowledge and that faith with which it has pleased a gracious Providence to bless our own country.

* * * * * * *

The new policies emanating from the Imperial Government influenced the actions of the colonial governments between 1838 and 1849 including the appointment of protectors, the encouragement of missionary and educational initiatives and the attempt to apply even handed justice.

INSTRUCTIONS ISSUED TO THE PROTECTOR OF ABORIGINES, WESTERN AUSTRALIA, ENCLOSED IN DISPATCH OF HUTT TO NORMANBY, 11 FEBRUARY 1840; *BPP: ABORIGINES: AUSTRALIAN COLONIES*, 1844, P. 372.

1. You will further encourage them to a close and intimate intercourse with yourself, in order that they may understand that they have in you a real protector and adviser, to whom they can appeal on every occasion of real or supposed injuries.
2. You will be particular in making yourself well acquainted with that part of the country which may be assigned to you as your particular district, in order that you may become intimate with the haunts, the movements, and, if possible, the intentions of the natives. Great good may be effected by this means in occasionally checking disturbances, as well as allaying any ill feeling that may exist amongst them, which will be greatly to their own benefit as well as to that of the white population.
3. You will receive all complaints wherein natives are concerned as the suffering party or as the offending party; also, when you can act as mediator, in general the law will point out the course to be pursued; in special cases, after having inquired immediately and fully, without waiting for further instructions, into all the circumstances connected therewith, you will, if you find it or deem it necessary, submit the same for the Governor's final consideration and decision.
4. You will be careful to impress upon the natives the determination of

the Government to treat them with the most strict and impartial justice; that whilst no one will be allowed to maltreat them under any pretence whatever, neither will they be allowed to transgress our laws and customs; that no offence committed by them will be passed over; that forgiveness will never be extended to any of them who may be guilty of murder or aggravated robbery; and that, however long a person may succeed in evading the hands of justice, he will, when taken, be made to bear the full penalty of his crime.

5. Your endeavours will be directed particularly to their advancement in the arts, and even the acquirement of the wants of civilization; and, however slight the first steps taken may be, it is of importance that they should be urged, and even compelled to these, rather than that any, the smallest prospect of success in the improvement of their condition should be allowed to escape. For this purpose it is the wish of the local Government,

- 1st That no native be allowed to appear in your presence, and within the limits of our townships or locations, without a cloak or some ample covering to his nakedness.
- 2nd That they do not, any of them, approach your own or other white people's habitations with their spears.
- 3rd That no fights among themselves be allowed within the boundaries of any township.

6. You will clearly make them understand that any native living with Europeans will be considered as one of the white community, and injury done to him will be severely punished, even though the injury shall have been inflicted in accordance with their own laws and customs.

7. In the event of a native being killed in collision with Europeans, or among themselves, under the circumstances above mentioned, you will perform, so far as the nature of the case will admit, the duty of coroner.

8. Perseverance in any industrious pursuit is hardly yet understood among them, but you may encourage them to perform occasional service for hire and reward; and you will discourage, as far as you can, the exercise of gratuitous charity. A savage is always a beggar, and neither he, nor any other man, will work if bread can be procured by mere asking and importunity.

9. You will carefully prevent the introduction of ardent spirits among them.

10. You will remember that it is the duty as well as the interest of the Government, acting for the public, to treat these people with kindness and conciliation, and that although a rigid enforcement of the rules here given may be desirable it is not meant that these rules may not be modified or relaxed according to circumstances. You will have it in

your power to confer presents of clothes, provisions or other useful articles on deserving individuals, and where you think that confidence may be thereby promoted among them, you are particularly desired to urge upon the Government the distribution among them of more ample and more substantial rewards.

11. Whenever education in any shape can be promoted among them, you will render every assistance on your part towards the advancement of this all-important branch of the general scheme of improvement.

12. You will report your proceedings quarterly, or oftener if desirable, to the Government through the Colonial Secretary. Independent of the amount of what you may have been actually called upon to perform as Protector of the Aborigines, you will include in the report such statistical details as you may have been able to collect, or may be relied upon, of the number of individuals forming the several families of particular tribes, the number of families forming the tribes, the portion of country occupied by them; any peculiar law, custom, idea or transaction which, as a tribe or collection of individuals, may be prevalent amongst them; together with the names, in the native language, of all portions of land, hills, rivers, lakes or springs.

* * * * * *

PROCLAMATION CONCERNING THE ESTABLISHMENT OF COMMISSIONERS OF CROWN LAND IN NEW SOUTH WALES, 21 MAY 1839. PUBLISHED IN *PP: THE ABORIGINES: AUSTRALIAN COLONIES*, 1844, PP. 20–1.

His Excellency the Governor desires to draw the attention of owners of stock throughout the colony, and the public in general, to the extensive powers by which an Act passed in a recent extraordinary session of the Legislative Council (2 Vict. No. 27), are now vested in the commissioners of lands acting beyond the boundaries of location, as well as to the fact that these commissioners are now magistrates of the territory; and as one of the principal objects which the Council had in view in passing the Act referred to, was to put a stop to the atrocities which have of late been so extensively committed beyond the boundaries, both by aborigines and on them. His Excellency deems the present a proper occasion to notify to the public, that he has received distinct instructions from Her Majesty's Government, to cause an inquest or inquiry to be instituted in every case wherein any of the aboriginal inhabitants may have come to a violent death in consequence of a collision with white men; and that his Excellency is determined to make no distinction in such cases, whether the aggressors or parties injured be of one or the other race or colour, but to bring all, as far as may be in his power, to equal and indiscriminate justice.

As human beings partaking in our common nature—as the aboriginal possessors of the soil from which the wealth of the country has been principally derived—and as subjects of the Queen, whose authority extends over every part of New Holland—the natives of the colony have an equal right with the people of European origin to the protection and assistance of the law of England.

To allow either to injure or oppress the other, or to permit the stronger to regard the weaker party as aliens with whom a war can exist, and against whom they may exercise belligerent rights, is not less inconsistent with the spirit of that law, than it is at variance with the dictates of justice and humanity.

The duties of the commissioners of Crown land, in respect of the aborigines, will be to cultivate at all times an amicable intercourse with them; to assist them in obtaining redress for any wrong to which they may have been exposed, and particularly to prevent any interference on the part of white men with their women. On the other hand, they will make known to them the penalties to which they become liable by any act of aggression on the persons or properties of the colonists. They will endeavour to induce the chiefs in their respective districts to make themselves responsible for the good conduct of their tribes, and they will use every means in their power to acquire such personal influence over them, as may either prevent aggression or ensure the immediate surrender of the parties who may be guilty of it.

His Excellency thinks it right, further to inform the public, that each succeeding despatch from the Secretary of State, marks in an increasing degree the importance which Her Majesty's Government, and no less the Parliament and the people of Great Britain, attach to the just and humane treatment of the aborigines of this country; and to declare most earnestly, and solemnly, his deep conviction that there is no subject or matter whatsoever in which the interest as well as the honour of the colonists are most essentially concerned.

* * * * * *

As a result of Imperial concern for the Aborigines there was a renewed emphasis on equality before the law. The question was thrust onto the centre of the political stage in 1838 when Governor Gipps of New South Wales decided to try a group of stockmen who were accused of mass murder of Aborigines at Myall Creek in northern New South Wales. Gipps described the events in a letter to his superiors in Britain.

DESPATCHES RELATIVE TO THE MASSACRE OF AUSTRALIAN ABORIGINES, *BPP*, 1839, PP. 34–5.

The first accounts of these deeds of blood reached Sydney about the end of the month of June. I despatched, with as little delay as possible, a stipendiary magistrate (Mr. Day), on whose activity and discretion I could rely, and a party of mounted police, in search of the murderers; and Mr. Day, after an absence of 53 days, reported to me in person, that having come unexpectedly to the cattle station of Mr. Dangar, he had succeeded in capturing no less than 11 out of the 12 persons who were known to have taken part in the massacre. When Mr. Day arrived at the spot, some few scattered human bones only were visible, great pains having been taken to destroy the whole remains of the slaughtered blacks by fire; but undeniable evidence was procured of more than 20 human heads having been counted on the spot, within a few days after the day of the massacre; and the best accounts lead me to suppose that the number of persons murdered, of all ages and both sexes, was not less than 28. The 11 persons apprehended by Mr. Day all arrived in this country as convicts, though of some of them the sentences have expired. The twelfth man, or the one who has escaped, is a free man, a native of the colony, named John Fleming.

The 11 men were all brought to trial on the 15th of November, on an information lodged against them by the Attorney-general, containing nine counts. The first four counts charged them in various ways with the murder of an aboriginal black, named Daddy, the only adult male who could be identified as one of the murdered party; the five other counts charged them (also in various ways) with the murder of an aboriginal male black, name unknown. The jury on this occasion acquitted the whole of the prisoners . . .

The Attorney-general immediately applied to have them detained on the further charge of murdering the women and children, none of whom had been comprehended in the first indictment; and this being done, seven of these men, on the 27th of the same month (November), were again brought before the Supreme Court, on the charge of murdering a child. On this occasion, the first five counts charged them simply with the murder of an aboriginal black child; other counts described the aboriginal child by the name of Charley . . .

The seven men were consequently two days afterwards, on the 29th November, put on their trial for the murder of the child, and found guilty on the first five counts, which described the child merely as a black aboriginal, but were acquitted upon the counts which charged them with the murder of a child named Charley, sufficient proof of the name of the child not being adduced . . .

The report of the judge (Mr. Justice Burton) who presided at the trial

GOVERNMENT POLICY 191

was received by myself and the Executive Council on Friday the 7th instant, when no mitigating circumstances appearing in favour of any of them, and nothing to show that any one of them was less guilty than the rest, the Council unanimously advised that the sentence of the law should take effect on them; they were accordingly ordered by me for execution, and suffered yesterday morning at nine o'clock.

* * * * * *

Imperial humanitarianism was usually applied in Australia in a half-hearted fashion. The weight of popular opinion was strongly opposed to meddling from overseas 'theorists'. Australian history had its own momentum. Any attempt to recognize Aboriginal rights to land was vociferously attacked. Assertions of equality met a growing swell of racism. The government superintendant at Port Phillip, J.J. La Trobe, catalogued the failure of the various measures in Victoria in the 1840s.

It is now thirteen years since the first permanent settlement of this portion of New Holland by Europeans was effected; and twelve since the infant Colony was taken under charge by the New South Wales Government; and from this time, if not from the earlier date, some influence, direct or indirect, must have been exercised over the Aboriginal tribes by the presence of the whites.

The appointment of a Chief Protector and four assistants, specially with the purpose of civilizing the tribes of Port Phillip, and affording them the protection they might require in the period of early intercourse with the whites, followed at the close of 1838.

In that year also the Wesleyan Missionaries undertook the duty of establishing a Mission in the country. In the year 1840, in addition to the Reserve on which they sat down, with the concurrence of the Colonial Government, four other Reserves were selected by the Chief Protector and his assistants, in the different quarters of the District, and homesteads established in order to facilitate the intercourse with the tribes in the respective vicinities, and their reclamation from their wandering habits, and savage life and propensities.

In 1841, a corps of Native Police was embodied from among the Melbourne and Western Port tribes, and placed under distinct management from the Protectorate.

Still later, in 1846, an Aboriginal School for children of both sexes was set on foot, mainly by the exertions of charitable individuals in the town and vicinity of Melbourne.

Although neither that Institution, nor the Mission established upon the

Barwon, were under the direct control of the Government, yet both the one and the other, have received no inconsiderable amount of Government aid.

The maintenance of the Mission station of the Barwon, as far as I have the means of ascertaining, from its establishment to the present time, has cost the Wesleyan Missionary Society, inclusive of Government aid, nearly six thousand nine hundred pounds.

I am informed that the outlay upon the Aboriginal School on the Merri Creek at this date, amounts to the sum of eight hundred pounds and upwards.

The cost of maintenance of the Protectorate, since its establishment, amounts to no less a sum than forty-two thousand two hundred pounds, and that of the Native Police to eleven thousand one hundred pounds—making a total expenditure of sixty-one thousand pounds in thirteen years.

The result of all this outlay may be stated in few words. Every one of these plans and arrangements made for the benefit of the Aboriginal Native, with exception of the last named, the Native Police, perhaps, has either completely failed, or shows at this date most undoubted signs of failure, in the attainment of the main objects aimed at.

The Protectorate, as I had occasion to state officially eighteen months ago, has totally failed to effect any of the higher and more important objects aimed at in its formation—and, I may again be allowed to repeat my opinion, that while it may not be justifiable to assert that it has been wholly inoperative, and has exercised no good influence upon the condition of the Aboriginal Native, still it may be believed, that if no such establishment had existed the state of the Aboriginal Native, within the District, would not have differed very greatly from what it now is—that the improved understanding to be remarked between the European settler and the Native is less the fruit of any influence which the Protectors have been in a position to exert, or have exerted, than of the altered position and circumstances of both parties, and the better appreciation that each possesses of the characters and powers of the other.

The Wesleyan Mission has failed. After labouring for ten years to inculcate the truth and lessons of Christianity upon the tribes within their reach, and to induce application to the arts of civilization, under circumstances of far greater promise seemingly than those which attended the formation and conduct of the several Government establishments, it is admitted that not a single individual has been either Christianized or civilized, and the Mission is now on the point of final abandonment.

The Aboriginal School is still carried on; at such times as the attendance of any of the Native children can be secured; but under such circumstances of discouragement, and with the appearance of so little real fruit for past exertions, that it is not hazardous to predict its ultimate failure also.

The Native Police had a specific object in view—and that object has been in a great measure successfully attained. But I cannot consider it in another light than affording an example of partial and temporary reclamation. Were it broken up, no doubt the great majority, if not all the men incorporated in it, would return to savage life.

The primary object of our exertions, and of all our schemes with regard to the Aboriginal Natives of the country, which under God's providence has become the theatre of European colonization, is, taking the higher view of the duties of a Christian people, to Christianize them. It is certainly true, that the history of the Heathen furnishes distinguished examples, of Christianization, through the simple preaching of the Gospel, preceding, and not following, the gradual adoption of those changes in the moral and physical character and habits, in which civilization consists; but is to be stated, I believe without fear of contradiction, that such example has never been afforded in any individual.

After Responsible Government

After 1856 responsibility passed from the British Government into the hands of the self-governing colonies. After federation the states continued to have the major say on Aboriginal policy although the Commonwealth government was responsible in the Northern Territory. During the 19th century policy differed in the various colonies. The ideas which evolved in England in the 1830s and 1840s had most influence in Victoria and South Australia. The ideals and objectives of Victorian politicians were expressed in the Report of the Select Committee on the Aborigines.

VLCV&P, 1858−9, NO. D. 8, PP. IV−V.

Your Committee are of opinion that great injustice has been perpetrated upon the Aborigines—that, when the Government of the Colony found it necessary to take from them their hunting grounds and their means of living, proper provision should have been made for them. Had they been a strong race, like the New Zealanders, they would have forced the new occupiers of their country to provide for them; but being weak and ignorant, even for savages, they have been treated with almost utter neglect.

With the exception of the Protectorate, which was an emanation of the

Imperial Government, and which seemed to have been only partially successful, little or nothing has been done for the black denizens of the country. Victoria is now entirely occupied by a superior race, and there is scarcely a spot, excepting in the remote mountain ranges, or dense scrubs, on which the Aborigine can rest his weary feet. To allow this to continue would be to tolerate and perpetuate a great moral wrong; and your Committee are of opinion that, even at this late period, a vigorous effort should be made to provide for the remnants of the various tribes, so that they may be maintained in comparative plenty. This is a duty incumbent upon the community, and clearly in accordance with the principles of advanced civilization and Christianity. The Committee regret that it has been so long neglected. They trust that your Honourable House will vigorously strive for some permanent provision for the poor oppressed and wandering natives, who have been so long left in abject want and misery; and that endeavours will be made, in the language of the Society for the Propagation of Christian Knowledge in Foreign Parts, 'for the conversion of the blacks, whose country God's Providence has given to the British Crown, and whose amelioration and happiness he has confided to British Christian benevolence'.

The only practical method of accomplishing the desired object, and the one most likely under all the circumstances of the case to succeed, would, in the opinion of your Committee, be to form reserves for the various tribes, on their own hunting grounds. Those ought to be of such a size as would enable each tribe to combine agricultural and gardening operations with the depasturing of a moderate number of cattle and sheep (such reserves in agricultural districts not to exceed 500 acres; but where the land is not capable of being used for agriculture, then the reserve to be materially extended, in order that it might unite pastoral with agricultural pursuits); and every effort should be made to induce the Aborigines to take an interest in the occupations of civilized life and give their aid in carrying out the various branches of industry. Those establishments ought to be under the charge of missionaries, clerical or lay, whose duty it would be to endeavour to teach the Aborigines the great principles of Christianity, as well as the elemental branches of secular education; and it is the opinion of the Committee, that ample supplies of provisions and blankets should be provided for these establishments until they could be made self-supporting, which your Committee trust might ultimately be the case.

In cases where grants for this object are made, the sites should be chosen in retired localities, and no licensed taverns should be permitted in their vicinity.

It was hoped that it might have been practicable to have settled the whole of the remnants of the tribes in one locality, and the first two witnesses, Mr. Thomas, Guardian of Aborigines, and the Rev. Mr.

GOVERNMENT POLICY

Spieseke, Moravian Missionary to the Aborigines, were examined at great length on the subject. The former gentleman expressed a decided opinion against the practicability of such a plan. The blacks would not leave their own hunting grounds, and would pine away at once if removed from them. The various tribes would never agree to go there; consequently the idea of settling them together was reluctantly abandoned by your Committee, in favour of the plan that all the witnesses appeared to agree in thinking the most likely to succeed. Your Committee hope that, in some measure, under the plan which they have suggested, the remnants of the Aborigines may be both civilized and Christianized.

* * * * * *

Queensland was at the opposite end of the policy spectrum. When responsible government was granted in 1859 there were only 20,000 Europeans who were certainly outnumbered by the Aborigines who also occupied more than half the land within the colonial boundaries. The colony was dominated by the pastoral industry and there was an overriding desire to catch up with the other colonies. Aborigines received little sympathy beyond an annual grant of blankets and an abortive attempt to establish a few reserves in the 1870s. Policy was dominated by the desire to 'disperse' the Aborigines from in front of the advancing tide of settlement. But by the end of the century the need for a comprehensive policy had become starkly apparent. In 1897 the colonial parliament swung to the opposite extreme, introducing protective legislation which remained virtually intact until 1965. Similar legislation was adopted in Western Australia and the Northern Territory.

THE ABORIGINALS PROTECTION AND RESTRICTION OF THE SALE OF OPIUM ACT, 1897.

Whereas it is desirable to make provision for the better protection and care of the aboriginal and half-caste inhabitants of the Colony: And whereas great and widespread injury is being caused to the aboriginal and half-caste and certain other inhabitants of the Colony by the consumption of opium: And whereas the restrictions heretofore imposed by law upon the sale and distribution of opium are found to be insufficient, and it is expedient to make more effectual provision for restricting such sale and distribution, and for preventing the evils arising therefrom: Be it therefore enacted by the Queen's Most Excellent Majesty, by and with the advice and consent of the Legislative Council and Legislative Assembly of Queensland in Parliament assembled, and by the authority of the same as follows:

Queensland, like the other colonies, gave blankets to the Aborigines on Queen Victoria's birthday. The ceremony was a public spectacle which everyone came to see. In this case the Protector of Aborigines at Herberton handed a blanket to King George of Cedar Creek, while townspeople looked on. Source: Annual Report of the Chief Protector of Aborigines, *Queensland Parliamentary Papers*, Vol. 3, 1912.

---

1. This Act shall be styled, and may be cited as, 'The Aboriginals Protection and Restriction of the Sale of Opium Act, 1897,' and shall commence and take effect on and from the first day of January, one thousand eight hundred and ninety-eight . . .
4. Every person who is—

(a) An aboriginal inhabitant of Queensland; or
(b) A half-caste who, at the commencement of this Act, is living with an aboriginal as wife, husband, or child; or
(c) A half-caste who, otherwise than as wife, husband, or child, habitually lives or associates with aboriginals;

shall be deemed to be an aboriginal within the meaning of this Act.

5. The Governor in Council may, by Proclamation, declare any portion or portions of the Colony to be a District, or Districts, for the purposes of this Act.

6. The Governor in Council may from time to time appoint, for the purpose of carrying the provisions of this Act into effect, fit and proper persons, to be severally called 'Protector of Aboriginals', who shall, within the Districts respectively assigned to them, have and exercise the powers and duties prescribed.

7. The Governor in Council may appoint such and so many Superintendents for the reserves, situated within such Districts as aforesaid, as may be necessary for carrying the provisions of this Act into effect.

8. Every reserve shall be subject to the provisions of this Act and the Regulations.

9. It shall be lawful for the Minister to cause every aboriginal within any District, not being an aboriginal excepted from the provisions of this section, to be removed to, and kept within the limits of, any reserve situated within such District, in such manner, and subject to such conditions, as may be prescribed. The Minister may, subject to the said conditions, cause any aboriginal to be removed from one reserve to another.

10. Every aboriginal who is—
    (a) Lawfully employed by any person under the provisions of this Act or the Regulations, or under any other law in force in Queensland;
    (b) The holder of a permit to be absent from a reserve; or
    (c) A female lawfully married to, and residing with a husband who is not himself an aboriginal;
    (d) Or for whom in the opinion of the Minister satisfactory provision is otherwise made;

shall be excepted from the provisions of the last preceding section.

11. It shall not be lawful for any person other than an aboriginal, not being a Superintendent or a person acting under his direction, and not being a person authorised under the Regulations, to enter or remain or be within the limits of a reserve upon which aboriginals are residing, for any purpose whatever.

Any person, without lawful excuse, entering or remaining or being upon such reserve as aforesaid, shall, for every such offence, be liable on conviction to a penalty not exceeding fifty pounds, or to imprisonment for any term not exceeding three months, and the proof of such lawful excuse shall be on the person charged.

12. A Protector may permit any aboriginal or half-caste who, before the commencement of this Act, was employed by any trustworthy person, to continue to be so employed by such person, and, in like manner, may permit any aboriginal or half-caste not previously employed to be employed by a like person . . .

13. The Governor in Council may from time to time, by Proclamation, make Regulations for all or any of the matters following, that is to say,
    (1) Prescribing the mode of removing aboriginals to a reserve, and from one reserve to another;
    (2) Defining the duties of Protectors and Superintendants, and any other persons employed to carry the provisions of this Act into effect;
    (3) Authorizing entry upon a reserve by specified persons or classes of persons for specified objects, and defining those objects, and the conditions under which such persons may visit or remain upon a reserve, and fixing the duration of their stay thereupon, and providing for the revocation of such authority in any case;
    (4) Prescribing the mode of distribution and expenditure of money granted by Parliament for the benefit of aboriginals;
    (5) Apportioning amongst, or for the benefit of, aboriginals or half-castes, living on a reserve, the net produce of the labour of such aboriginals or half-castes;
    (6) Providing for the care, custody, and education of the children of aboriginals;
    (7) Providing for the transfer of any half-caste child, being an orphan, or deserted by its parents, to an orphanage;
    (8) Prescribing the conditions on which any aboriginal or half-caste children may be apprenticed to, or placed in service with, suitable persons;
    (9) Providing for the mode of supplying to any half-castes, who may be declared to be entitled thereto, any rations, blankets, or other necessaries, or any medical or other relief or assistance;
    (10) Prescribing the conditions on which the Minister may authorize any half-caste to reside upon any reserve, and limiting the period of such residence, and the mode of dismissing or removing any such half-caste from such reserve;
    (11) Providing for the control of all aboriginals and half-castes residing upon a reserve, and for the inspection of all aboriginals and half-castes, employed under the provisions of this Act or the Regulations;

(12) Maintaining discipline and good order upon a reserve;
(13) Imposing the punishment of imprisonment for any term not exceeding three months, upon any aboriginal or half-caste who is guilty of a breach of the Regulations relating to the maintenance of discipline and good order upon a reserve;
(14) Imposing, and authorising a Protector to inflict summary punishment by way of imprisonment, not exceeding fourteen days upon aboriginals or half-castes, living upon a reserve or within the District under his charge who, in the judgment of the Protector, are guilty of any crime, serious misconduct, neglect of duty, gross insubordination, or wilful breach of the Regulations;
(15) Prohibiting any aboriginal rites or customs that, in the opinion of the Minister, are injurious to the welfare of aboriginals living upon a reserve;
(16) Providing for the due carrying out of the provisions of this Act;
(17) Providing for all other matters and things that may be necessary to give effect to this Act.

The Meaning of Protection

Most Aborigines experienced highly authoritarian controls on their lives during the first half of the 20th century. Officials controlled where they could live, who they married, what they did with their money and whether they could keep their own children.

Reserves were often used as places of permanent incarceration for Aborigines who had committed crimes, were considered dangerous or had been 'cheeky' to an official or an employer. The Queensland Protector listed those removed to reserves and the reasons for his action in the annual report to parliament.

ANNUAL REPORT OF THE CHIEF PROTECTOR OF ABORIGINES, *QVP*, 2, 1903, P. 14; 1, 1905, P. 16.

'Antoni', 'Tiger', 'Billy', 'Paddy', 'Jacky', and 'Peter'. Antoni (his second sentence for a similar offence), and Tiger, are already serving sentences of six months for housebreaking. The police reported that these boys had banded themselves into a gang under the leadership of Antoni, and that their removal from the district was very desirable.

'Tommy', for the murder (by stabbing), of aboriginal 'Albert', at Mareeba, on 9 March. 'A drunkard and an opium smoker. All the aboriginals in the district are afraid of him. He generally camps by himself, but when he gets drink he goes into camp, where he nearly always causes trouble. Both he and deceased have given more trouble to the police than all the aboriginals in the district. The legal evidence against him on the capital charge was too slight to secure a conviction.'

'Papa' (partly deaf and dumb). For the murder of 'Ningi', at Liverpool Creek (Geraldton), on 7 July 1902. The murder was committed in conjunction with 'Mick', still at large and witnessed by a female half-caste, 'Annie' (whose removal to Yarrabah has since been effected). There were some peculiar circumstances connected with the case in that the tomahawk which was used for the purpose was alleged by the blacks to have been borrowed for the purpose by a white settler. Owing to the prisoner being partly deaf and dumb, it would be impossible to explain the nature of the charge to him. He subsequently appears to have escaped from Fraser Island, whither he was deported.

'Harry', on the complaint of the Pentland (Deep Lead) miners to Mr. Geo. Jackson, M.L.A., that he has been repeatedly stealing from their camps. Since then he stole eighteen sovereigns from a wagonette at Cape River Siding.

'Toby', on the complaint of the manager of Lawn Hills. The police reported that Toby has been the cause of many fights between different blacks, and the organiser of all depredations committed by the tribe of which he is 'king'. Before the Minister's warrant for his removal to Mapoon was received, he was convicted at Burketown (7-7-3), with a six months' sentence, of having meat illegally in his possession.

'Mallin', on the requisition of the Herberton justices, was sentenced to two months' imprisonment in Cairns gaol for assaulting a white woman.

'Hero', an incorrigible horse-thief from Maytown. In connection with this case Protector King reports that this practice of deporting such characters has a far more deterrent effect on the blacks than sending them to gaol. He has since made his escape from Fraser Island.

'Friday', continually thieving from the camps of the Cape River fossickers, by whom he is even more dreaded than his mate 'Harry' (see above); he obstructed the police, with a tomahawk, when they were arresting the latter.

'Marabo', at present serving six months' imprisonment with hard labour at Stewart's Creek; sentenced at Geraldton (1-7-3) for assaulting a young white woman. About twenty-two years of age, and has been a noted thief in the district for the past two years. 'After the expiration of his sentence, it would be of the utmost service to the district to have him deported, as if he is allowed to return he will be looked upon as a hero among the other aboriginals, and perhaps continue in his depredations.'

The Protector could control all travel by Aborigines while their compulsory savings were held by him. Aboriginal workers had to ask the Protector to have some of their money. In this picture the station employees have come into Charters Towers for Christmas and are with the local protector. 'Station Aborigines in Charters Towers for Christmas, c. 1920' *North Queensland Register*, 5 December 1921.

'Toby' and 'Jack'. On the application of the local Protector at Cairns. Two incorrigible thieves, of Atherton, now in the Herberton cells. 'Toby escaped from Herberton gaol in March last year . . . '

'Missie', of the Starcke River. First reported on by Constable Kenny to his sub-inspector on 20-7-00. 'Daring and treacherous disposition; believed to be the murderer of the civilized aboriginal Fred Fooks, on the Starcke last October. A great deal of influence over his tribe, and quite capable of using it against white men as well as aboriginals.' The Minister gave the order for his removal to Fraser Island on 4-1-01. 'Missie' however managed to elude capture by Kenny until the beginning of last March.

'Charlie Bushman', of Barrow Point. Two or three murders of others than members of his own tribe—as well as threats to Europeans—are recorded against him. (His removal has not yet been effected.)

'Paddy', a myall belonging to Camooweal country. Charged with having murdered his gin 'Rosie'; one white witness to the fact. Was charged before the Normanton Supreme Court last September (1901);

remanded to the next court (March) and a *nolle prosequi* entered. 'His own tribe fear him, and the white people consider him dangerous.'

'Darkie' was arrested at Cairns for escaping from Fraser Island. It would appear that he had served nine years at St. Helena for murdering a European (Hobson) in the neighbourhood of Cairns, but was released during Jubilee conditionally on his remaining at Fraser Island. His return to his native country was fraught with great danger.

'Jimmie Donga', 'Toby', 'Jerry', 'Tommy Neil' (ex-tracker, and leader of the gang), 'Paddy' and 'Jack', all from Atherton. The first three have already been caught. The trouble with them is that they have been continually breaking into, and stealing from the settlers' huts, and then hiding away in the scrub. The three captures have declared their intention of not doing any work, but of continuing to steal what they can. All have been in the habit of camping by themselves away from the other blacks, so it may prove some little time before the other three are arrested. To prevent any subsequent trouble or collusion, it has been arranged that two are to be deported to Fraser Island, two to Durundur, and two to Deebing Creek...

* * * * * *

Reserves and other institutions were also used as places to receive Aboriginal children whose circumstances were deemed to be unsuitable. The variety of situations in question was illustrated in a Queensland report of 1905.

REPORT OF THE CHIEF PROTECTOR OF ABORIGINES, *QPP*, 1, 1905, P. 461.

The following are notes concerning the half-caste and other helpless aboriginal children and young women who have been forwarded during the course of the year to Yarrabah (Y), Mapoon (M), and Cape Bedford (C.B.):

A little aboriginal girl, four years, with C—, of Georgetown, in whose service the mother (a Croydon native) used to be. C—, who had reared it ever since its mother died (two years ago), 'wished to be relieved of the child on account of his wife not taking kindly to it'. As the child's mother did not belong to any of the Etheridge tribes, he did not feel disposed to send it to the camp, and run the risk of its being killed. (M.)

'Harry Brown', half-caste, twelve years, from Cloncurry, for alleged indecent practices. It was rather an account of the filthy surroundings in which this child had been living, and the treatment to which he had been subjected, that I recommended the removal. His employer's wife puts this boy on a chain occasionally, when he misbehaves himself.' (M)

'Dolly', half-caste, about thirteen years, lately in service with Mrs. M— in whose employ she has been for ten years past. Before leaving for Cooktown, Mrs. M— asked permission from Protector Galbraith to send the girl to a neighbouring station, as she feared the responsibility of taking her away with her to Cooktown, where she proposed residing, but never mentioned or hinted anything concerning her condition. Permission being refused, Dolly was accordingly handed over to the police, who had her examined by the doctor, when she was found to be seven months pregnant. The girl having been with her mistress so many years without receiving any wages, and only possessing the two articles of clothing which she stood up in, the Protector asked Mrs. M— what she was prepared to do for her, but could get no satisfaction. (Until the Amending Act of 1901 received the Royal Assent in May 1902, I had no power to insist on the fulfilments of agreements, the payments of wages, &c., in the case of children already in employment at the time of the passing of the original (1897) Act.) Dolly was thereupon ordered to Yarrabah, but gave birth to a daughter soon after reaching Cooktown on her way south. The child died before the mother resumed her journey. I instructed the local Protector not to allow Mrs. M— any aboriginals, and to refer her to me if she applies for a permit. (Y.)

'Tommy', half-caste female, about sixteen years, who has been travelling over the country dressed as a boy, in the company of a stockman, W.J. Smith, for eight years past. In her evidence before the police court (See Harbouring), where Smith was charged with 'harbouring', she admitted camping at night with defendant. (Y)

'Dora', half-caste, about ten years, amongst the McIvor blacks. 'It is a pity to see her grow up in camp. Could you not have her removed? I think it would be good for her if she could be taken away soon. Her mother's husband is Matji, the rain-maker.' (C.B.)

'Lily', half-caste, five years, in good health and condition, living with her mother in the McKinlay camp. 'She is fairly well looked after; but of late is inclined to visit the Chinese camps.' (Y.)

'Flora', half-caste, about eight years. 'Given to Mr. W— about twelve months ago by Mr. M—, of N— Station. She has lately become unmanageable by her employers.' (M.)

'Lucy', half-caste, eleven years, has been living with the Etheridge blacks up to a month or two ago, when a Mrs. S—, of Georgetown, applied for permission to employ her. The child was then stolen by the blacks, with whom she did not wish to stay, and so got into the hands of the police. (M.)

Complete Isolation

Aboriginal policy of the early 20th century was aimed at segregating the Aborigines from European society—for their own good and advancement. Dr. W. Roth, Queensland's Chief Protector, provided his justification for this policy while discussing his reasons for attempting to stop Aborigines from competing in professional athletics or pedestrianism as it was called at the time.

REPORT OF CHIEF PROTECTOR OF ABORIGINES, *QPP*, 1, 1905, P. 20.

Professional Pedestrianism. Applications from individuals wishing to employ aboriginals for professional running purposes continue to be received, and invariably refused. My objection to allowing blacks to compete as professional pedestrians is based upon a sincere regard for their preservation and welfare. A similar difficulty arose at the Cape Bedford Mission two years ago, when attempts were made to force the Rev. Mr. Schwartz to arrange for some cricket matches to be played against the whites. While giving them every opportunity of playing amongst themselves, this gentleman remained firm in his resolve to put down any attempt at competition with Europeans, or in any way to make a 'show' of their performances. After seventeen years' continuous residence amongst these blacks, the Rev. Mr. Schwartz recognizes that the two main factors in preserving the aboriginal—if he is to be preserved at all—lie in giving him every legal protection when living in contact with the European, but making the isolation complete when once removed from it. I may take this opportunity of stating that the general principle here enunciated—the isolation of, and restricted intercourse between, the weaker race and the stronger, so long as the preservation of the former continues to be the goal to which, as humanitarians, we are striving—is one that was accepted by the late Herbert Spencer after long study of ethnical and historical problems. 'It seems to me,' says the philosopher, 'that the only forms of intercourse which you may with advantage permit, are those which are indispensable for the exchange of commodities—importation and exportation of physical and mental products. No further privileges should be allowed to people of other races, and especially to people of the more powerful races, than is absolutely needful for the achievement of these ends.'

With regard to professional pedestrianism in particular, I cannot do better than quote some very pertinent remarks recently expressed by an old friend of mine who has for the past ten or twelve years given abundant practical proof of his interests in the betterment of the blacks in connection with more than one of the Southern aboriginal settlements. On behalf of the inmates of a certain mission station he writes as follows: 'We find that this kind of thing disorganizes the work, demoralizes the people, and destroys our influence over those whom we are seeking to uplift and make a self-supporting people. Our aim has been to reach them and uplift them through moral and religious influences and regular employment, with a view to their becoming a self-supporting community, and I am confident that this can be done . . . They are being gradually turned into good farm workers, but the racing men will not work. They will not be subject to authority, but go away to their supporters for a time, and then come back and loaf on the station. If we deny them rations, they become a kind of martyrs, live on the others, and spread discontent. Their friends have to be maintained, and they themselves, making plenty of money for a few years on behalf of the betting fraternity who run them, come back to us wrecks, as a rule, and a nuisance and a burden upon the rest. Through them these men set us at defiance, and go their own way. The workers say: "Why should we be tied down, and get nothing such as what they do?"'

I entirely concur with the above opinion, in which I was confirmed by facts which came under my direct notice in Brisbane during the last Third Queensland Hundred. Blacks flocked into town, brought women with them; they obtained grog, and some attempted—fruitlessly, however—to get me to provide railway passes for their return journey home. One of these applicants came to my office, and told me that he could always get work on a station at 5s. a week and found, but that being as good as a white man he wouldn't take it; that he had already won several money prizes as a pedestrian, but had never given, nor intended to give, any portion of the moneys won to the settlement which was his home, and where his wife was being supported; that as the Government had taken the land from him, they were bound to give him a railway pass, &c.

I made attempts to prevent aboriginal pedestrians entering into competition with Europeans at all such race meetings, but without success, and the evil still continues. Of course, the instructions given to the various local Protectors throughout the State are not intended to apply to aboriginals in legal employment—i.e., under proper permit and agreement (as required by the Act), as the *bona fide* servants and employees of pastoralists, selectors and others; there is no objection to these boys taking part in the local annual sports meetings, &c.

The Menace of Colour

For two generations between the 1880s and the 1940s Australia was obsessed by the threat of colour—by the fear of invasion, of 'swamping' by immigrants and by the growth of a 'half-caste' population in north Australia. The Queensland, Western Australian and federal governments all adopted policies aimed at controlling the 'breeding of half-castes'.

ANNUAL REPORT OF THE PROTECTOR OF ABORIGINES, *QPP*, 1, 1933, PP. 9–10.

As seen by the census returns on 30 June 1932, the increase of 16 only in the half-caste population is gratifyingly small. Allowing for the number of deaths of half-castes recorded, approximately 200, this would only indicate an actual birth record of 216, or 1.6 per cent of the total aboriginal population, even if such births were proved to be the result of miscegenation; but, as a good proportion of such children are the progeny of crossbred women honestly married to men of their own colour, the percentage of illegitimates is much lower. Nevertheless, the problem of the increase of the half-caste population is a matter that in all States has caused grave concern. It is difficult to see how this social blot can be erased as long as the white and black races are allowed in contact, no matter how stringent the laws may be made. Only complete segregation of the black races, which is financially impracticable at present, or, as even suggested by some, sterilisation of the females, an absolutely unacceptable solution, will prevent the results of intercourse.

The efforts of this Department have in the past been directed to the checking of this evil, by sternly preventing miscegenation, as far as the limited machinery made possible. The marriage of whites and aboriginals, unfortunately not discouraged in earlier years, has been absolutely prohibited, and every encouragement given to these women to marry amongst their own race.

Regulations have been framed to ensure strict control of females in employment, keen prosecution of maintenance cases, and removal to settlements of women found to be promiscuous. Additional legislative power to deal with normal abuses and check procuring, trading and prostitution by the aboriginals themselves, has been provided in proposed amendments of the Acts and should, when approved, assist still further.

The above policy has naturally resulted in the mating of the half-castes, removed to the reserves, with other half-castes or aboriginals and the birth of half-caste children, but it is claimed that this is a less evil than the promiscuous intercourse of these crossbreeds with the lower elements of the white population.

In past reports the important question of the future of the crossbreed element has frequently been considered, on which considerable variance of opinion exists. One view—that they should be separated from the aboriginal class and educated for absorption into the white races—appears to overlook certain serious difficulties.

In this State probably not more than 30 per cent are of European extraction, the others being of Asiatic or Polynesian breed. This latter element, or the progeny by their further crossbreeding, already present a serious social evil, especially around certain Northern coastal towns, because of their freedom from protective control.

* * * * * *

The 1937 Canberra Conference of Aboriginal authorities was a major attempt to co-ordinate state and federal policy. One of the major concerns was the growth of the 'half-caste' population in the north. The conference adopted two strategies—to segregate 'full blood' and 'tribal' Aborigines on the assumption that they were destined to die out. 'Half-castes' were to be encouraged to 'raise their status' so that they would be absorbed in the white population— they would, in effect, be bred out.

ABORIGINAL WELFARE: INITIAL CONFERENCE OF COMMONWEALTH AND STATE ABORIGINAL AUTHORITIES, CANBERRA, 1937, P. 3.

Destiny of the Race
That this Conference believes that the destiny of the natives of aboriginal origin, but not of the full blood, lies in their ultimate absorption by the people of the Commonwealth, and it therefore recommends that all efforts be directed to that end.

Financial Assistance from the Commonwealth
That the Commonwealth give financial assistance towards the States most requiring it to assist them in the care, protection and education of natives which, unless extended, will bring discredit upon the whole of Australia.
This resolution is put forward for the following reasons:
(1) That the principle adopted by this Conference of the ultimate absorption of the native race into the ordinary community can only be achieved by a considerably extended programme of development and education.
(2) That the work of the States is already a saving to the Commonwealth of a very considerable sum by reason of the fact that there is being maintained at the cost of the States a large number of people who would otherwise be in receipt of the invalid or old-age pension or other assistance directly from the Commonwealth for which they are now ineligible.
(3) That the people of all the States are already contributing the whole cost of the care of natives in the Northern Territory, and it is only

equitable that the people of Australia should also assist in other parts of the Commonwealth.
(4) That following the precedent in other British dominions, it is reasonable that the Commonwealth Government should bear a considerable part of the cost.

Uniformity of Legislation
That the details of administration, in accordance with the general principles agreed upon, be left to the individual States, but there shall be uniformity of legislation as far as possible.

Education and Employment
That, subject to the previous resolution, efforts of all State authorities should be directed towards the education of children of mixed aboriginal blood at white standards, and their subsequent employment under the same conditions as whites with a view to their taking their place in the white community on an equal footing with the whites.

Supervision of Full-blood Natives
That this Conference affirms the principle that the general policy in respect of full-blood natives should be—
  (a) To educate to white standard, children of the detribalized living near centres of white population, and subsequently to place them in employment in lucrative occupations, which will not bring them into economic or social conflict with the white community.
  (b) To keep the semi-civilized under a benevolent supervision in regard to employment, social and medical service in their own tribal areas. Small local reserves selected for tribal suitability should be provided in these tribal areas where unemployable natives may live as nearly as possible a normal tribal life, and unobjectionable tribal ceremonies may continue and to which employees may repair when unemployed. The ultimate destiny of these people should be their elevation to class (a);
  (c) To preserve as far as possible the uncivilized native in his normal tribal state by the establishment of inviolable reserves; each State or Territory determining for itself whether mission activities should be conducted on these reserves and the conditions under which they may be permitted.

Racial Problems
Realizing that the pursuit of this policy and its ultimate realization, unless subject to enlightened guidance, may result in racial conflict, disastrous to the happiness and welfare of the coloured people, this Conference is of opinion that the Commonwealth should take such steps

as seem desirable to obtain full information upon racial problems in America and South Africa for submission to a further conference of Chief Protectors to be held within two years.

Policy in the Post-War World

Many changes influenced policy after 1945—the discrediting of racial ideology, the anti-colonial current sweeping the world, the growth of federal power and responsibility, third-world interest in the fate of the Aborigines, the Aboriginal renaissance. Federal and state authorities moved gradually towards a policy of assimilation in the 1950s and then edged away from it in the following decade, Aboriginal policy paralleling that adopted toward post-war immigrants. The question of assimilation was discussed at meetings of state and federal ministers in 1951, 1961 and 1965.

NATIVE WELFARE CONFERENCE OF COMMONWEALTH AND STATE MINISTERS QUOTED IN G.F. GALE AND A. BROOKMAN, EDS., *RACE RELATIONS IN AUSTRALIA—THE ABORIGINES*, MCGRAW-HILL, SYDNEY, 1975, P. 71.

The Commonwealth and States, having assimilation as the objective of native welfare measures, desire to see all persons born in Australia enjoying full citizenship. We recognise that some of the barriers against the enjoyment of all the privileges of citizenship today are not legal but social barriers. These citizens will only enjoy the privileges of citizenship if they can live and work as accepted members of the community.

Commonwealth Parliamentary Papers, 3, 1962-3, p. 651.
The policy of assimilation seeks that all persons of Aboriginal descent *will choose* to attain a *similar* manner and standard of living to that of other Australians and live as members of a single Australian community—enjoying the same rights and privileges, accepting the same responsibilities and influenced by the same hopes and loyalties as other Australians. Any special measures taken are regarded as temporary measures, not based on *race*, but intended to meet their need for special care and assistance and to make the transition from one stage to another in such a way as will be favourable to their social, economic and political advancement.

STATEMENT BY C.E. BARNES, MINISTER FOR TERRITORIES, ABORIGINAL WELFARE CONFERENCE, JULY 1965, QUOTED BY C.D. ROWLEY, *OUTCASTS IN WHITE AUSTRALIA*, PENGUIN, RINGWOOD, 1972, P. 403.

The policy of assimilation means that all Aborigines and part-Aborigines will attain the same manner of living as other Australians and live as members of a single Australian community enjoying the same rights and privileges, accepting the same responsibilities, observing the same customs and influenced by the same beliefs, hopes and loyalties as other Australians. Any special measures taken for Aborigines and part-Aborigines are regarded as temporary measures, not based on race, but intended to meet their need for special care and assistance to protect them from any ill effects of sudden change and to assist them to make the transition from one stage to another in such a way as will be favourable to their social, economic and political advancement.

Into a New Era

The pace of change quickened in the 1970s and particularly during the period of the Whitlam government, 1972–75. Many items on the current political agenda were first initiated during those three years. The ideals and objectives of the government were outlined by the Prime Minister in a speech to the Aboriginal Affairs Council in April 1973.

QUOTED BY G.F. GALE AND A. BROOKMAN, OP. CIT., PP. 100–2.

The basic object of my Goverment's policy is to restore to the Aboriginal people of Australia their lost power of self-determination in economic, social and political affairs. The Minister for Aboriginal Affairs, Mr Bryant, will be introducing into Parliament, I hope during the budget session, legislation to enable Aboriginal groups and communities to incorporate for the conduct of their own affairs. We see these incorporated societies, set up for purposes chosen by their Aboriginal members, determining their own decision-making processes, choosing their own leaders and executives in ways they will themselves decide as the primary instruments of Aboriginal authority at the local and community level.

The Government will also set up, on the advice of Aborigines, procedures for the election of freely-chosen Aboriginal representatives from the various regions of Aboriginal population to form a consultative council with which the Government will confer on matters affecting Aborigines. Mr Bryant has already convened initial meetings towards the establishment of this body.

Traditional Aboriginal societies have had close associations with specific areas of land, and there are many Aboriginal communities which have maintained that association substantially unbroken. In respect of land reserved for Aboriginal use and benefit it is the firm policy of the government to vest such lands in the Aborigines, as far as practicable in ways which accord with traditional Aboriginal law and practice. Mr.

Of all the reforms initiated by the Whitlam government perhaps the most significant was the acceptance of the principle of land rights. Mr Justice Woodward was given the task of preparing for land rights in the Northern Territory and legislation was introduced into Parliament just before the change of government in 1975. The Fraser government enacted the legislation in 1976. In August 1975 Whitlam handed over a lease to Wave Hill Station to Vincent Lingiari, who had led the strike on the station in the 1960s. As he poured the soil into Lingiari's hand Whitlam said:

> Vincent Lingiari, I solemnly hand to you these deeds as proof in Australian law that these lands belong to the Gurindji people and I put into your hands this piece of earth itself as a sign that we restore them to you and your children forever.

Australian Information Service, 26 August 1975. Photographer: Penny Tweedie.

Justice E.A. Woodward has been commissioned to confer with Aboriginal communities concerned and to advise the legislative and administrative actions required. His enquiry will also, of course, extend to land outside reserves. The Government will await with interest his recommendations in respect of those situations where traditional association can be established for such land outside reserves.

In the meantime, my Government plans, as opportunity offers, to purchase or acquire land which it will vest in the resident Aboriginal communities and you will be aware that it has undertaken to provide $5 million per year for the next 10 years for this purpose. In this way my Government hopes to restore as far as possible the traditional association of Aboriginal communities with their land and also provide them with a base for their economic and social development.

This policy of re-establishing the traditional association of Aboriginal communities with the land is linked with support for the preservation and development of Aboriginal languages and culture generally. A start has already been made in basing the education of Aborigines on literacy first in their own tribal tongue. Increasing support will be given to Aboriginal arts and Aborigines will be helped where they wish to do so to maintain the active ceremonial life on which these arts were traditionally based.

An opportunity for self-determination and independent action would serve little purpose if Aborigines continued to be economically and socially deprived. The Government therefore plans to help them as individuals, groups or communities, in crafts, trades and professions and as business entrepreneurs. To this end programs of socially valuable special work projects, vocational training and grants and loans in support of enterprises, will be actively promoted.

More generally, my Government is anxious that 200 years of despoliation, injustice and discrimination have seriously damaged and demoralised the once proud Aboriginal people. The Government, on behalf of the Australian people, accepts responsibility for their active and progressive rehabilitation.

We will legislate to outlaw all forms of discrimination and will allocate greatly increased resources to overcome the handicaps under which Aborigines now labour and to improve their health and capacity generally. We will not rest until they have taken up, as a distinctive and honoured component in the Australian society, the position to which their rights as the first Australians entitles them.

* * * * * *

The most significant development since the election of the Hawke Labour government in 1983 has been the Prime Minister's commitment to the drawing up of a treaty between Aborigines and white Australians. He outlined his objectives in a speech at the Barunga Sports and Cultural Festival in the Northern Territory in June 1988. The Prime Minister agreed to five proposals put to him by Aboriginal leaders. The Government, he said:

1. affirmed that it is committed to work for a negotiated Treaty with Aboriginal people;
2. saw the next step as Aborigines deciding what they believe should be in the Treaty;
3. would provide the necessary support for Aboriginal people to carry out their own consultations and negotiations: this could include the formation of a Committee of seven senior Aborigines to oversee the process and to call an Australia-wide meeting or convention;
4. stood ready to negotiate any proposals the Aborigines might present;
5. hoped that these negotiations could commence before the end of 1988 and would lead to an agreed Treaty in the life of that Parliament.

In his speech the Prime Minister outlined the following objectives.

UNPUBLISHED PRESS STATEMENT ISSUED BY PRIME MINISTER'S DEPARTMENT, 12 JUNE 1988.

Those proposals that they have put and with which I have agreed are these. Firstly, that there shall be a treaty negotiated between the Aboriginal people and the Government on behalf of all the people of Australia. Secondly, that the next step is that you the Aboriginal people should decide what it is that you want to see in that treaty. The third step is that I have agreed that we should provide you with assistance to establish those consultation processes and in particular that there should be a committee of seven of your traditional elders who will have the responsibility for organising those consultations with the view to organising at the end of the consultations an Australia-wide convention which will represent the culmination of your own negotiations and discussions. Fourthly, that when you have conducted these processes of consultation that we as a government should then be prepared to receive and to consider the results of your thinking and your consultation. And fifthly, that we agreed that these processes should start before the end of this year and that we would expect and hope and work for the conclusion of such a treaty before the end of the life of this Parliament.

Those are the five considerations that your elders put to me and to which I agreed. So now what we expect to happen is that on your part, as I on behalf of the Government, having agreed that you will now start these processes of talking amongst yourselves under the leadership of that committee of seven of your elders, to work out just what it is that you want to see. As you do that I give you the commitment of the preparedness, the willingness, the desire of my Government to respond positively.

At the end of this process when these things are done my fervent wish that I expressed, as you'll recall last year, my fervent wish is that at the end of that process a position will have been reached in which the non-Aboriginal people of Australia will recognise the injustices of the past, will recognise the obligations that we have to create an Australia in which your culture and traditions will not only be able to survive but to flourish, in which you the aboriginal people will have the opportunity of living in dignity, living in an environment in which you will have the opportunity for self-management, in which your law and tribal customs will be able to apply to the maximum possible extent, that these things will be done, that you will have that sort of Australia in which to live and that you on your part will accept then that Australia has accepted and will continue to discharge its commitment.

When those things are done, when that agreement can culminate in that treaty, compact—call it as we will decide—that then after this 200 years that truly we will have an Australia within which the Aboriginal and the non-Aboriginal Australia will be able to live together truly in peace and in dignity in the situation in which we will respect one another and in an Australia in which you and all other Australians will be able to live the life that you desire.

It's been too long, far too long in achieving or even being able to think that we will reach that position and I do truly believe that as a result of what's been happening recently, and a large part of what we've been able to do to day it's my belief that really now for the first time we can expect that sort of outcome to which I have referred.

So to all of you that had any part in creating this positive atmosphere in which we can expect this outcome, I repeat my thanks and deep gratitude and give you my commitment, the commitment of my government and certainly the commitment of my minister that we will now stand ready to respond to these processes to which we have agreed today.

SELECTED SECONDARY SOURCES

There is a vast literature about Aborigines and their relations with the Europeans. Bibliographers will provide the easiest guide to it. See for instance:

Hill, M. & Barlow, A., *Black Australia: An annotated bibliography and teacher's guide to resources on Aborigines and Torres Strait Islanders*, AIAS, Canberra, 1978.

There is much useful material in books written by explorers, colonists and visitors. Consult the following:

Bartlett, T., *New Holland etc.*, London, 1843.
Byrne, J.C., *Twelve Years Wanderings in the British Colonies From 1835 to 1847*, 2 vols., London, 1848.
Collins, D., *Account of the English Colony of New South Wales, 1798-1804*, 2 vols., London, 1798-1802.
Dawson, R., *The Present State of Australia*, London, 1830.
Grey, G., *Journals of Two Expeditions of Discovery in North-Western Australia*, London, 1841.
Mitchell, T.L., *Journal of an Expedition into the Interior of Tropical Australia*, London, 1846.
Stokes, J.L., *Discoveries in Australia*, 2 vols., London, 1846.
Tench, W., *Sydney's First Four Years: Tench's Narrative and Complete Account*, edited by L.F. Fitzhardinge, Angus & Robertson, Sydney, 1962.
Wilson, T.B., *Narrative of a Voyage Round the World*, London, 1835.

Much information about the early stages of frontier contact can be found in the reminiscences of pioneer settlers. See for instance:

Bull, J.W., *Early Experiences of Life in South Australia*, Adelaide, 1884.
Bunbury, H.W., *Early Days in Western Australia*, London, 1930.
Curr, E.M., *Recollections of Squatting in Victoria*, Melbourne, 1883.

Daly, D., *Digging, Squatting and Pioneering Life in the Northern Territory of South Australia*, London, 1887.
Eden, C.H., *My Wife and I in Queensland*, London, 1872.
Hill, W.R.O., *Forty-five Years' Experience in North Queensland*, Brisbane, 1907.
Hodgson, C.P., *Reminiscences of Australia*, London, 1840.
Kirby, J., *Old Times in the Bush of Australia*, Melbourne, 1894.
Landor, E.W., *The Bushmen, or Life in a New Country*, London, 1847.
Major, T., *Leaves from a Squatter's Notebook*, London, 1900.
De Satge, O., *Pages from the Journal of a Queensland Squatter*, London, 1901.
Searcey, A., *In the Australian Tropics*, London, 1907.

Of the many books published about the Aborigines in the 19th century the following are the most interesting:
Curr, E.M., *The Australian Race*, 3 vols., Melbourne, 1886.
Fraser, J., *The Aborigines of New South Wales*, Sydney, 1982.
Gribble, J.B., *Black But Comely*, London, 1884.
Hale, M.B., *The Aborigines of Australia*, London, 1889.
Lang, G.S., *The Aborigines of Australia*, Melbourne, 1865.
Lumholtz, C., *Among Cannibals*, London, 1889.
Parker, E.S., *The Aborigines of Australia*, Melbourne, 1854.
Sadlier, R., *The Aborigines of Australia*, Sydney, 1883.
Smyth, R.B., *The Aborigines of Victoria*, 2 vols., Melbourne, 1878.
Taplin, G., *The Folklore, Manner, Customs and Languages of the South Australian Aborigines*, Adelaide, 1879.
Westgarth, W., *A Report on the Condition, Capabilities and Prospects of the Australian Aborigines*, Melbourne, 1846.

Of 19th century historical works the following are the most relevant:
Bennett, S., *The History of Australasian Discovery and Colonization*, Sydney, 1867.
Bonwick, J., *The Last of the Tasmanians*, London, 1870.
McCombie, T., *The History of the Colony of Victoria*, Melbourne, 1858.
Melville, H., *History of Van Diemen's Land*, London, 1835.
Rusden, G.W., *History of Australia*, 3 vols., London, 1883.
Sutherland, A.G., *Victoria and Its Metropolis*, Melbourne, 1888.
West, J., *History of Tasmania*, 2 vols., Launceston, 1852.

BIBLIOGRAPHY 217

Our understanding of Aboriginal history has been transformed in the past 20 years. Many excellent books and articles are now available. Among them you should refer to:

Beckett, J., *Torres Strait Islanders: Custom and Colonialism*, Cambridge UP, Cambridge, 1987.

Biskup, Peter, *Not Slaves, Not Citizens: The Aboriginal Problem in Western Australia 1898-1954*, Uni. of Qld. Press, St Lucia, 1973.

Blainey, Geoffrey, *The Triumph of the Nomads*, Macmillan, Melbourne, 1975.

Broome, Richard, *Aboriginal Australians: Black Responses to White Dominance 1788-1980*, Allen & Unwin, Sydney, 1982.

Christie, M.F., *Aborigines in Colonial Victoria 1835-86*, SUP, Sydney, 1979.

Evans, R., Saunders, K. & Cronin, K., *Race Relations in Colonial Queensland*, UQP, St. Lucia, 1988.

Harris, S., *'It's Coming Yet': An Aboriginal Treaty Within Australia Between Australians*, Aboriginal Treaty Committee, Canberra, 1979.

Hasluck, P. *Shades of Darkness, Aboriginal Affairs, 1925-1965*, MUP, Melbourne, 1988.

Jenkin, G., *Conquest of the Ngarrindjeri*, Rigby, Adelaide, 1979.

Loos, N., *Invasion and Resistance: Aboriginal-European Relations on the North Queensland Frontier*, ANU Press, Canberra, 1982.

McGrath, A., *Born in the Cattle*, Allen & Unwin, Sydney, 1987.

Marcus, A., *Blood From a Stone*, Allen & Unwin, Sydney, 1988.

Marcus, A., *From the Barrell of a Gun: The Oppression of the Aborigines, 1860-1900*, Victorian Historical Association, Melbourne, 1974.

Miller, J., *Koori: A Will To Win*, Angus & Robertson, Sydney, 1985.

Read, G., *A Nest of Hornets, The Massacre of the Fraser Family at Hornet Bank etc.*, OUP, Melbourne, 1982.

Read, P., *A Hundred Years War, The Wiradjuri People and the State*, ANU Press, Canberra, 1988.

Reece, R.H.W., *Aborigines and Colonists: Aborigines and Colonial Society in New South Wales in the 1830's and 1840's*, Sydney UP, Sydney, 1974.

Reynolds, H., *The Other Side of the Frontier*, Penguin, Ringwood, 1982.

Reynolds, H., *Frontier, Aborigines, Settlers and Land*, Allen & Unwin, Sydney, 1987.

Reynolds, H., *The Law of the Land*, Penguin, Ringwood, 1987.
Rowley, C.D., *The Distinction of Aboriginal Society*, Penguin, Ringwood, 1972.
Rowley, C.D., *Outcasts in White Australia*, Penguin, Ringwood, 1972.
Rowley, C.D., *The Remote Aborigines*, Penguin, Ringwood, 1972.
Rowley, C.D., *A Matter of Justice*, ANU Press, Canberra, 1978.
Rowley, C.D., *Recovery, The Politics of Aboriginal Reform*, Penguin, Ringwood, 1986.
Ryan, L., *The Aboriginal Tasmanians*, Uni. of Queensland Press, St Lucia, 1981.
Stanner, W.E.H., *After the Dreaming*, ABC, Sydney, 1969.
Wright, J., *The Cry for the Dead*, OUP, Melbourne, 1981.
Wright, J., *We Call for a Treaty*, Collins/Fontana, Sydney, 1985.
Yarwood, A.T. & Knowling, M.J., *Race Relations in Australia*, Methuen, Australia, 1982.

INDEX

Aboriginal Affairs Council, 210-12
Aboriginal atrocities, in Tasmania (1830-31), 34-8
Aboriginal children, bible instruction, 172-3; kidnapping, 142-4; raised by missionaries, 170-4; removal by authorities, 202-3
Aboriginal embassy (Tent Embassy) (1972), 22
Aboriginal ideology and philosophy of land, 88-92
Aboriginal kings, Araluen Billy, 85; George (Cedar Creek), 196; 'King Mickey Johnson', 117
Aboriginal labour, agricultural, 131-2; pearl divers, 140; pioneer townships, in, 138; stations, on, 133-5, 136-7; value, 136-7; Western Australia, in, 138-40
Aboriginal languages, 19
Aboriginal Protectorate (Victoria), 192, 193
Aboriginal reserves, 81-3, 191, 199-203; Crown Lands, 87
Aboriginal rights movement, 19
Aboriginal society, principles, 89
Aboriginal Welfare Conference (1965), 209-10
Aboriginal women, kidnapping of, 51, 143-4
Aboriginals Protection and Restriction of the Sale of Opium Act 1897 (Queensland), 195-9
Aborigines, Arnhem Land tribes, petition to Parliament (1963), 85-6; agricultural labourers, 131-2; attacks on, by Queensland Native Mounted Police, 48-52; attacks on frontier settlers, reasons for, 27-31; attacks on gold fields, 32-3; attacks on settlements, settlers' response, 38; attempts to settle or locate, 127-8; attitudes to work, 127-33; British subjects, 182-3; 'coming in' to white society, 124-7; compensation to, 83-4; contribution to development of Australia, 135-40; conversion to Christianity, 164-70; decline in population, 17-18; defiance of traditions, 164-6; image of, 96-122; Imperial government policies, 186-91; 'keeping them in their place', 63-5; marksmen, 140; massacre at Myall Creek, 189-91; protection, meaning of, 199-203; Protectors of, 81, 129, 186-8, 196, 206-7; rejection by white society, 148-52; reserves *see* Aboriginal reserves; Royal Commissions, 147, 152; segregation, government policy, 204-5; settlers' first impressions, 101-4; 'taming' of, articles by 'H.7.H.', 56-60; Tasmania, list of atrocities in (1830-1831), 34-8; Tasmanian, 112-13; Baudin Expedition, 99-101; trackers, 140; use of military forces against, 44-6; white society, in, 123-54; World Council of Churches report on (1981), 180
Aborigines Advancement League, petition to United Nations, 86-8
Aborigines Protection Society, 5, 73-5, 81, 183
Adelaide, Government House, 149-50
Age, The, 9-10
American Indians, 115
'Amicitia', 55-6, 70-1
'Amicus Nigrorum', 60-1
'Aneas', 108-9
Anti-slavery movement in Britain, 76, 183
Araluen Billy (Aboriginal king), 85
Armit, Inspector, 50
Arnhem Land tribes, petition to Parliament (1963), 85-6

Arthur, Governor, 184
Arukun, 21
Ashley-Montagu, M.F., 120-1
Assistant-Protector of Aborigines, Port Phillip, 114
Australian Constitution, 20
Australian Journal of Science, 124-7

Bains, C.E., 209-10
Balamumu people, 85-6
Barwon Mission, 191-2
Bathurst, third Earl of, Secretary of State for Colonies, 67, 104
Batman, John, treaty with Port Phillip Aborigines, 75, 87
Battle of Pinjarra, 44-6
Baudin expedition, 98; Tasmanian Aborigines, 99-101
bauxite mining, 88
Beagle, The, 151
Bennilong (Bennelong), 73
Bentinck Island, 25
Bible, justification for settlement, 5-9; racial equality based on, 111
Bible instruction, Aboriginal children, 172-3
Bible stories, translation into Aboriginal dialect, 173
Bicentenary, 1
black politics, 84-92
Blackburn, Justice, 68
Blainey, Geoffrey, 19
Bock, Thomas, 112-13
Bonwick, J., 172
Bonwick Transcripts, 73
Bora (Queensland), 50
Bourke, Governor Sir Richard, 87
Boyer lectures (1968), xii
Brennan, M., 84-5
Bristow, G.A. (Miranda Downs), 136
Britain, anti-slavery movement in, 76, 183
British Colonial Office, 78
British Empire, 23, 111
British Government, policies toward Aborigines, 186-91
British subjects, 182-3
Bronlee, 84
Brown, Peter, 129
Bruny Island, 100
Bryant, G., 210
Bungaree, 149
Bunjel Creek, 154

Burt, S. (Attorney-General), 142
Buxton, T.F., 183

Cairns, 160
Canberra Conference of Aboriginal Authorities (1937), 207-9
Cape Bedford, 202, 204
Cape York Peninsula, 131; bauxite mining on, 88
Carnegie, D.W., 142
caste barrier, 144-7
cattle stations, Cooper district, 137; employment of Aborigines on, 133-5, 136-7; Lower Thomson district, 137
Cawthorne, W.A., 79
Charleville, 152-5
Charters Towers, 201
Cheshunt Station, 137
Chief Justice Stephen, 67
Chief Protector of Aborigines (Queensland), 196, 204-5
Chinese gold miners, 35
Christian marriage, imposition of, 163-4
Christian philanthropy, 111-14
Christianity, conversion of Aborigines to, 164-70
church, *see* Bible; Bible instruction; Bible stories; Christian marriage; Christianity; Church Missionary Society; Methodist Missionary Society, report for (1826), 2-3; Missionaries; Missions; Wesleyan Mission School (Perth); Wesleyan Missionary Society; World Council of Churches
Church Missionary Society, 166, 172-3
Church News, 169-70, 173
Cilento, R., 172
Cock, Robert ('A Tenant'), 80-1
Coe, Paul (Coe v. Commonwealth of Australia), 93-5
Collins, Lieut.-Governor David, 73
Colonial Literary Journal, The, 108-9
Colonial Office, 78
colonies, responsible government of, 193
Colonist, The, 6, 76
Colonization Commission *see* Commissioners on Colonization of South Australia
colour, threat of, 205-9
'coming in' (to white society), 124-7
Commissioners of Crown Land (New South Wales), establishment, 188-9

INDEX

Commissioners on Colonization of South Australia, first report, 78–9, 80, 82; third report, 80
compensation for Aboriginal land, 83–4
Condamine River, 149
Conference of Aboriginal Authorities, Canberra (1937), 207–9
conquest, right of, 11–13
Constitution, Australian, 20
Cook, Captain James, 4, 94, 98
Creen Creek (Queensland), 50
cricket, 178
Crossland, J.M., 178
Crown Lands, Aboriginal reserves, 87
Crown Lands Commissioners, 129, 188–9
Cunningham, Peter, 106–7
Curr, Edward, 25–7, 124
Currie, Robt. (Marine Plains), 137

Dagworth Station (Queensland), truce at, 63
Dallatite or Devil's River, 31
Dampier, W., 97–8
Darling, Governor Sir Ralph, 183
Darlington Point, 158–9
Darwin, 124
Darwin, Charles, application of evolutionary theories, 9–11, 114–19
Darwinism, Social, 9–11, 114–19
Devil's River or Dallatite, 31
Dhaluayu tribe, 85–6
Dillon, Protector, 137
dispossession, compensation for, 83–4; reality of, 76–7; Victorian Aborigines, 84
Djambarrpuynu tribe, 85–6
Djapu tribe, 85–6
dog on tucker-box nine miles from Gundagai, 18
Dredge, James (Assistant-Protector of Aborigines, Port Phillip), 114

Earle, Augustus, 125
Eipper, Rev. Christopher, account of German mission to Aborigines at Moreton Bay, 113
Eldershaw, F., 42–4
Elkin, A.P., 120
England, 23
Enlightenment, philosophy of, in Antipodes, 104–7
Epworth, John (Delta Downs), 136

equality, racial, based on bible, 111; refusal to recognise, 191
Eureka Stockade, 22
Europe (occupied), 121
evolution, Charles Darwin's theories, 9–11, 114–19
Examiner, The, 144–6
exploration of land, 24–65 *passim*
Eyre, Edward, 27

'Fidelis', 53
Fijians, 115
Fitzhardinge, L.F., 101–4
Fitzmaurice River, 124
Fletcher, C.J., 168
Flinders Island, 172
Forrest, Lord, 140
Fraser government, 211
Fraser Island, 33
fringe camps, conditions in, 152–4
fringe dwellers, 103, 124–7, 152–4
frontier realism, 14–17
frontier settlers, attacks by Aboriginals, 27–31
frontier violence, 14–17, 22, 141; legacy of, 63–4
Fulford, Lieutenant, 149

Galbraith, Protector, 136–7, 143
Galpu tribe, 85–6
Gapinyi people, 85–6
Gardner, Rev. John, 163
Garren, A., 75
Gawler, George (Governor of South Australia), 81
George III, King, 94
George of Cedar Creek (Aboriginal King), 196
Georgetown, 50
German mission to Moreton Bay Aborigines, 113–14
Germany, Nazi, 121
Gibbs, Justice, 93–5
Gilberton, 35
Gipps, Governor Sir George, 189–91
Gladstone, 138
Glenelg, Lord, Secretary of State for the Colonies, 78
Goat Island (Me-mel), 73
gold fields, Braidwood, 84–5; Gilberton, 35; Palmer River, 32–3
Gondarra, Djiniyihi, 180–1
Gould, William Buelow, 112–13

222 DISPOSSESSION

Gove Land Rights Case (Milirrpum v. Nabalco Ltd.), 68; petition to Prime Minister, 86
Gove Peninsula, 85-6; bauxite mining on, 88
government policy, 182-214
Governor Arthur, 184
Governor Bourke, 87
Governor Darling, 183
Governor Gawler, 81
Governor Gipps, 189-91
Governor Grey, 144, 151
Governor Hutt, 128, 186-8
Governor Macquarie, 104-6, 146-7
Governor Phillip, 22, 94, 102, 183
Great Chain of Being, 107
Green, J., 147
Grey, Governor Sir George, 144, 151
Gribble, J.B., 156-9
Griffith, C.J., 130-1
Griffith, S.W., 4
Guardian of Aborigines (Victoria), 133, 194
Gumaitj tribe, 85-6
Gundagai, dog on tucker-box nine miles from, 18
Gunther, James, 166, 174-5
Gurindji people, 88, 211

'H.7.H.', articles on settlement of North Australia by, 56-60; replies to critics, 61-3
Hale, Bishop Matthew, 149-50, 178
Haly, Emmanuel, 31
Hammond, J.H., 138-40
Hardie, Rev. A., 157
Hawke Government (1983-), 212-14
'heathenism', missionaries' conflict with, 160-70
Hillcoat, Reginald (Bonnarra), 137
Hobbes, Thomas, 97
Hodgson, C.P., 5
Hope Vale, 169
House of Commons Select Committee on the Native Inhabitants of British Settlements, 183-6
Hutt, Governor John, Western Australia, 128, 186-8

identity, 85-6
Illawarra, 'King Mickey Johnson', 117
Imperial Government, policies toward Aborigines, 186-91

Indians, American, 115
Innes, James M., 113
International Labor Conference, 87

Jerilderie, 157-8
Johnson, 'King Mickey', 117
Journal of the Royal Geographical Society (South Australia), 160
Jukes, J.B., account of Aboriginal attack, 38-40; survey voyage in H.M.S. *Fly*, 38

Kandwillen, Samuel, 178
Kelly gang, 22
Kevin, J.C.G., 17
kidnapping, Aboriginal children, 142-4; Aboriginal women, 51, 143-4
Kyly, John, 31

La Perouse, encampment at, 19
La Trobe, J.J., 191-3
Lack, C., 122
land, dispossession, reality of, 76-7; exploration, 24-65 *passim*; philosophy, 88-92
land question, 66-95
land rights, growing awareness, 72-6; the Makarrata, 92; Milirrpum v. Nabalco Ltd. (Gove Land Rights Case), 68; National Aboriginal Conference pamphlet, 88-92; recognition, 78-81; refusal to recognise, 191; United Nations, petition to, 191; *see also* land question; *Terra nullius*
land settlement, 24-65 *passim*
Landor, E.W., 12
Lang, Andrew, 126
Lang, Dr John Dunmore, 5, 73-5
Lang, G.S., 40-1
Launceston Advertiser, 11-12
law of nations, 68-70
Legge, J.G., 67-8, 77
Lingiari, Vincent, 211
'Lover of Justice, A', 80
Lower Murray tribe, 164

Macallister, D., 114-15
Mackay, 167
Maclean, Ross (Magowra), 137
Macquarie, Governor Lachlan, 104-6, 146-7

INDEX

Madarrpa tribe, 85–6
Magarrwanalinirri tribe, 85–6
Makarrata, the, 92
Mangalili tribe, 85–6
Maoris (New Zealand), 115
Mapoon, 202
Maranoa River, 153
Marrakulu tribe, 85–6
marriage, Christian, imposition of, 163–4
Maryborough, 33
Matthews, D., 160
Matthews, J., 147
Maymil tribe, 85–6
McConnell, David, 4
McConnell, F., 4
McConnell, John, 4
McConnell, Mary E., 4
McLaren, D., 81, 82–3
McLaren, J., 131–2
Me-mel (Goat Island), 73
Melbourne, history, 10
Melbourne Review, 114–15
Merri Creek, Aboriginal School, 192
Meston, A., 152–4
Meston, H., 134
Methodist Missionary Society, report for (1826), 2–3
Miago, 151
Milirrpum v. Nabalco Ltd. (Gove Land Rights Case), 68; petition to Prime Minister, 86
military forces, use against Aborigines, 44–6
Miliwurrwurr people, 85–6
Milson, J.V. (Forest Home), 137
missionaries, 155–81; Rev. Christopher Eipper, 113; J.B. Gribble, 156–9; Salvation Army, 162; Rev. Schwartz, 204; Rev. Spieseke, 195; George Taplin, 163–6, 175; Lancelot Edward Threlkeld, 77, 110–11; Francis Tuckfield, 84
missionary endeavour, reassessment, 179–81
Missionary Notes, 160–3
Missions, Barwon, 191–2; Cape Bedford, 202, 204; German mission to Moreton Bay Aborigines, 113–14; Poonindie, 175–7, 178; Warangesda, foundation, 156–9; Wellington Valley, 174–5; Yarrabah, 160–3, 167, 168, 177–9, 202, 204

Mitchell, 153–4
Mitchell, R.B., 138
Mitchell, Thomas, 22
Moore, G.F., 44–6
Moorhouse, M., (Protector of Aborigines, South Australia), 129
Moreton Bay, Crown Lands Commissioner, 129; German mission to Aborigines at, 113
Moreton Bay Courier, 5, 12, 48–9, 110
Moreton Bay Friends of the Aborigines, 5
Morinish, New Township of, 49–52
Morisset, E.V., Commandant, Queensland Native Mounted Police, 47–8
Mort, Henry, 4
Mundy, G.C. 76
Murdoch, Walter, xi
Murray River, 156
Murrell, Jack Congo, 77
Murrumbidgee River, 157–8
Myall Creek, massacre of Aborigines at, 189–91

Nabalco Ltd.; Milirrpum v. (Gove Land Rights Case), 68; petition to Prime Minister, 86
Nannultera, 178
Narandera (Narrandera), 159
Narrinyeri people, 163–4
Narrkala people, 85–6
National Aboriginal Conference, call for treaty, 93; pamphlet on land rights, 88–92
National Outlook, 180–81
Native Mounted Police, Queensland, *see* Queensland Native Mounted Police
Native police, Victoria, 191–3
Native reserves *see* Aboriginal reserves
Native Welfare Conference of Commonwealth and State Ministers, 209
Nazi Germany, 121
'Never-Never', 15
New Zealand, Maoris, 115; treaty of Waitangi, 92
Newland, Rev. Ridgway William, 113–14
Noonkanbah, 21
Northern Protector of Aborigines (Queensland), 136–7, 143
Northern Territory, 124

occupancy, right of, 13
Oceania, 120–121
official violence, 44–52
origin, 87–88
Ouriaga (native of Bruny Island), 100

Palmer, Sir Arthur Hunter (Colonial Secretary), 141–2
Palmer River gold field, Aboriginal attack on, 32–3
Papua, 92
pearl divers, 140
Peingdestre, Inspector, 50
Penny, Richard, 144
Peron, François, 98–101
Pfalzer, Missionary, 169–70
'Philanthropus', 54–5
philanthropy, Christian, 111–14
Phillip, Governor Arthur, 22, 94, 102, 183
philosophy of enlightenment, 104–7
phrenology ('scientific racism'), 107–11
Pinjarra district, 138; Battle of, 44–6
Plomley, N.J.B., 99–101
political violence, 21–3
politics, black, 84–92
Poonindie Mission, 175–7, 178
population, Aboriginal, decline in, 17–18
Port Denison Times, 52, 64–5
Port Douglas, 160
Port Lincoln, 175
Port Phillip, 87, 166, 191
Porteus, S.D., 120
post-World War II policy, 209–10
Privy Council, sanctions principle of *Terra nullius*, 68
protection of Aborigines, 199–203
Protector Dillon, 137
Protector Galbraith, 136–7, 143
Protector of Aborigines (Queensland), 196, 206–7
Protector of Aborigines (South Australia), 129
Protector of Aborigines (Western Australia), 186–8
punitive expeditions by settlers, 40–4, 56–60

Queensland, Chief Protector of Aborigines, 196, 204–5; gold fields, Aboriginal attacks on, 32–3; policy following self-government, 195–9

Queensland Guardian, 12
Queensland Native Mounted Police, 46; attacks on Aborigines, 48–52; commandant's instructions (1858), 47–8; E.V. Morisset, Commandant, 47–8; public opinion divided over, 48, 52–6; Select Committee on, 148–9
Queenslander, The, 15–17

racial equality, based on bible, 111; refusal to recognise, 191
'racism, scientific', 103; *see also* phrenology
reassessment of missionary endeavour, 179–81
religion, *see* Bible; Bible instruction; Bible stories; Christian marriage; Christianity; Church Missionary Society; Methodist Missionary Society; missionaries; missions; Wesleyan Mission School (Perth); Wesleyan Missionary Society; World Council of Churches
reserves *see* Aboriginal reserves
responsible government of colonies, 193
Reynolds, Henry, 21
Ridley, W., 148–9
right of conquest, debate concerning, 11–13
right of occupancy, 13
Rirritjinu tribe, 85–6
Riverina, the, 156
Roberts, John T. (Pastoral Inspector, Bank of N.S.W.), 137
Rockhampton Bulletin, 49–52
Rodius, Charles, 103
Roma, 154
Royal Commission on the Aborigines (1877–1888), 147, 152; (1915), 147

Salvation Army missionaries, 162
Saunders, Rev. John, 76, 111
savage, noble, 96, 97
savages, '– and civilized', 118–19; European image, 97
Schwartz, Rev., 204
Science of Man, 118–19
'scientific racism', 103; *see also* phrenology
Secretary of State for the Colonies, Earl of Bathurst, 67, 104; Lord Glenelg, 78
segregation of Aborigines, government policy, 204–5

INDEX

Select Committee on the Aborigines and the Protectorate, 130–1
Select Committee on the Aborigines Bill, 143–4
Select Committee on the Aborigines (Victoria), 193–5
settlement of land, 24–65 passim
settlements, Aboriginal attacks on, reasons for, 27–31; settlers' response, 38
settler violence, 124
settlers, attacks on, by Aboriginals, 27–31; first impressions of Aborigines, 101–4; punitive expeditions by, 40–4, 56–60; response to Aboriginal attacks, 38
sexual relations between Aborigines and whites, 146–7
Shelley, W., 146–7
Shoalhaven, 84
Simpson, S., (Crown Lands Commissioner at Moreton Bay), 129
Simpson, Thos. A. (Carpentaria Downs, Forest Home and Magowra stations), 136–7
slavery, abolition, 111, 183; movement against, in Britain, 76
Social Darwinism, 9–11, 114–19
South Australia, Charles Sturt (Land Commissioner), 81, 82–3; Commissioners on Colonization of, first report, 78–9, 80, 82; third report, 80; Governor George Gawler, 81
South Australian, The, 14–15
South Australian Register, 82–3
Southern Australian, The, 71–2, 80
sovereignty, 93–5
Spencer, Herbert, 204
Spieseke, Rev., 195
Stanley, A.W., 128
Stanley, Lord (14th Earl of Derby), 128
Stanner, W.E.H., xii, 17, 124–7
stations, Aboriginal labour on, 133–5, 136–7; Chadshunt (Queensland), 137; Dagworth (Queensland), 63; Wave Hill, 211
Stephen, Chief Justice, 67
Stephen, S., 77
Strzelecki, Sir Paul Edmond de, 75–6
Sturt, Captain, 6
Sturt, Charles (Land Commissioner), 81, 82–3
Surat, 149

Sutherland, Alexander, history of Melbourne and Victoria, 10–11
Swan River, 151; settlement, 44–6
Sydney Gazette, 53, 54–6, 70–71
Sydney Herald, 72

Taplin, George, 163–6, 175
Tasmania, Aboriginal atrocities in, 34–8; Aborigines, 112–13; Baudin Expedition, 99–101
'Tenant, A' (Robert Cock), 80–1
Tench, W., 101–4
Tent Embassy, (1972), 22
Terra nullius, 67–8; Milirrpum v. Nabalco (Gove Land Rights Case), 68, 86; sanctioned by Privy Council, 68
'Theodoric', 61
Thomas, William, 111, 133
Thorn, Daniel, 137
Thorpe, Constable R.C., 143
Threlkeld, Lancelot Edward, 77, 110–11
Townsville Herald, 56–63
trackers, Aboriginal, 140
treaty, between Aborigines and white Australians, 92–3, 212–4; Waitangi, New Zealand, 92
Tuckfield, Francis, 84, 166–7
Turnbull, J., 101
Turner, H.B., history of Victoria, 9
Tweedie, Penny, 211
twentieth century attitudes to race, 119–22
twentieth century debate on white settlement, 17

Uhr, Sub-Inspector, 52
Underwood, A.H. (Midlothian), 137
United Nations, petition by Aborigines Advancement League, 86–8

Vattel, Emerichde, Swiss jurist, 68
Victoria, Aboriginal Protectorate, 192, 193; failure of measures for advancement, 191–3; history, 9, 10–11
Victoria, Queen, 196
Victorian native police, 191–3
Vinegar Hill, 22
violence, frontier, 14–17, 22, 141; legacy of, 63–4; official, 44–52; political, 21–3; settler, 124

'W.B.', 14-15
Waitangi, New Zealand, treaty of, 92
Walker, W., 73
Wangurri tribe, 85-6
Warangesda Mission, foundation, 156-9
Warramirri tribe, 85-6
Watson, R., 73
Watson, W., 172-4
Wattie Creek, 88
Waugh, David, 31
Wave Hill Station, 211
Weekend Australian, 19-21
Weipa, 88
Wellington Valley Mission, 174-5
Wesleyan Mission School (Perth), 170-2
Wesleyan Missionary Society, 192
West, John, history of Tasmania (1852), 6-7, 34
Western Australia, Aboriginal labour in, 138-40; Constitution Act (1889); 83-4; Governor John Hutt, 128, 186-8; self-government (1890), 83-4
white Australia, guilt of, 1

white settlement, 24-65 *passim*; Bible as justification, 5-9; moral problems, 2-4; twentieth century debate, 17
white society, Aborigines in, 123-54
Whitlam government (1972-1975), 210-12
Wiley, W. Ormsby (Milgarra), 136
Willis, Justice, 68
Windeyer, Richard, 5
Woodward, Justice E.A., 211
World Council of Churches, report on Aborigines (1981), 180
Wright, J., 92
Wright, W. (Wallabadah), 136
Wroth, Dr W., 204-5
Wyndham, 124

Yarrabah, 160-3, 167, 168, 177-9, 202, 204
Yirrkala people, 88; petition to Parliament (1963), 85-6; petition to Prime Minister (1971), 86